SERIES IN INTERNATIONAL COMMUNICATION

...ity of Southern California (USA)

From democratization to terrorism, economic development to conflict resolution, global political dynamics are affected by the increasing pervasiveness and influence of communication media. This series examines the participants and their tools, their strategies and their impact. It offers a mix of comparative and tightly focused analyses that bridge the various elements of communication and political science included in the field of international studies. Particular emphasis is placed on topics related to the rapidly changing communication environment that is being shaped ... the evolving world

...ience (UK)

Kurdish Identity, Discourse, and New Media

Jaffer Sheyholislami

palgrave
macmillan

KURDISH IDENTITY, DISCOURSE, AND NEW MEDIA
Copyright © Jaffer Sheyholislami, 2011.

All rights reserved.

First published in 2011 by PALGRAVE MACMILLAN® in the
United States—a division of St. Martin's Press LLC, 175 Fifth Avenue,
New York, NY 10010.

Where this book is distributed in the UK, Europe and the rest of the world,
this is by Palgrave Macmillan, a division of Macmillan Publishers Limited,
registered in England, company number 785998, of Houndmills,
Basingstoke, Hampshire RG21 6XS.

Palgrave Macmillan is the global academic imprint of the above companies
and has companies and representatives throughout the world.

Palgrave® and Macmillan® are registered trademarks in the United States,
the United Kingdom, Europe and other countries.

ISBN: 978–1–137–56387–3

The Library of Congress has cataloged the hardcover edition as follows:

Sheyholislami, Jaffer, 1960–
    Kurdish identity, discourse, and new media / Jaffer Sheyholislami.
        p. cm.—(Palgrave Macmillan series in international political
communication)
    Includes bibliographical references and index.
    ISBN 978–0–230–10985–8 (alk. paper)
    1. Mass media—Political aspects—Kurdistan. 2. Mass media and
nationalism—Kurdistan. 3. Internet—Political aspects—Kurdistan.
4. Group identity—Kurdistan I. Title.

P95.82.K87S54 2010
302.230891'597—dc22   2010046032

A catalogue record of the book is available from the British Library.

Design by Newgen Knowledge Works (P) Ltd., Chennai, India.

First PALGRAVE MACMILLAN paperback edition: October 2015

10 9 8 7 6 5 4 3 2 1

To
Dr. Amir Hassanpour,
whose groundbreaking research into
Kurdish language and media inspired
and informed this study, and

To
Narmin, Hauna *and* Sarah,
whose love and support helped me to complete it.

CONTENTS

Figures, Maps, and Tables

Figures

Maps

Tables

Acknowledgments

The author and publisher thankfully acknowledge the followings for permission to use copyright materials:

1. Amir Hassanpour (1992). *Language and nationalism in Kurdistan*. San Francisco: The Edwin Mellon Press. Map: Major Dialect Groups, p. 22; Map: Major Kurdish Principalities, p. 51.
2. Behzad Naghib Sardasht, for screenshot of www.koord.com homepage.
3. Barozh Akrayi, for the cover image, of the town of Akrê in Kurdistan-Iraq, taken in 2005.

TRANSLITERATION

Since this study is addressed to audiences who may not be familiar with Kurdish and other Middle Eastern languages, transcription and transliteration are reduced to a minimum. English translation of Kurdish texts is provided without transcription of the original text whenever possible. Anglicized names have not been transliterated; for example, the name of an Iranian Kurdish filmmaker has been written as Ghobadi instead of its romanized Kurdish transliteration *Qubadî*. However, when the same name (i.e., Ghobadi) is part of a transliterated text, the Kurdish version of the name (i.e., *Qubadî*) is used. To transcribe Kurdish texts, I have used the Latin-based writing system that has been in use since the 1930s predominantly among Kurds from Turkey and Syria. This system has been used for the transcription of personal and geographical names, title of publications, television programs and websites, and parts of texts that are transliterated for the purpose of illustrating specific aspects of textual analysis. Romanization is done according to the following list of transliteration.

Table i.i Transliteration

Consonants		Vowels and diphthongs	
ء	'	ا، ئ	A, a
ب	B, b	ه	E, e
پ	P, p	ۆ	O, o
ت	T, t	ێ	Ê, ê
ج	C, c	وو	Û, û
چ	Ç, ç	و	U, u
ح	Ḥ, ḥ	یی، ی	Î, î
خ	X, x	ی، ێ	i
ر	R, r		
ڕ	Ř, ř		
ز	Z, z		
ژ	J, j		
س	S, s		
ش	Ş, ş		
ع	‘		
غ	Ġ, ğ		
ف	F, f		
ڤ	V, v		
ق	Q, q		
ک	K, k		
گ	G, g		
ل	L, l		
ڵ	Ļ, ļ		
م	M, m		
ن	N, n		
و	W, w		
وو	Ŭ, ŭ		
ه	H, h		
ی	Y, y		

CHAPTER 1

Introduction

Although a number of scholars predicted the demise of nationalism and nation in the age of globalization[1] (Appadurai, 1996; Hobsbawm, 1990),[2] nationalism has been identified as "one of the most powerful forces in the modern world" (Hutchinson & Smith, 1994, p. 3, see also Anderson, 1991; Billig, 1995; Hall, 1993; Malešević, 2006). Whereas previously nationalism was primarily viewed as the architect of the modern nation-state from the late eighteenth century onward (Deutsch, 1966, 1953; Gellner, 1997, 1983; Hobsbawm, 1990, 1988; Kedouri, 1993; Smith, 1998), its surge in recent decades has been seen as a response to the need for collective identities. Many scholars believe that nationalism is a force and resource promoting national identities both in nation-states (Billig, 1995; Calhoun, 1997; Madianou, 2005; Wodak, de Cillia, Reisigl & Liebhart, 2009) and also among nations without states (Castells, 1997; Kane, 2000; Guibernau, 1999, 1996).

Morley (1992) has suggested that "the construction and emergence of national identities cannot properly be understood without reference to the role of communications technology" (p. 267, see also Silverstone, 1999, pp. 19–27; Hroch, 2006). Research on the place of communication in general (Deutsch, 1953, 1966), and mass communication in particular, in the processes and practices of building modern nation-states started almost half a century ago (Anderson, 1991; Innis, 1951; McLuhan, 1962, 1964). In recent decades, more studies have focused on the place of media in forming and sustaining national identities in nation-states (Billig, 1995; Drummond, Paterson & Willis, 1993; Madianou, 2005; Price, 1995; Wodak et al., 2009) and also among stateless nations and national minorities (Castells, 1997; Guibernau, 1999; Hassanpour, 1998; Higgins, 2004; Law, 2001).[3]

The question to be asked then is why are the media deemed so important in this respect? In other words, how does media use contribute to the formation and maintenance of national identities? This is the question that is not often asked; rather, it is assumed that the links between media, nationalism, and national identity are there and all researchers have to do is to take the links for granted and map them out (Schlesinger, 1991; Law, 2001). Despite the fact that a number of studies have aimed at delineating the interrelationship between national identity and media, Schlesinger (1991) has noted that, in communication studies, the nation and national identity have not been sufficiently theorized; at the same time, "in the nationalism literature, the mass media are usually quite untheorized" (p. 156). In 1991, Schlesinger called for a reassessment of the relationship between media and nationalism. However, as Law (2001) notes, "little progress has been made since" (p. 299).[4] This study contributes to this line of research.

The study is also a contribution to a more recent approach to national identity: Critical discourse analysis (Billig, 1995; Wodak et al., 2009; Wodak, 2006b). In addition to focusing on the crucial role of the media in the practices of collective identity construction, a discourse analytical approach elucidates the ways identities are constructed discursively in each specific local context. Wodak (2006b) identifies a need for more interdisciplinary research in order to better address the complexity of national identity formation:

> Although…discourse analytical approaches [e.g., CDA] have been adapted and applied to other cultures and the study of national identities elsewhere, more interdisciplinary research is needed that would make the historical and contextual specificities of each social group/collective/community under investigation more explicit. Moreover, the interdependence of local, regional, national and global dimensions has to be studied in their vast complexity. (pp. 114–115)

The Kurdish case qualifies as a complex instance of identity formation, a context within which the complex interrelationship between identities, discourses, and media can be examined.

KURDS AND KURDISTAN: AN OVERVIEW

The Kurds are the largest people claiming the status of a non-state nation (Gunter, 2005; Kreyenbroek & Allison, 1996; Mojab, 2001; Vali, 2003). Estimated at about 25 to 30 million people,[5] Kurds predominantly live in the Middle East, in an area called Kurdistan, which comprises parts of Turkey, Iraq, Iran, and Syria (henceforth, the four states) (see map 3.1).[6] Although there has not been a state called Kurdistan (van Bruinessen, 1992), the term Kurdistan has been in use since the twelfth century, and as McDowall (2004) suggests, today "Kurdistan exists within relatively well-defined limits in the minds of most Kurdish political groups" (p. 3) and also a great number of Kurdish intelligentsia and masses.[7]

The history of Kurdish dynasties and principalities goes back as far as the eighth century (Hassanpour, 1992, p. 50) (See map 3.1). There were 40 Kurdish principalities by the end of the seventeenth century, but by the mid-nineteenth century, no Kurdish self-governing entity remained in the region, as a result of the division of Kurdistan by the Ottoman and Persian empires. Kurdistan was further divided among the four countries of Turkey, Iraq, Iran, and Syria following the European powers' (i.e., Britain and France) re-mapping of the Middle East immediately following the First World War.

Kurdish nationalism emerged at the turn of the last century mainly as a reaction to the denial of Kurdish identities by the four states (Vali, 1998, 2003).[8] However, to this day, Kurdish nationalism has failed to create a strong cross-border or trans-state[9] Kurdish identity because of both external and internal obstacles. There were more than 20 Kurdish movements and revolts involving armed struggle in the twentieth century (Romano, 2002), but not one was successful.[10] The reactions of the four states to Kurdish demands for cultural and political autonomy and rights have been fierce and violent, accompanied by imprisonment, torture, disproportionate military campaigns, and acts of genocide (Fernandes, 2007). Kurdish national liberation movements have been ineffective because they have been too parochial (Vali, 1998), and they have often been used as pawns against each other by the four states and the superpowers involved in the politics of the region (Romano, 2006).[11] Since the First World War, the dynamics and patterns of Kurdish identity formation have been determined not only by its own internal factors but also by various nation-building policies and practices of different states straddling Kurdistan (Vali, 1998). Kurdish identity within each state has taken a different shape.

For decades Kurds remained deeply fragmented territorially, politically, culturally, and linguistically, and these fragmentations made communication difficult among the Kurds.[12] Less than two decades ago, it would take weeks if not months for news concerning major events in Kurdistan to reach most of the Kurds who were not directly affected by those events.[13] Two examples from Iraqi Kurdistan should suffice. In 1988, the Iraqi regime embarked on the infamous *Anfal*[14] campaign in Iraqi Kurdistan, during which about 100,000 people were killed and disappeared (Black, 1993). A report by the Human Rights Watch-Middle East (HRW-ME) designated the perpetuated atrocities against Iraqi Kurds "crimes against humanity and genocide" (1995, p. 20). Next to *Anfal,* one can recall the town of Halabja where the Iraqi regime's warplanes gassed 5,000 Kurds on March 16, 1988 (Randal, 1997). According to Bulloch and Morris (1992), the Halabja incident "did more than any other single incident in seventy years of rebellion against central authority to remind Kurds everywhere of their separate Kurdish identity" (p. 43).

Despite this, both the Anfal campaign and Halabja incident generated very little, if any, reaction among the Kurds in Turkey, Syria, and Iran.[15] Even many Iraqi Kurds did not realize the magnitude of the atrocities perpetuated by the Iraqi regime until months and years later. Kurds had no means to communicate with each other sufficiently; they lacked a collective identity even in Iraqi Kurdistan, let alone across the borders of four nation-states. To have a collective identity requires having not only the means of articulating it (i.e., in discursive practices) (Billig, 1995), but also communicating it dialogically among the members of a prospective community.[16] Kurds could not enjoy this communication for almost a century; their identities remained greatly fragmented.

However, there have been suggestions that a strong Kurdish cross-border identity has begun to emerge since the mid-1990s (van Bruinessen, 2000a; Romano, 2006). Several major events in recent years point to some substantial changes in the state of communication between Kurds of different countries. Among these events are the abduction of the Kurdish rebel leader Abdullah Öcalan by Turkey in 1999, which sparked a swift and spontaneous worldwide protest by the Kurds in the four states and diasporic communities (Romano, 2002; Siddiqui, 1999; BBC, 1999).[17] Solidarity was also expressed worldwide in 2004 for the Kurdish uprising in the town of Qamişli (Al Qamishli in Arabic) in Syria and its violent repression by the state (O'Leary & Salih, 2005, p. 15). The appointment of Masoud Barzani as the Iraqi Kurdistan's president in 2005 was a cause for celebrations throughout Kurdistan and diasporas[18] (AFP, 2005; Institut Kurde de Paris, 2005).

A strengthening cross-border Kurdish identity has started to emerge since the mid-1990s due to some significant political developments in the region but more importantly because of an increasing and effective use of digital broadcasting satellite (DBS) among the Kurds. Kurds themselves have viewed Kurdish satellite television as a catalyst. When the first Kurdish satellite television, MED-TV, was launched in 1995, a Kurdish newspaper wrote that the step was "more important than all [Kurdish] armed revolutions" (as cited in Hassanpour, 1998, p. 44). MED-TV's director, Hikmet Tabak, has been quoted as saying that Kurds all over the world were excited about the station because "they think this is the first step on the last, long part of the road to the *formation of a Kurdish state*" (Ryan, 1997, p. 5, my emphasis). The Turkish state managed to jam MED-TV in September 1996 (Hassanpour, 2003a), but since then more than ten Kurdish satellite TV stations have been launched. This is in addition to the proliferation of the Internet and its publishing, communication, and broadcasting facilities. Christiane Bird, after travelling throughout Kurdistan in 2002, wrote:

> The Kurds remain a fractured people on many levels—torn between countries, regions, political parties, tribes, families, dialects, outlooks, the old, and the new.
> And yet, and yet…Modern technology, coupled with oppression, has changed everything. Through satellite communications and the Internet, the Kurds have their own television shows, radio broadcasts, publications, and websites, all of which are theoretically available to every Kurd anywhere in the world…The Kurds may not have their own physical nation, but they do have an international cyberspace state, along with a quickening sense of national identity that, decades from now, may yet give rise to Pan-Kurds unification—perhaps in the form of a federated Kurdish nation-state. (Bird, 2004, p. 373)

Bird, however, like many commentators who have heralded this development, offers no analysis as to how this "modern technology" might "give rise to pan-Kurd unification."

The suggestion that the new media technologies can foster "pan-Kurd unification" is built on the assumption that when people connect and communicate, they begin sharing a sense of belonging and identity. The assumption tends to ignore messages, what is communicated. Communication among the members of a prospective community is essential for the creation and maintenance of a collective identity, but it is doubtful if connection or even communication alone can create a collective sense of belonging. When human beings come into contact, they do not just begin sharing similarities, they also notice differences because communication technologies carry messages that may or may not concur with the ideas and beliefs of audiences (Connor, 1994). Sameness and difference coexist in complex ways, as if as a unity of opposites, for example, dialectically. There is clearly more to the media than their technological attributes, namely the messages they disseminate. For example, Connor observes that ethnic consciousness in most of the world "involves not the nature or density of the communication media, but the message" (p. 38). Kurds have lived under different hegemonic cultures (e.g., Arabic, Turkish, Persian) for at least a century. Seeing their fellow Kurds on television or communicating with them on the Internet after all this time might make them realize how different they are from each other instead of bringing them closer. More communication might actually cause them to abandon aspirations for the establishment of a greater Kurdistan state or belonging to a cross-border Kurdish identity. Thus, for instance, Iranian Kurds might realize that they share more with the rest of the Iranians than with Kurds from Turkey or Syria.

The belief that the new media technologies by themselves may create "pan-Kurd unification" not only ignores the messages that these technologies disseminate but also the sociocultural and historical contexts that bear upon the use of the media and the production and consumption of their messages. One cannot ignore the issue of media ownership when studying Kurdish satellite television channels. The vast majority, if not all, of these stations belong to political organizations that advocate cultural or/and political autonomy for the Kurds of each part of Kurdistan within the respective states where they reside. For example, the Kurdistan Democratic Party (KDP), which owns Kurdistan Television (KTV), openly aspires not to establishing a greater Kurdistan state but to securing regional autonomy for Iraqi Kurdistan within a federal Iraq. This begs the question: how and why does the existence of KTV or its broadcasts contribute to "pan-Kurd unification," when its owner, KDP, is not a pan-Kurdish organization? The issue of ownership, along with other important issues such as access, need to be taken into consideration also when looking at the Internet and its use and impact on the processes of identity reproduction and construction. Individuals, small groups and alternative voices can access the Internet, not only as recipients of information, which is often the case with television, but also as producers and distributors of information. Does this mean that the Internet makes a different contribution to the process of identity formation, as opposed to television?

A comprehensive examination of the place of communication technologies in the processes of identity formation requires investigation at least at three levels: (1) messages: describing strategies of identity construction and their materialization in linguistic and other semiotic forms (e.g., images); (2) the medium: interpreting the significance of these semiotic realizations of identity against relevant discourse practices that constrain or facilitate the consumption of media messages (e.g., media type used for the dissemination of messages); (3) context: contextualizing the discursive constructs and practices of identity formation socioculturally, politically, and historically.

I submit that KTV's discourse practices are carried out within the ideological framework and political interests of its owner, the KDP, an organization that aspires to regional autonomy for Iraqi Kurdistan as opposed to establishment of Greater Kurdistan. Representations of pan-Kurdism are often subtle on KTV. The Internet, on the other hand, provides alternative communicative spaces for explicit and overt construction and reproduction of a cross-border and pan-Kurdish identity. Although there is not one single Kurdish identity, it can be said that within the last decade or so, Kurds from many places have started to learn more about themselves and their "Others" than they had ever known. This change, however, cannot be entirely attributed to the new media technologies. In recent years, various sociopolitical developments, from the U.S.-led war in Iraq and Turkey's bid for membership in the European Union, to the expansion of Kurdish diasporas, have transformed Kurdish communities. It is within this sociopolitical and historical context that the new communication technologies have enabled Kurds to begin overcoming the geographical and political barriers that have kept them apart and fragmented. As a result, since the mid-1990s, alongside several regional Kurdish identities, a pan- or cross-border Kurdish identity has been strengthening. The implications of this development can be significant for Kurds and the entire region. Finally, investigating the interrelationship between collective identity, discourse, and media can lead to more general observations. Far from being agents of only homogenizing the world, satellite television and the Internet have enabled non-state actors and marginalized minorities to reify both their regional and cross-border identities in multimodal discourses. Finally, I suggest that the nation-state ideology which primarily conceives of a national identity as culturally and linguistically homogenous may no longer be tenable especially in the context of emerging or newly established nation-states.

The statement above leads to the following questions.

- Why is it that, in the case of the Kurds, it is only recently that this strong connection has been made between a collective Kurdish identity and the mass media? What are satellite television and the

Internet capable of doing for the Kurds that other media have failed to do?[19]

- How do the Kurds use satellite TV and the Internet to construct, articulate and negotiate their identities? What are the discursive strategies and practices used in this process?
- What Kurdish identities are constructed, who constructs them, and why?
- What might be the sociocultural and political implications of these Kurdish identity formations?
- What can be learned from the Kurdish case for our understanding of the interrelationships between identity, discourse, and media?

DEFINITIONS AND THEORETICAL CONSIDERATIONS

Nation, Nation-State, Ethnic Group

A nation is a group of people who unite for the purpose of creating or maintaining a state of their own, and who continue to recreate a set of pre-existing or/and invented geographical, cultural, historical, and sociopolitical characteristics (e.g., territory, language, landscapes, flags, maps, stereotypes, myths, and so forth) that they believe set them apart from other peoples. This conceptualization of nation refutes an essentialist view of the nation as a perennial entity that has existed from time immemorial (Geertz, 1973; van den Berghe, 1995). It also challenges the extreme modernist view, which claims that no nation could have emerged prior to the emergence of modern nation-states in the late eighteen century and that there is no nation without a state of its own (Hobsbawm, 1990; Gellner, 1983). For one thing, according to Hastings (1997), as early as the beginning of the fourteenth century, "English felt themselves to be a nation" (p. 15). Second, as Castells (1997) suggests, "nations are, historically and analytically, entities independent from the state" (Castells, 1997, p. 30; see also Billig, 1995, pp. 24–26). Thus, here nation and nation state are understood as being different (see Guibernau, 1996).

Whatever the definition of the nation, almost all theorists consider the nation-state a modern phenomenon. Then, one might ask: how does a nation-state differ from a nation? Guibernau makes the following useful distinction:

> The main differences between a nation and a nation-state...are that, while the members of a nation are conscious of forming a community,

the nation-state seeks to create a nation and develop a sense of community stemming from it. While the nation has a common culture, values, and symbols, the nation-state has as an objective the creation of a common culture, symbols and values. (p. 47)

From this perspective, it is conceivable to talk about those nations without state that, along with their nationalism, as Castells (1997) observes, "did not reach modern nation-statehood (for example, Scotland, Catalonia, Quebec, Kurdistan, Palestine), and yet they display, and some have displayed for several centuries, a strong cultural/territorial identity that expresses itself as a national character" (pp. 29–30).

Taking the position that nations can exist without a state distinguishes the definition adopted here from another major approach in the literature of nation and nationalism: ethnosymbolism (Smith, 1998), which does not distinguish between the semantics of nation and nation-state. However, this study concords with Smith (1999, 1998) that nations, regardless of how recent or old they are, often have ethnic roots. The two terms "ethnic group" and "nation," however, should not be used interchangeably, unless the people in question choose to do so. When a group of people is called an "ethnic group" by an outsider, including a researcher, it is implied that that people should stay within a nation-state without having rights to political autonomy or independence, but calling a group of people a "nation" acknowledges their rights to rule themselves culturally and politically (Calhoun, 1993, pp. 220–221; see also Billig, 1995). The labeling or naming of concepts, peoples, or places is not neutral; it is the expression and reinforcement of an ideological position which shows the speaker's stance on a sociocultural or political issue (Fowler et al., 1979; Bourdieu, 1991), for example, whether a group of people should have the right to self-rule or not.

A nation might consist of one ethnic group or of a multi-ethnic population that collectively aspires to the same nationalist goal of achieving political and cultural rights. This is particularly true of nations without states. Schlesinger (1991), suggests that "the stateless nation is judged to be of special significance as a prototype of potentially innovative forms of post–nation-state affiliation, as an exemplar of flexible networking, and as offering multiple identities and allegiances to its inhabitants" (p. 267). The question then is: in the absence of a state what force fosters the imagination of the nation? The answer is: nationalism.

Nationalism

There is really no consensus on the definition of nationalism. A quick look at the labels that theorists have chosen for the phenomenon testifies to this: "a common bond of sentiment..." (Weber, 1948, as cited in Smith, 1983, p. 174), a set of "sentiments..." (Guibernau, 1996, p. 47), "a state of mind..." (Hans Kohn, 1944, as cited in Smith, 1983, p. 174), "a form of collective consciousness" (Habermas, 1994),[20] "a political principle..." (Gellner, 1983, p. 1), a "political movement..." (Breuilly, 1993, as cited in Smith, 1998, p. 84), "a theory and practice..." (Hastings, 1997, p. 3), "a doctrine..." (Kedouri, 1993, p. 9), and finally "a way of thinking, an ideological consciousness" (Billig, 1995, p. 10), or in Collins' (1990) words, "a belief system or ideology" (p. 11).

In this study, following Smith (1998), I understand nationalism as both an ideology[21] and a social or political movement aimed at the establishment and maintenance of self-government and/or the creation and reconstruction of collective cultural/national identity for a group of people who believe themselves to be a nation or proto-nation.[22] Viewing nationalism as both an ideology and a movement synthesizes many of the major definitions and conceptualizations of nationalism. Whereas the term "ideology" refers to the cultural, ethnic, and linguistic aspects of nationalism (with the aim of preserving one's culture and identity and not necessarily pursuing political independence—e.g., Catalans in Spain), the term "political movement" refers to nationalism's political nature (with the explicit agenda of pursuing some sort of regional autonomy or independence, for example, Québec nationalism) (Smith, 1999). Conceptualizing nationalism in the sense of an ideology in addition to a social and political movement will encompass both categories of nationalism (Hutchinson & Smith, 1994).

Whatever nationalism might be, it is unmistakably a modern phenomenon (Anderson, 1991; Gellner, 1983; Hobsbawm, 1988, 1990; Smith, 1998). According to Deutsch (1953), among other things, modernity is also marked by an increasing "self-doubt." In the modern world, because people are uprooted from their small towns, traditions, and context-dependent meaning systems (e.g., face-to-face interaction), more than ever the answer to the question "who am I?" is illusive (p. 184, see also Dascal, 2003, p. 160). In a similar vein, Hall (1992) speaks of "crisis of identity" in the sense of "fragmenting the modern individual as a unified subject" (p. 274). According to Deutsch (1953), in the search for themselves, people discover those who are similar, and "they may discover once again the connection between ethnic nationality and the capacity for fellowship" (p. 184).[23] In the 1990s, however, national identities are said to be threatened by globalization (Guibernau, 1999).[24] Thus, the realization and maintenance of cultural fellowship and collective identity has been one of the reasons for the surge of nationalism and its objective (Billig, 1995; Guibernau, 1996; Smith, 1998).

IDENTITY

Identity is conceptualized primarily in relation to social actors' experience and also the representation of these experiences in narratives and discourses that are shared publicly, for example, through mass media (Brubaker, 2004). In similar veins, Castells (1997) defines identity as "people's source of meaning and experience" (p. 6). It is what combines people's names, languages, cultures, behaviors, ways of living, and ways of relating to others. Thus, for the purpose of this study, "identity, as it refers to social actors...[is understood as] the process of construction of meaning on the basis of a cultural attribute, or related set of cultural attributes, that is/are given priority over other sources of meaning" (p. 6). Others have consistently defined identity in terms of meaning making in the sense of shared understanding among social actors (Ainsworth & Hardy, 2004; Hall, 1992; Triandafyllidou & Wodak, 2003). Ainsworth and Hardy contend that "the construction of identity in discourse is also the construction of meaning and relationships" (p. 237).

Meanings and relationships, including identities, are formed and acted out in contexts. From a sociological perspective, all human identities are social and socially constructed (Triandafyllidou & Wodak, 2003).[25] Construction, however, does not occur in a vacuum. To capture the complexity of identity construction, Castells (1997) suggests that we need to ask: "how, from what, by whom, and for what" identities are constructed (p. 7; see also p. 32). These questions call attention to the importance of context. Every group and collective entity constructs identity according to its available social, cultural, and historical resources and within their "space/time framework" (Castells, 1997, p. 7). This context-based construction of identities applies to national identities as well: "[T]he various discursive constructs of national identity are given different shapes according to the context and to the public in which they emerge" (Wodak et al., 2009, p. 3).

Castells (1997) proposes three kinds of identity building: legitimizing identity,[26] project identity,[27] and resistance identity. The latter is particularly relevant to this study. It is "generated by those actors that are in positions/conditions devalued and/or stigmatized by the logic of domination, thus building trenches of resistance and survival on the basis of principles different from, or opposed to, those permeating the institutions of society" (Castells, 1997, p. 8). I would submit that the struggle of minority nationalism against the assimilationist majority nationalism is an example of resistance identity (see also Kymlicka & Straehle, 1999; Williams, 1999). According to Castells (1997), "*identity for resistance*, leads to the formation of *communes*, or *communities*" (p. 9), or what Anderson (1991) has famously called "imagined communities." This kind of identity, for Castells, is the most important type of identity building because "it constructs forms of collective resistance against otherwise unbearable oppression usually on the basis of identities that were, apparently, clearly defined by history, geography, or biology, making it easier to essentialize the boundaries of resistance" (Castells, 1997, p. 9).[28] A clear example of resistance identity seems to be national identity the construction of which, as discussed earlier, is the fixation of all sorts of nationalisms.

NATIONAL IDENTITY

National identity denotes shared feelings of belonging to a cultural or national group, but at the same time it denotes differences from other groups and national identities (Billig, 1995; Riggins, 1997; Wodak et al., 2009). All identities are relational and national identity is no exception. National identity is primarily a social construct; however, it has historical and ethnic roots, even if such roots are invented (Smith, 1998). According to Castells (1997), "most successful nationalisms presume some prior community of territory, language, or culture, which provide the raw material for the intellectual project of nationality" (p. 29). In other words, nationalist ideologies use history and memory, territory and landscape, language, and a great number of other cultural and political symbols and myths, with the aim of strengthening national ties (Smith, 1999; Hobsbawm, 1988; Wodak et al., 2009). It should also be stressed that national identity is dynamic; it is neither primordial nor will it remain the same forever. It is context-dependent, which means that "the various discursive constructs of national identity are given different shapes according to the context and to the public in which they emerge" (Wodak et al., 2009, p. 3).

National identity and discourse

The construction of national identity is discursive in crucial ways. As Billig (1995) suggests, "to have a national identity is to possess ways of talking about nationhood" (p. 8). Ways of communicating about nationhood, especially in the age of television and the Internet, include not only verbal language but also audio-visual means of communication. To encompass this multimodality of the new media I use the term discourse. Discourse and discursive practices contribute to the construction, reproduction, and maintenance of national identities (Wodak, 2006b). Therefore, the "study of identity should involve the detailed study of discourse" (Billig, 1995, p. 8). Components of a nationalist discourse often include the discursive construction of a common culture, language, territory, symbols, history, and a shared present and future.

Discourse of National Identity and Media

Collective identities are understood primarily in terms of shared meanings and understandings among social actors. It follows that discursive constructs of national identity need to be disseminated and negotiated among prospective members of a community (Ainsworth & Hardy, 2004; Hall, 1992; Triandafyllidou & Wodak, 2003). Mass media have proven to be excellent tools and sites for the dissemination and articulation of national identity discourses (Anderson, 1991; Billig, 1995; Bishop & Jaworski, 2003; Chouliaraki, 1999; Madianou, 2005). For nations without states, such as the Kurds, which lack institutions like their own schools, ministries of culture, and the military, mass communication technologies are important sources of mediation and negotiation of discursive identity constructs.[29]

Media technologies, however, differ with respect to their degree of reach, accessibility, resourcefulness for creating semiotic and discursive constructs, and, finally, the messages and images they disseminate. Communication scholars such as Deutsch (1966) and McLuhan (1962, 1964) and a number of nationalism scholars such as Gellner (1983) have emphasized the form and technological characteristics of the media and have ignored the content of media. In contrast, other scholars, notably discourse analysts, concerned with the interface between media and nationalism, have paid little attention, if any, to the technological characteristics of the media and, instead, have focused on the content of the media (Billig, 1995; Wodak et al., 2009). Many scholars of nationalism have also confirmed the importance of media content and messages (Smith, 1998; Connor, 1994). This study proposes a more balanced approach to the role of the media discourse in the processes of identity construction. The medium matters, but so does the content. Of great importance also are the sociocultural contexts that bear upon the construction and consumption of media products.

METHODOLOGICAL CONSIDERATIONS[30]

Data

The television data consists of approximately 168 hours of Kurdistan Television (KTV) broadcasting, from August 6–12, 2005. The Internet data was accumulated over a decade of observation of Kurdish online activities and sources, such as web directories, websites, chatrooms, weblogs, forums, and social networking tools (e.g., YouTube). The data are enriched by email interviews and personal communication with television viewers and Internet users and also by drawing on various media outlets reporting on the discourse practices and sociocultural aspects of the media under investigation.

Method of Data Analysis

To explicate the interface between national identity, discourse, and media, this study is informed by the interdisciplinary approach of Critical Discourse Analysis (CDA), an interdisciplinary approach in the sense that it blends social theories with theories of language and discourse. According to Chouliaraki and Fairclough (1999), CDA facilitates a dialogue between various social and linguistic theories (p. 16). Discourse is a social practice, simultaneously constitutive of and constituted by social structures, relations, and identities. For example, national identities are reflected and articulated in the use of language and discourse, and at the same time, they are constructed, reproduced, and sustained through discursive practices. However, two points need to be clarified. First, discourses do not construct identities on their own; they do so because they are produced and used by human beings who subscribe to certain ideologies and worldviews (Weiss & Wodak, 2003). The second point is that national identities do exist outside discourse; however, they are constantly mediated by and through discourse.[31]

The CDA framework that is proposed here for studying media discourse consists of three interrelated dimensions: text, discourse practices, and sociocultural practices. At the text level, CDA involves detailed analysis of text properties, such as linguistic elements and audiovisual signs. At the discourse practice level, issues of text production and consumption are addressed. Analysis at the sociocultural level attempts to explain how social, cultural, and political contexts influence the ways texts are produced, distributed, and consumed.

CHAPTERS OVERVIEW

Chapter 2 is devoted to theory and method. It illustrates how national identities are discursive constructs. To be effective, however, these linguistic and semiotic images and meanings must be disseminated and negotiated among the prospective members of a nation. For people without a state of their own, the new electronic media such as satellite TV and the Internet have proven to be among the most practical and effective means of producing and disseminating discursive constructs of identities. To understand how discursive constructs in the case of the Kurds are mediated and what implications such discourse practices might have a discourse analytical framework is developed.

There are three main sections to this chapter. In the first section, the instrumentality of language in identity construction is illustrated with a survey of studies that have a discourse analytical orientation in investigating discursive constructions of national identities. While it is noted that identity constructs are not exclusively discursive, the chapter suggests that having an identity entails the ability to articulate it in language and other semiosis. Thus, the study of identity needs to involve the study of discourse. The second section illustrates the significance of communication technologies, from the printing press to the Internet, in the projects of identity construction. It is argued that, in order to be effective, discursive constructs of identity must be disseminated and negotiated among people. Emphasis here is not only on the form and technological characteristics of media, which has been the prime focus for the vast majority of scholars on nation and media (e.g., in works by Karl Deutsch, Marshall McLuhan, Benedict Anderson, David Morley, and Philip Schlesinger), but also their content, the linguistic and audio-visual constructions that the media articulate and disseminate. In the third section, the methodological approach, Critical Discourse Analysis (CDA), is defined and explained. This methodology enables analyses at three levels: (1) text (micro-analysis of various modes of texts such as language and images), (2) discourse practices (production and consumption of texts), and (3) sociocultural, political and historical contexts that bear upon media texts under analysis.

Chapter 3 focuses on Kurdish identity. The purpose here is to illustrate the diversification and fragmentation of Kurdish identity along political, cultural, territorial, and linguistic lines. The chapter begins with a history of the Kurds, ancient and contemporary. It continues by examining Kurdish nationalism, its origins at the turn of the last century and the reasons for its failure to create a cross-border Kurdish identity. I discuss both external and internal barriers to the formation of a pan-Kurdish identity. The chapter reports that in recent years, several scholars of Kurdish studies have suggested that a Kurdish cross-border identity has been strengthening and that satellite television, in particular, has been a catalyst in this respect. I first question whether media should be credited with fostering this development singlehandedly. Various cultural and political developments, from the Barzani revolt to the latest reforms in Turkey, are discussed as potential contributors to an increase in communication and ethnic awareness among the Kurds. Then I note that, to this date, no detailed analysis of the place of new Kurdish media has been conducted. We need to examine why in the case of the Kurds only recently this strong connection has been made between a collective Kurdish identity and the mass media. The chapter also calls for an investigation into what satellite television and the Internet have been capable of doing for the Kurds that other media have failed to do.

Based on established research suggesting that mass media have been foundational to most, if not all, nation-building projects, Chapter 4 extrapolates why traditional media have not been able to do the same for the Kurds. A brief history of Kurdish media is presented to illustrate why none of the press, radio, or cable television has been able to become the Kurdish mass medium, capable of creating a truly imagined Kurdish community. Finally, the history of Kurdish satellite television and Internet is presented partially in light of several studies that have been devoted either entirely or partially to these two Kurdish communication technologies. The main objective here is to establish the argument that with the emergence of satellite television and Internet the Kurds for the first time have started to communicate dialogically and spontaneously in unprecedented ways. It is further surmised that this change in communication among the Kurds cannot be without influence on the ways Kurdish identities are constructed and disseminated. What remains to be done, however, is to investigate what the Kurds actually do with these new media in their disposal.

Chapter 5 is devoted to an overview of Kurdistan TV and the empirical data collected from KTV programs recorded during a one-week period (168 hours). Following the triad framework of media discourse analysis introduced earlier, this chapter focuses on analysis at the discourse practices level. After organizing the data into several categories, the types of programs that KTV broadcasts are identified. Guided by several research questions, then, further descriptions are provided to identify practices of media text production and consumption as they pertain to regional or cross-border Kurdish identities. These questions are: (1) Are there shows that are devoted to the history, demography, and geography of other parts of Kurdistan? (2) Does KTV address current issues related to all parts of Kurdistan or of Iraqi Kurdistan only? (3) Whose culture, that of Iraqi Kurdistan alone or all Kurds, is reflected on KTV? (4) Do Kurds other than the Kurds of Iraq contribute to the production of TV programs (e.g., as hosts or hostesses, producers, and directors)? (5) Do non-Iraqi Kurds participate in shows and programs as guests, callers, interviewees?

Reworking the Wodak el al. (2009) method of analyzing discursive construction of national identity, in Chapter 6 a micro-analysis (verbal and visual) of KTV texts is carried out to show how various components of the discourse of national identity (such as history/past, present and future, language, national symbols, and territory and homeland) are constructed and reproduced. Micro-analysis of television texts is illustrated through analyzing a weather program, illustrating how the mental image of a greater Kurdistan is reconstructed on a daily basis through renaming geographical places and symbolically redrawing the map of a greater Kurdistan through moving images in the weather forecast. The analysis illustrates that KTV, which belongs to a regional Iraqi Kurdish organization, overtly remains Iraqi Kurdish but subtly and implicitly contributes to the reconstruction of a cross-border Kurdish identity. The final section of this chapter takes a multimodal analysis approach to a Kurdish patriotic song frequently aired on KTV. The objective here is to show how various ingredients of national identity discourse are reconstructed in the three main modes of this audio-visual text: verbal language, visual images, and music. The analysis reveals at least two Kurdish political identities competing within the same text, a regional Southern Kurdistani (read Iraqi) identity and a pan-and cross-border Kurdish identity. Reasons and implications of this complex identity formation are discussed in the last chapter.

Chapter 7 illustrates that the Internet has provided crucial communicative spaces not only to powerful Kurdish political organizations but to individual Kurds and marginal groups, such as women who, theoretically, could construct Kurdish identities different from those of Kurdish political parties, who also happened to own and control all the Kurdish satellite television stations, arguably the most powerful medium in Kurdistan and among Kurdish diasporic communities. To illustrate this, I will first present the Internet data collected for this study. This is followed by a description of the Kurdish Internet constituents, for example, websites, chat-rooms, blogs, forums, and other social networking tools like YouTube and Facebook. The origins of the Internet among the Kurds and the extent to which they have been used are reported. Observations will be based on my active observation of Kurdish online activities for more than a decade, and correspondence and interviews with people who have been involved in both production and consumption of Kurdish Internet texts. It is then asked: what discursive and semiotic constructions of Kurdish identities are present online?

Chapter 8 is devoted to textual analysis of the content of various constituents of Kurdish Internet. Encompassing both linguistic and visual modes, the analysis maps out identity discursive constructs and the kind of Kurdish identities articulated. For example, the chapter reports on the blogging activities of two Kurdish women. By interviewing the bloggers and also analyzing their posts, the study reports on their motivations for blogging in Kurdish and how they see this as an expression of their ethno-national identity. Originally from Iran, where Kurdish has no official status, the two women write about their deeply emotional experience of learning to write in their mother tongue for the first time thanks to blogging. The Internet has provided them with a communicative space where they can express their sense of belonging to a cross-border and collective Kurdish identity.

In the final chapter, discussion and conclusion, I attend to the third part of the framework of this study: sociocultural practices. Here I explain the findings at the other two levels (textual and discourse practices) within the sociocultural and political contexts that bear upon the production and consumption of the discourses analyzed. The focus here is on why at this point in time these social actors are engaged in such particular identity constructions illustrated in the study, and what the possible implications of these discursive activities might be for the Kurds and also the region. Could the new media strengthen a pan-Kurdish identity and the desire for the establishment of an independent greater Kurdistan? Could the two media have different influences in this process of identity formation and what they might be? Exploring possible answers to these questions is followed by a summary of the overall findings of the study and a discussion of some of the implications of this study for further studies of the interrelationship between collective identities, discourses, and communication technologies in other contexts.

CHAPTER 2

Discourse, Media, and Nation

To have a national identity is to possess ways of talking about nationhood...the study of identity should involve the detailed study of discourse.

Billig, 1995, p. 8

...the construction and emergence of national identities cannot properly be understood without reference to the role of communications technology.

Morley, 1992, p. 267

The objective of this chapter is to outline this study's main theoretical and methodological underpinnings. While it is noted that identity constructs are not exclusively discursive, it is suggested that having an identity entails the ability to articulate it in language and other semiosis. Thus, the study of identity must involve the study of discourse (Wodak, 2006b). The second part of the chapter illustrates the significance of communication technologies, from the printing press to the Internet, in the projects of identity construction. It is argued that in order to be effective, discursive constructs of identity must be disseminated and negotiated among people. Emphasis here is not only on the form and technological characteristics of media, which has been the prime focus for the vast majority of scholars on nation and media (e.g., in works by Karl Deutsch, Marshall McLuhan, Benedict Anderson, David Morley, and Philip Schlesinger), but also their content, the linguistic and audio-visual constructions that the media articulate and disseminate. The third section of the chapter brings together insights from the two other sections and suggests that an approach to media discourse needs to take into consideration not only the content and forms of media, but also the sociocultural contexts that bear upon the production and consumption of media products. The approach must be interdisciplinary, in that it should account for theories of group identity and nationhood, discourse and language, and media. To this end, I draw upon the research approach of Critical Discourse Analysis (Fairclough, 2003, 1995a; van Dijk, 2001; Wodak, 2006a; Wodak & Meyer, 2001) to present a particular analytical framework for studying media discourse (Fairclough, 1995b) that informs this study.

Discursive Construction of National Identities

Although Anderson's (1991) publication in 1983, *Imagined Communities: Reflections on the Origin and Spread of Nationalism*, was the first major work on nation and nationalism from a discourse constructivist approach, we had to wait another decade to witness a series of studies that started to engage in the detailed analysis of the language and discursive practices of the construction of national identities. The two pioneer works in this respect are Billig (1995) and Wodak et al. (1999).[1] While a few studies have specifically drawn upon Wodak et al. (e.g., Ricento, 2003; Karner, 2005; Higgins, 2004), these studies and more have been influenced by Billig (1995) (e.g., Bishop & Jaworski, 2003; Dixon & Durrheim, 2000; Law, 2001; Sutherland, 2005; Yumul & Uzkirimli, 2000).

Employing the Viennese Critical Discourse Analysis (CDA) approach, Wodak et al. (2009) have studied the discursive construction of national identity in Austria. In addition to interviews and focus-group discussions, the bulk of their data encompasses media products: newspaper articles, posters, slogans, and direct mail in time of election campaigns, and politicians' speeches, most of which are mediated by the media. The findings in this study illustrate that discourses facilitate the construction of national identities. Wodak et al. identify three components of discourse and textual analysis: thematic contents, strategies, and linguistic means and forms of realization (p. 30).

Contents can be viewed as the meaning-making sources for the discourse of national identity. Wodak et al. (2009) identify the following thematic contents:

1. The linguistic construction of the homo *Austriacus*
2. The narration and confabulation of a common political past
3. The linguistic construction of common culture
4. The linguistic construction of common political present and future

5. The linguistic construction of a "national body" (p. 30)

Similar to Billig's (1995) study, these thematic contents outlined by Wodak et al. (2009) are based on a study of an established nation-state, Austria. When studying the identity of stateless people, one expects the above list to be modified accordingly. For example, whereas language in Wodak et al. is treated as only one part of culture, in the case of the Kurds, language needs to be viewed as one of the most important identity markers. Since Austria shares its language with another national identity, Germany, it is not surprising that language is not on top of the list. Whereas language in the case of Austria is a sign of similarity with the "Other," in the case of the Kurds, language is perceived to be the most salient sign of difference with Turks, Persians, and Arabs, the three dominant ethnic groups in the states where Kurds reside. Thus, the thematic contents, or what can be called meaning resources for discourse of national identity, for this study have been modified as follows (for further details, see Appendix 1):

1. The discursive construction of a common past and history
2. The discursive construction of a collective and shared present and future
3. The discursive construction of a common language
4. The discursive construction of national symbols and "invented traditions"
5. The discursive construction of a common culture
6. The discursive construction of a common territory

The thematic contents upon which discourses of identity draw are packaged through strategies.[2] National identity discourses employ a number of strategies to represent and materialize the semantic areas in terms of language and other discursive means (e.g., images). Wodak et al. identify the following macro-strategies: constructive, perpetuating, transformational, and destructive. Constructive strategies refer to the attempts aimed at constructing and establishing "a certain national identity by promoting unification, identification and solidarity, as well as differentiation" (p. 33). Perpetuating strategies "attempt to maintain and to reproduce a threatened national identity, i.e., to preserve, support and protect it" (p. 33). This involves strategies of justification, which are "employed primarily in relation to problematic actions or events in the past which are important in the narrative creation of national history" (p. 33). Transformational strategies "aim to transform a relatively well-established national identity and its components into another identity the contours of which the speaker has already conceptualised" (ibid.).

Finally, destructive strategies "aim at dismantling or disparaging parts of an existing national identity construct, but usually cannot provide any new model to replace the old one" (p. 33).

The last dimension of Wodak et al.'s analytical framework is means and forms of realization (2009, p. 35). Although the study acknowledges that the list is by no means complete, the focus is on lexical units and syntactic devices that "serve to construct unification, unity, sameness, difference, uniqueness, origin, continuity, gradual or abrupt change, autonomy, heteronomy and so on" (p. 35). Similar to Billig (1995), Law (2001), and Higgins (2004), Wodak et al. (2009) underscore deixis (personal, spatial, and temporal references) as "the most important" linguistic devices of national identity discourse.[3] In addition to deixis, they pay close attention to euphemisms, linguistic slips, metaphors, rhetorical questions, passive versus active voice, agency and personification (pp. 35–42). This study uses a selection of these analytical tools (See Appendix 1).

Among the findings in Wodak et al. (2009) the following are particularly important for this study. First, national identities are engendered and reproduced through discourses. The study, however, reiterates that the formation of national identities is not exclusively discursive. In substantial ways, extra-discursive (e.g., institutional and material social) structures influence the way national identities are constructed. For example, Wodak et al. confirms Higgins's (2004) findings that political functions and affiliations of both the addressers and the addressees could affect the kind of national identity that is imagined and projected (Wodak et al., 2009, pp. 188–189). Second, the study demonstrates that "there is no such thing as *one* national identity in an essentialist sense" (p. 186, emphasis in original). Discourses of national identity are susceptible to the context within which they are formed, negotiated, and disseminated. Context here refers to the extent to which a discourse is exposed publicly, the situation and mode of the exposure and the addressees, among other things (pp. 186–187). For example, the study shows that, whereas the public discourse of Austrian national identity does not excludes minorities, the semi-public and quasi-private interviews (e.g., individual interviews) excluding ethnic minorities, in the sense of not considering them as "Austrians," is a "constitutive element of national identity" (p. 192). Third, the study highlights the importance of intertextual connections (p. 189). Some examples are:

> literal repetitions of passages from commemorative addresses and text extracts from books and articles by historians, political scientists and

essayists, and hackneyed formulations transferred from the areas of politics and the media into semi-public formulations transferred from the areas of public and the media into semi-public and quasi-private areas (recontextualisations). (p. 189)

Fourth, the study shows that Austrians perceive their language to be an important feature of their national identity (p. 193). Since they realize their language is also German, similar to their neighbor, Germany, Austrians tended to emphasize the differences between the two varieties of German. Most Austrians also wanted to distinguish themselves from Germany, especially in relation to the "common Nazi past" (p. 192). Assigning such importance to language in defining national identity is in line with most prominent theories of language and national identity (Edwards, 2009; Fishman, 1989; Joseph, 2004; Kymlicka & Patten, 2003).

Fifth, the study illustrates that the discourse of an Austrian national identity encompasses both state-based and culture-based (*Staatsnation* and *Kulturnation*) features of national identity. State-based features include citizenship, the country's social and economic progress, and its "neutrality" (Wodak et al., 2009, p. 190). Culture-based features include culture, sport, language, and "a frequently invoked 'Austrian mentality', and 'typical Austrian ways of behaviour'" (p. 190). Wodak et al.'s final finding compares the discursive identity constructs produced by the politicians and media elites, on the one hand, and the semi-public and quasi private situation, on the other. The study concludes that

> the discursive national identification "products" offered by these political and media élites to their targeted audiences was influenced partly by the demand of these target groups for images to reinforce their national confidence. At the same time, these élites endeavoured to satisfy such demands for national identity, at times by creating, emphasising, or—as illustrated by the myth of permanent neutrality— by playing down particular features of this identity. (p. 202)

Put differently, the discourses of the elites, including media, not only reinforce the national identity that is desired by the public, but they also modify, reshape, and rearticulate that identity.

Focusing on the discursive identity constructs promulgated by the media elites is more prominent in Billig (1995) and other works that have drawn upon that study. Billig introduces the term banal nationalism "to cover the ideological habits which enable the established nations of the West to be reproduced" (p. 6). Refuting the suggestions of some observers that the age of nationalism in the West is over, Billig argues that the ideological habits of banal nationalism are embedded in the daily lives of the citizenry to the extent that albeit quietly but persistently and effectively "the nation is indicated, or 'flagged'" (p. 6). Billig illustrates that different kinds of British newspapers, right or left wing, spreadsheet or tabloids, discursively and symbolically "flag" the nation and homeland daily. Banal nationalism, in contrast to "hot" or "ethnic nationalism," often

> operates with prosaic, routine words, which take nations for granted, and which, in so doing, inhabit them. Small words, rather than grand memorable phrases, offer constant, but barely conscious, reminders of the homeland, making 'our' national identity unforgettable. (p. 59)

For example, both journalists and politicians quoted in the newspapers use, reinforce, and redefine the word "nation" constantly (p. 116). The nation is often reproduced through the use of non-designated nouns such as "the nation," "the country," "the region." These flag the British national identity as a given, a context within which the daily life is carried out. In contrast, 'other' places and nations are explicitly identified, for example the United States, France and so on.

This routine reproduction of national identity is also, and more frequently, carried out by deixis, encompassing some of "the most basic things we do with utterances" to point at things, people, spaces, and time (Yule, 1996, p. 9). Some examples of deixis are "here" versus "there" (spatial), "we" versus "they" (personal), and "now" versus "then" (temporal). According to Fowler (1991), deixis "links a text with the time and place of communication and with the participants, which 'orient' speaker and addressee to the context of the discourse" (p. 93). Billig (1995) shows that in newspapers, for example, editorials routinely use the syntax of hegemony and unity by using words like "we" and "us," which encompass not only the paper, the writers, and the readers, but also the entire "nation" (pp. 114–115). The discourse of the media, according to Billig (1995), presents England as the homeland, center of the continent of Europe, and the nation to be appreciated by its citizens. He observes that when reporting the weather, papers display a map of Europe with England placed in the center, and in this way, emphasize the prominence of the "homeland" (p. 117). The nation is "here" and the rest of the world is "there."

Billing (1995) observes that focusing on and validating the nation and homeland is also achieved by the national news coverage, compared to international stories in the British press (p. 117). Whereas focus on the national news could flag the nation, national identity could also be reinforced through foreign news coverage. Home news (ours) is always more than the international (theirs). Thus, a "'biased' interest in 'ourselves'" is reinforced (p. 84). Other studies have come to the same conclusion. For example, a study of the Greek newspapers' coverage of the Macedonian question in 1992–1993 shows that the Greek press contributed to the flourishing of Greek nationalism by adapting an ethnocentric outlook towards the foreign news (Demertzis, Papathanassopoulos & Armenakis, 1999; also see Chouliaraki, 1999).

Billig's research further demonstrates that whereas the flagging of the nation concerning the editorials and the news sections of the press is implicit, when it comes to the sports section, the national flag is waved quite explicitly. Bishop and Jaworski (2003), analyzing news reporting in the British press of a soccer game between England and Germany, also conclude that sport reportage in the British press formulates English nationalism and reproduces the nation-state as a sovereign and homogeneous entity. This unified entity, in turn, constrains the behavior of its citizens within the boundaries defined by the values and the ideology of nationalism.

Bishop and Jaworski (2003) identify three strategies used by the British press to reproduce English national identity: separation, conflict, and typification. Separation refers to the rhetoric of "us" versus "them" through which self-representation is contrasted with other-negative-representation. The differences between "us" and "them" is intensified through the portrayal of war imagery. Through the use of a military metaphoric language, past animosities between Germany and Britain are invoked and "our" nation's victories are glorified to say that we have to "beat'em" again. Finally, typification strategy reproduces the nation as both homogeneous and timeless. Through the use of modals with high probability, a national future is projected, as in these examples: "there *will* always be an Ingerland," or, "[the England's victory] was a moment to savour and one which, while it may not lead to England winning this competition, *will* be remembered for years to come" (p. 255, my emphasis). This way, the continuity and eternity of the nation is heralded. Similar observations have been made in different parts of the world, for example in Turkey (Kösebalaban, 2004), where the Turkish press's sports reportage has been investigated for its discursive practices in reproducing a collective national identity. Replicating Billig's methodology, Yumul and Uzkirimli (2000) have further researched the Turkish newspapers' sports coverage. They have concluded that "the discourse used by the Turkish press is crammed with the constituent elements of the nationalist ideology" (p. 15).

Law (2001) and Higgins (2004), investigating the Scottish press and Scottish national identity, primarily draw upon Billig's study, and confirm the importance of deixis in reproducing national identities in Scotland. However, they make several useful observations in relation to Billig's study. Law observes that "unlike banal British national-ism, able to sink around England vitally unnoticed in the shadows of deixis, national identity in Scotland is more explicitly enunciated" (p. 314). I expect this to be the case with Kurdish identity as well, since Kurdistan, similar to Scotland, more or less, is a stateless nation. This compels Law (2001) to call for a revision to Billig's approach when applied to stateless nations (p. 300). In the case of Scotland and Kurdistan, in addition to the small words, one also needs to look for the more obvious and discernible symbols and discursive practices of national identity.

Unlike Law (2001), Higgins (2004) wants to find out "what dis-tinctions may be made between" Scots (p. 466), instead of looking for commonalities among them. Investigating several Scottish newspa-pers' coverage of 1999 elections for the Scottish parliament, Higgins analyzes the language choices of the papers in naming the location of the elections, for example, Britain versus Scotland. He concludes that "various newspapers engage in particular textual strategies of articu-lating nation and politics, based upon a politically charged distinction between Scotland and Britain" (p. 469). Thus, Higgins highlights the influence of media's political affiliations on their discourse of national identity. The findings show that the newspapers' stance on the constitutional arrangement between Britain and Scotland at the time (whether they favored the mutual arrangement as opposed to total independence for Scotland) seemed to determine the tex-tual choices made in the papers with respect to naming locations. A valuable outcome of this study, especially for studying Kurdish media, is that lexical choices and other discursive practices related to national identity are often politically and ideologically charged. Thus, it will be interesting to see if the discourse of the Kurdish TV sta-tion under investigation names locations the same way or differently. It is well known in the political circles that the Patriotic Union of Kurdistan (PUK), the Kurdish party affiliated with the current Iraqi president, Jalal Talabani, avoids indications of separating Kurdistan from Iraq. Conversely, KDP, which is affiliated with Masoud Barzani, the president of Kurdistan Iraq, portrays itself as more nationalist, more Kurdistani[4] and less Iraqi. It will be interesting to see whether these different political positions are reaffirmed in the TV stations' discursive identity constructs.

These studies (i.e., Bishop & Jaworski, 2003; Law, 2001; Higgins, 2004), in their own ways, confirm Wodak's (2006b) assertion that "discourses serve to construct national identities" (p. 112). The place of language and discourse in the construction of national identity is well explicated by Billig (1995): "an identity is to be found in the embodied habits of social life. Such habits include ways of thinking and using *language. To have a national identity is to possess ways of talking about nationhood*" (p. 8, my emphasis). Possessing "ways of talking about nationhood" can mean at least two things. First, it means as Fishman (1989) says, that "nationalist beliefs, like all societally patterned beliefs, are language dependent" (p. 287). In other words, defining one's identity and its continuous remaking is done through language, not entirely of course, but in very significant ways. Second, "possessing ways of talking of nationhood" also means having access to ways of producing and disseminating discursive constructs of national identities, for example, having access to mass communication technologies. As Michael Mann has suggested, if an ideology, such as nationalism, is "to spread, [it] must be organized through specific channels of communication" (as cited in Spencer & Wollman, 2002, p. 47).

Billig (1995) and other studies discussed here have underscored the crucial role of communication technologies in the formation, reproduction, and articulation of national identities. These studies, however, have been more concerned with the language, messages, and contents of the media rather than their technological characteristics per se. As I will discuss in the next section, focusing on both aspects of media is important because identity discursive constructs of a stateless people are mostly shaped and distributed through communication technologies. Among the most important technologies are satellite television and the Internet, for reasons that I will present shortly.

Media and the Articulation of Discourses of Identity

Traditional Media as the "Architect of Nationalism"

Contrary to Billig (1995), Wodak et al. (2009), and other researchers with a discourse analytical orientation reviewed in the previous section, some prominent scholars have deemed mass media of communication as important in the emergence of nationalism and formation of national identities, not because of their content but because of their technical characteristics or their forms (Deutsch, 1966; McLuhan, 1962, 1964; Gellner, 1983). For these scholars, communication technologies enable people from far away distances to connect and interact, regardless of their messages. This interaction, over time, especially when it is in the same language, brings about commonality, unity, homogeneity or sameness, and, finally, loyalty to a collective entity, the nation.

McLuhan (1962, 1964) posited that print technology was the architect of "nationalism" in Western Europe and gave birth to the nation in a deterministic way: "What we call 'nations' did not and could not precede the advent of Gutenberg technology" (McLuhan, 1962, p. ix). Traces of this claim can be found in the writings of Innis (1951): "By the end of the sixteenth century the flexibility of the alphabet and printing had contributed to the growth of diverse vernacular literatures and had provided a basis for divisive nationalism in Europe" (p. 55).[5]

McLuhan (1964) speculated that printing turned vernaculars into an "extensive mass medium" (p. 177) that engendered homogenization in the sense of being able to communicate in one single code or language. Because print fostered "uniformity" and then "repeatability" of such unified forms, it prompted the standardization of vernaculars by codifying the spelling, syntax, and pronunciation of vernaculars of the masses (p. 175). As a result of printing, "visual images of group destiny and status" (p. 177), started to disperse with unprecedented speed over vast territories (p. 177). Because these images were in the same code[6] for a large group of people living on the same territory, they fostered commonalities and similarities. This, according to McLuhan, resulted in "political unification," centralization, and, thus, the establishment of nation-states (p. 175).

Aside from the social and cultural effects, print also caused significant political changes. According to McLuhan, as products of "the printed book and the printed page, uniformity and repeatability gave to the political ruler a new instrument of centralism and homogeneity" (1960, p. 571). Within the boundaries of the vernacular, the ruler could use printed materials to spread the same information to different corners, and this enabled him to mobilize the population. Since nationalism has often been identified as a political and, at the same time, mass movement (Gellner, 1983; Smith, 1998), this capability of printing must have been crucial in the success of the nationalism project. The printed words, as also noted by Anderson (1991), brought about fraternity and loyalty to a common sovereign, something that nationalism is meant to achieve. It is from this perspective that McLuhan sees nationalism as the child of print.

McLuhan's perspective, which attributes a direct causal role to media, for example print, as the creator of nationalism, has been identified as "technological determinism." McLuhan's "technological determinism," which suggests that a technology on its own can be the cause of social change apart from social, economic, political, or institutional workings of that technology, may have not been all that convincing to scholars of nationalism (e.g., Deutsch, 1966; Gellner, 1983; Anderson, 1991;[7] Smith, 1998; Hobsbawm, 1990) or of cultural studies (Williams, 1974, pp. 126–134). However, his famous saying, "the medium is the message," has enjoyed popularity with commentators on the relationship between media and nationalism. For example, Gellner (1983), who unlike McLuhan adopts a socio-economic approach to nationalism and the invention of the nation, sounds unmistakably McLuhanian when he comments on the role of modern communication technology with regards to nationalism:

> The media do not transmit an idea which happens to have been fed into them. It matters precious little what has been fed into them: it is the media themselves, the pervasiveness and importance of abstract, centralized, standardized, one to many communication, which itself automatically engenders the core idea of nationalism, quite irrespective of what in particular is being put into the specific messages transmitted. (p. 127)

This position of Gellner can be traced back to one of McLuhan's most famous sayings which was written about 20 years earlier: "The medium is the message," which more closely resembles another statement by Gellner: "The most important and persistent message is generated by the medium itself" (Gellner, 1983, p. 127).[8] Both scholars believe that the content of media, the messages they carry, should matter very little, because, as Gellner contends, "the 'content' of any medium blinds us to the characteristics of the medium" (p. 9; see also Deutsch, 1966, p. 90).

However, there is clearly more to the media than their technological attributes, namely the messages they disseminate. For example, Connor (1994) observes that ethnic consciousness in most of the world "involves not the nature or density of the communication media, but the message" (p. 38). The idea of "self-determination" is an example in point. Although this idea goes back to the mid-nineteenth century, it started to be viewed as a "universal truth" after the Second World War when it was publicized to mean that "any self-differentiating people, simply because it is a people, has the right, should it so desire, to rule itself" (p. 38). The idea, as Connor sees it, has been a "catalyst" for "ethnic" nationalist movements: "The spreading of effective communications has had an evident impact upon ethnic consciousness, but the full impact of the communications media did not precede the message of self-determination" (p. 39). Thus, one can suggest that in the projects of creating national identities, mass media of communication are important because they carry messages that inject new ideas and values or reinforce old myths and memories, which can instigate national awareness, start or intensify nationalist movements, or preserve and reconstruct national identities.

In addition to privileging the technological aspect of media over their contents, traditional conceptualizations of the place of media in projects of nationalism have tended to privilege print over other forms of communication (Smith, 1998). Even in the era of tremendous technological advances (e.g., radio, television, satellite, Internet) Anderson (1991) only briefly alludes to television in his major work on nations and nationalism: "advances in communications technology, especially radio and television, give print allies unavailable a century ago. Multilingual broadcasting can conjure up the imagined community to illiterates and populations with different mother-tongues" (p. 135).[9] What seems to be evident to Anderson is that the electronic media are only new allies for print rather than being media capable of doing what print has done, namely facilitating the standardization of languages, engendering horizontal comradeship, and creating mass audiences who could simultaneously experience and imagine belonging to the same collective identity called the nation. It is, however, important to note Anderson's appreciation for the significance of the new media among the "illiterates and populations with different mother-tongues." Although he sees new media as only good to "conjure up," not to imagine or create the community that is already imagined supposedly by print, it can point one to the right direction: focusing on the significance of electronic media in the processes of constructing and maintaining national identities.

Electronic Media as New Communicative Spaces

According to McLuhan (1962), whereas print gave birth to nationalism, electronic media would go against it: "What we call 'nations' did not and could not precede the advent of Gutenberg technology any more than they can survive the advent of *electric circuitry with its power of totally involving all people in other people*" (p. ix, my emphasis, also see McLuhan, 1964, p. 67). In recent years, too, some scholars have seen electronic media at the forefront of cultural globalization (e.g., Appadurai, 1996). Although the connection between globalization and electronic media cannot be denied, it has also been suggested that the same technologies, in different contexts, have been fostering the articulation of regional and national identities (Drummond, Paterson & Willis, 1993; Fisk & Hartley, 2003; Hartley, 2004; Hassanpour, 2003a, 1998; Morley, 2004, 1992; Price, 1995; Thussu, 2000; Yoshimi, 2003). The multilayered connection of cable and satellite television with globalization, nationalism, and regionalism is well captured in this quote from Straubhaar (2002):

> Overall, within an increasingly internationalized world of television, we find a fairly compelling argument for looking at global, regional and national levels fairly equally...Now the new technologies of cable and satellite television present a new level of globalization, simultaneous global exposure to some channels delivered by satellite. These media also present an equal if not larger opportunity for a new level of regionalization, channels targeted at geolinguistic groups across national borders. (p. 202)

Thussu (2000, p. 168) believes that television is essential to what Stuart Hall has called "global mass culture" and suggests that "this mass culture may be influencing the way people think about their regional or national identities, as they are increasingly exposed to global, which in most part are American, messages" (p. 168). In other words, the concern seems to be over the domination of a homogenous American culture and the withering away of other national and regional identities. In 1996, 82 percent of webpages in the world were in English (Warschauer, 2000, p. 156), and this led to some premature predictions that, as a result of this overwhelming domination by English, thousands of languages will be lost. It is, however, estimated that in the first decade of 2000s, the percentage of English webpages will decrease from 80 percent to 40 percent (p. 156).[10] According to Warschauer (2000),

> the Net is now growing fastest in developing countries...Web browsers are being adapted for an increasing number of languages and character sets. Thus, while Internet users around the world still must use English for global communication, today they are increasingly turning to their own language to reach websites or join discussion in their own country or region. (p. 157)

Smith (1998) suggests that "the electronic media serve to rein-force old ethnic identities or encourage the (re-)creation of new ones" (p. 215). For example, studies of ethnic communities in diasporas have shown that the new electronic media, such as satellite television, can in important ways "enhance and consolidate subcultural identities based on location, ethnicity…language and nationality" (Naficy, 1993, p. xvi). Further, the nationalist movements of minorities, such as Kurds, whose demands for cultural or political autonomy often have been silenced within the borders of the nation-states in which they live (van Bruinessen, 2000a; McDowall, 2004), have been altered in important ways because of the utilization of these media (Erikson, 2007; Romano, 2002; Ryan, 1997). Of the new media that are believed to facilitate the processes of identity and community formation, satel-lite television and the Internet have enjoyed most attention.

Television
Television has become an integrated part of both theoretical and empirical investigations into the constructing, reproducing, and sus-taining of collective identities concerning different parts of the world and at different levels of global, regional, or local. Within the nation-state context, Hartley, in 1978, suggested that "television…is one of the prime sites upon which a given nation is constructed for its mem-bers" (p. 124, as cited in Morley, 1992, p. 267). During the 1990s and 2000s, the significance of television broadcasting in the pro-cesses of defining and changing national identities has been reiterated (Ashuri, 2005; Drummond et al., 1993; Griffiths, 1993; Madianou, 2005; Price, 1995).

Ashuri (2005), for example, illustrates that television networks from different countries, when attempted to produce documenta-ries of the same "global" story, ended up framing the event within the discourses of their own national identities. The most globalized stories in the media are often nationalized so that they might reso-nate with national audiences and also fit the hegemonic national dis-course. As Martin and Wodak (2003) have observed, "media produce and reproduce ideologies, beliefs and also histories. Elites depend on the media, and the media are used for the construction of histories and the past" (p. 11). It is usually within the frame of the nation, in the eyes and ears of the national audiences, that narratives of the past can turn into shared memories.

In another study, Griffiths (1993), focusing on a Welsh soap opera on television, looks into the "ideological effect" of this TV produc-tion in "offering definitions and re-definitions of a 'Welshness' and contributing to (re)formations of cultural identity" (p. 9). He finds that textually the program serves the definition and re-making of Welshness. Further, audiences' reflections on their viewing experience of the program indicate "a sense of national pride and desire for cultural autonomy" (p. 22). Investigating the ways in which television mediates national identity construction in Greece, Madianou (2005) analyzed 473 news stories. The author observes that "the nation, the common 'we', is continually invoked both through the text and the form of the news" (p. 5). In addition to conducting a qualitative analysis of the news, Madianou conducts interviews with audiences to investigate the ways in which viewers interpret the news and draw on the contents and themes of the news to articulate their own identities. Underscoring the different interpretations of the discourse of identity among audiences due to a variety of factors such as ethnic background, age, class, and gender, Madianou makes two crucial observations. First, she reports that "most interviewees [audiences] challenged the national in the news and the dominant identity discourses it projected" (p. 131). This rejects the assumption that banal nationalism in the established nations is too implicit and at the same time has permeated the society for too long and in too many ways to be contested (Billig, 1995). Second, and in line with the previous finding, Madianou observes that discourses of national identity are not monolithic and unvarying (p. 139). This is not to suggest that people can switch their identity from Greeks to Turks overnight, but it means that identities are always in making, and they are, to various degrees, susceptible to change (Wodak et al., 2009).

Drummond et al. (1993) suggest that since television discourse is the site of identity negotiations, television production and programs provide a convenient context for studying and understanding the ways in which the new identities (European, national, and ethnic) are defined, are changing, and are coexisting. By extension, one could suggest that discursive practices of Kurdish television can be convenient contexts for studying the ways in which Kurdish identity is articulated. However, for the Kurds and many other minorities who do not have an easy access to cable television, it might be more appropriate to focus on satellite television.

If there has been a strong connection between print and television and national identity in Europe, there might be a similar, if not a stronger, connection between satellite television and national identities among peoples without states (see also, Hartley, 2004; Jones, 2007; Cormack & Hourigan, 2007; Lysaght, 2009). The Kurds, for example, have better and easier access to satellite television than print or even cable television. One of the main reasons is that satellite television can cross borders of nation-states more freely, since the messages and images it disseminates cannot be easily prevented from reaching potential audiences. Investigating the utilization of a satellite television, Med TV, by the Kurds from Turkey, Hassanpour suggests:

> As an audiovisual medium, television is more effective than radio and print media [in the practices of centralizing political power and nation-building]. Televisual messages generally cross the social boundaries of illiteracy, language, regionalism, age, gender, and religion. Combining visuality with sound and language, both spoken and written, television is a powerful vehicle for creating national culture and identity. (1998, p. 53)

As Poster posits, "digital information may be transported without regard to the posts the nation established to monitor and control its movement" (Poster, 1999, p. 235). This way, satellite television technology fosters cross-border reproduction and formation of cultural artifacts, including discursive constructs of national identities. Unlike print, radio, or cable television, satellite television has, not entirely but in significant ways, overcome the political constraints that nation-state or majority nationalism imposes on discursive practices of minority identities. For example, Kurdish audiences in Turkey, who had their language banned for decades, and still cannot freely broadcast in their language, have been able to receive television programs beamed at their homes from Europe since 1995 (Hassanpour, 2003a, 1998; Karim, 1998; Price, 2001; Ryan, 1997).[11]

Internet
Similar to satellite television, the Internet is also endowed with this quality of disrespect for nation-state borders. Further, utilization of the Internet among the minorities and diasporic communities tends to be more common than satellite television. The main reason is that the Internet is more accessible. Karim (2003) states:

> The extensive use by diasporic groups of online services like the Internet...is allowing for relatively easy connections of members of communities residing in various continents. As opposed to the broadcast model of communication which, apart from offering little access to minority groups, is linear, hierarchical and capital-intensive, online media allow easier access and are non-linear, largely non-hierarchical and relatively cheaper. (p. 13)

The Internet is more accessible than other types of broadcast media such as print, cable, and satellite television. Several years later, this observation is still applicable. However, a few points can be added here. First, in many parts of the developing world, the majority of people do not use the Internet. For example, Bargh and McKenna (2004) report that, "in 2001, only 1 in 250 people in Africa was an Internet user" (p. 574). Limited use of the Internet has also been reported among diasporic communities, such as the Salvadoran immigrants in the Washington, D.C., area (Benítez, 2006). Benítez identifies several factors that could contribute to this condition, such as "level of education, technological skills, family and cultural capital as well as the socio-economic conditions in the local economic structure" (p. 195). In a similar vein, Ackah and Newman (2003) report on the scarce use of the Internet among the members of a Ghanaian diaspora. They suggest that "the assumption that ICTS inherently will be beneficial certainly cannot be taken for granted" (p. 207).

Notwithstanding these difficulties with respect to accessing the Internet, many commentators have found the Internet more accessible to those groups and individuals whose access to traditional communication technologies such as print and television for various reasons (e.g., financial and political) is limited. The use of the Internet for producing and distributing information is relatively cheap, but at the same time it can be done much more freely since the medium is not so easy to control or regulate. Anyone who wants to and has the technical means (e.g., access to a computer and Internet service) can produce or/and retrieve a tremendous amount of information. The point here is not to praise the Internet as an agent of social change, a position akin to technological determinism, but to simply say that it is cheap, and it bypasses state or market regulations and constraints (Poster, 1999).

Being more accessible than the more traditional media, the Internet provides the social space for dissenting voices, particularly those of individuals and smaller groups (Mautner, 2005, p. 813) that might be different from the voices of the states, commercial enterprises, mainstream media, and political parties (see also Bargh & McKenna, 2004, p. 573). As Hargreaves suggests, "what we are witnessing here is the emergence . . . of the voices of those who have previously been unheard, neglected, rejected, ignored—the voices of those who have been marginalized and disposed" (as cited in Almasude, 1999, p. 117; see Bernal, 2006; Cunliffe, 2007; Danet & Herring, 2007; Honeycutt & Cunliffe, 2010; Muhamad-Brandner, 2009).

One of the first dissenting voices amplified on the Internet was that of the Zapatistas in Chiapas, Mexico, in the mid-19990s (Castells, 1997; Knudson, 1998). According to Castells, "[t]he Zapatistas ability to communicate [primarily through the Internet] with the world, and with Mexican society, and to capture the imagination of people and of intellectuals, propelled a local, weak insurgent group to the forefront of world politics" (p. 79). Everyone may not believe in a deterministic role of the Internet in any social movement, including that of the Chiapas. However, many analysts have praised this utilization of the Internet as a progressive development, not just because it helped a minority's voice to be heard but also because it helped the Zapatistas to shed more ink than blood in making themselves heard and having their indigenous rights recognized (Knudson, 1998).

Another minority group that has managed to utilize the Internet to its advantage is the Imazighen people from North Africa (Almasude, 1999).[12] According to Almasude, prior to the 1990s and the use of the Internet, the Imazighen demands for the recognition of their distinct cultural and linguistic identity were largely ignored internally (e.g., in Morocco) and were unheard of internationally. However, according to the author, with the establishing of the first online Amazigh forums in 1992, "the Amazigh cause took an international dimension," and the Imazighen in Morocco, Algeria, Tunisia, and Mali joined voices to articulate their distinct identity and started "to perceive themselves as one community" (p. 124). Only then, according to Almasude, did North African countries start to recognize Imazighen as a distinct cultural identity and respect their distinct language; they were pressured to do so after the utilization of the computer technology by the Imazighen.

The Internet has been credited with accommodating the revitalization of other minority languages, for example, Hawaiian indigenous languages (Warschauer, 2001, 2000). According to Warschauer, "the Internet is proving to be effective for linking together learners of minority languages and is being used extensively in language revitalisation programs in Hawaii and elsewhere" (2001, p. 58). According to Warschauer (2000), "Hawaiian-language computing took on an important symbolic value, allowing them to say to themselves and to the world that they are Hawaiian and proud of it" (p. 167). At the same time, the Internet seems to be a fertile ground for the growth of English as an international language, since it is the language used the most on the Internet (Crystal, 1997). While fostering the development of a *lingua franca* (i.e., English) for business and professional communication at the international level, the Internet has also facilitated personal communication in the mother-tongue and local speech varieties.[13] For example, Warschauer (2001) observes that Egyptian professionals conduct most of their email communication in English, even among themselves, but they switch to the Egyptian colloquial Arabic (as opposed to Standard Arabic, which is formal) when it comes to face-to-face communication (pp. 54–55). Thus, the Internet has provided the means to access the language of power (i.e., English), and, at the same time, it has fostered the language of the soul and the self to express one's individual identity and feelings of belonging to collective and group identities. In other words, the Internet has provided a social space for resisting the homogeneity of English and other dominant languages.

Dissenting voices have used the Internet also to reveal the multiplicity and hybridity of national identities, and to question and contest the nationalist discourse of the status quo, which presents national identity as uniform and homogenous. An example of this kind of dissenting voices is described in Chan's (2005) study of the use of the Internet by Chinese workers and immigrants in Singapore. She observes that the Internet provides a liminal space for the Chinese in Singapore to oppose various discourses of national identities perpetuated from the homeland, such as "the hegemonic discourse of state as nation," "the pan-Chinese identity," and "the dominant Han national identity" (p. 362). They also reject the marginalization practices directed at them in the host country, Singapore. These Chinese immigrants and workers cultivate a national identity discourse that they prefer, which is different from both the Chinese and the Singaporean states. Their online activities enable them "to produce an online imaginary of China as a superpower and an empire" (p. 362), which could compensate for China's current weakness. Such a fanaticized China could not only stand up to the hegemony of another superpower, the United States, but also to the marginalizing and "disciplining practices" of the host country.

In summary, both satellite television and the Internet provide communicative spaces for the articulation of identities, spaces that to a large extent cannot be controlled and regulated by the states and powerful commercial enterprises. These media amplify dissenting but otherwise unheard or ignored voices (Sheyholislami, 2009a; see also, Seib, 2007). However, I have tried to highlight a difference, among others, between the two technologies. Production on the Internet, notwithstanding its technological challenges, is much cheaper than television. For example, among the minorities such as the Kurds, it is only the most powerful political parties that can operate a satellite television station. But, almost every individual, small groups, and alternative voices can access the Internet, not only as recipients of information, which is often the case with television, but also as producers and distributors of information. Individuals and marginal groups can use the Internet to contest dominant nationalist discourse of states or political parties and to construct their own cultural or individual identities. It is important to see if discourses of Kurdishness disseminated on the Internet by individuals and small groups are different from those of the satellite television stations that are owned by the dominant Kurdish political parties. If there are differences, it is important to see what the implications of these differences might be for the processes of Kurdish identity constructions.

An Interdisciplinary Approach to Media Discourse: CDA

It is both useful and productive to employ a discourse approach to the study of discursive identity construction as mediated by communication technologies. Such an approach encapsulates the notion that discourses serve the construction and maintenance of national identities (Wodak, 2006b). Since discursive practices of identity construction are at the forefront of nationalism projects (Billig, 1995), a discourse approach can provide an understanding of the discoursal aspects of nationalist ideologies and nationalist discourses. A discourse approach is also useful in investigating the place of the media in the articulation and circulation of discourses of identities. As Mcdonald (2003) suggests, "discourse acknowledges more readily than other analytical concepts that the media are now at the best partial originators of ideas and values" (p. 2). The use of the term media discourse (the combination of the two terms discourse and media) signals the fact that there is much more to media than their technological characteristics and forms. Such an approach emphasizes the idea that the importance of the media is owed as much to the content and messages they disseminate as to their technological characteristics (Madianou, 2005). A discourse approach also sets it apart from a top-down or a hypodermic needle model approach to media, the view that media are all powerful and capable of influencing weak audiences in manipulating ways. Finally, a discourse analytical approach to media enables analysts to map relations both between and across various media.

The type of discourse approach that has been employed in this study is called Critical Discourse Analysis (CDA) (van Dijk, 2001; Fairclough & Wodak, 1997; Luke, 2002; Wodak, 2006a), a type of discourse analysis that takes the view that discourse is a social practice, is simultaneously constitutive of and constituted by social structures, relations, and identities, and is ideological. Language and other semiotic elements (e.g., images) not only represent the world, realities, and identities but also contribute to their formation and maintenance. One of the areas that CDA has addressed is construction and reproduction of national identities (Billig, 1995; Ricento, 2003; Wodak et al., 2009; Wodak, 2006b). From a CDA perspective, national identities are reflected and articulated in the use of language and discourse, and at the same time, they are constructed, shaped, and sustained through discursive practices, including those of the media. CDA is not a unified and single theory or methodology (Bell & Garret, 1998; Martin & Wodak, 2003); it is, rather, an interdisciplinary (Weiss & Wodak, 2003), multidisciplinary, or transdisciplinary (Chouliaraki & Fairclough, 1999) approach to discourse, in general, and language use, in particular. CDA is interdisciplinary in that it blends social theories with theories of language and discourse. It aims to make transparent the link between language/discourse and the social. This objective stems from the assumption that what is happening socially happens linguistically and no linguistic use happens outside the social (p. 113). According to Chouliaraki and Fairclough (1999), CDA facilitates a dialogue between various social and linguistic theories (p. 16). Thus, they see a CDA theory as "a shifting synthesis of other theories," and continue to suggest that what CDA "itself theorises in particular is the mediation between the social and the linguistic" (p. 16). From this perspective, CDA is useful in combining theories of nationalism and national identities, discourse and media, the three main areas with which this study is concerned. A CDA approach to the study of identity construction is specifically helpful in exploring *how* identities are constructed, *who* construct them and *why* they are constructed.

Now, I will outline the CDA framework that I have found useful in the study of media discourse (Fairclough, 1995b). From a CDA perspective, media discourse "is a recontextualizing principle for appropriating other discourses and bringing them into a special relation with each other for the purposes of their dissemination and mass consumption" (Chouliaraki, 1999, p. 39). Fairclough's (1995b) framework for analyzing "communicative events" such as media discourse consists of three interrelated parts:

- Text (verbal language, images and other textual elements)
- Discourse practices (processes of producing, disseminating, receiving and interpreting texts)

- Sociocultural practices (social, historical, and political contexts and processes that bear upon the production and consumption of media texts)

According to Fairclough (1995b), showing, or attempting to show, systematic links between text, discourse practices, and sociocultural practices constitutes discourse analysis (pp. 16–17). Systematic links between these three parts of a communicative event are made by three kinds of analyses: description, interpretation, and explanation. Whereas description of the textual elements corresponds to the microanalysis of text, interpretation and explanation of the results of microanalysis correspond to macroanalysis.

Text: Microanalysis at the Text Level

Texts could be written, spoken, or multimodal (e.g., visual, music, sound), for instance in the case of television and the Internet. At the text (textual) level, discourse analysis involves detailed analysis of text properties. These properties could include linguistic elements (e.g., lexicon, grammar, sound, and accent) in the case of spoken and written text; images and graphics in the case of still images (Kress & van Leeuwen, 1996), camera shots, sound effects, voiceover, and music in the case of film or television (Iedema, 2000); and some or all of the above, depending on the text—for example, a multimodal web page, in the case of the Internet (Lemke, 2002). In order to illustrate the meaning-making potential of text properties, however, an analyst is not only concerned with multisemiotic elements that are present in a text but also with what has been implied. As van Dijk (1988) states, "what is not said may even be more important, from a critical point of view, than what is explicitly said or meant" (p. 17; see also Huckin, 2002).

Another important consideration that an analyst needs to keep in mind when dealing with multimodal texts is the meaning-making interplay between the verbal language and other semiosis (e.g., images). Engaging in textual analysis without considering the multimodality of texts, especially when dealing with modern advertising or television (Fairclough, 2001, p. 27) and the Internet (Lemke, 2002) is unrealistic and the effort may not be as productive as hoped for. According to Lemke, "the specificity and precision which is possible with an imagetext [—combination of verbal text and image—] is vastly greater than what is possible with text alone or with image alone" (p. 303).

Consideration of all the meaning-making semiosis in a text, however, bears its own challenges. The main challenge facing the analyst is "how…other semiotic modalities [such as images and music] interact with language in producing meanings, and how such interactions define different aesthetics for different media" (Fairclough, 1995b, p. 58). Kress and van Leeuwen (1996) suggest that "the visual component of a text is an independently organized and structured message—connected with the verbal text, but in no way dependent on it: and similarly the other way around" (p. 17). This means two things, at least. First, each semiotic mode (e.g., verbal language) has its own meaning-making potential and, thus, deserves distinct analysis. Second, despite being independently organized, the two modes of verbal and visual (and other modes, for that matter) are connected in the contents and meanings they carry. As Fairclough (2001) puts it, "very often visuals and 'verbals' operate in a mutually reinforcing way which makes them very difficult to disentangle" (p. 28). We need to keep in mind, as well, that sometimes the verbal part of a text may tell a different story from the visual aspect of the same text. Nonetheless, different modes of a text have meaning-making potentials in relation to each other. Different modes of a text may have two kinds of relations: elaborative or extensive (van Leeuwen, 2005, p. 77). The relation is elaborative when messages and content in one mode are restated in another mode for the purpose of explaining the content, exemplifying or summarizing it (p. 77). The relation between different modes is *extensive* when the content expressed in one mode is expanded and added to by another mode. Thus, the final verdict on the relationship between different modes of text (e.g., image, verbal, music) seems to be that while each has its own distinct meaning-making potential, and, as such, each deserves to be described and analyzed in its own terms, the final analysis of a text as a whole rests on explicating the connections between those modes and the ways they contextualize (Lemke, 2002, p. 322) each other and the ways they create a multimodal meaning-making system.

Discourse Practices

In addition to microanalysis, which involves detailed description of textual elements, there is also macroanalysis. Macroanalysis has two dimensions: discourse practices and sociocultural practices. The primary concern at the discourse practices level is with the ways texts are produced and consumed. It is based on the analyst's understanding of text production and consumption that the findings established at the micro level can be properly interpreted. For example, when discussing media discourse, we deal with texts that are distributed through communication technologies. The differences various media have in their channels of communication "have significant wider implications in terms of the meaning potential of the different media" (Fairclough, 1995b, p. 38). Having different meaning potential, primarily due to possessing different technological attributes, could result in having different impact on social behaviors and relations (Meyrowitz, 1985). Compared to print, television is much more personal, here and now, immediate, and with a much wider appeal and larger audience (Fairclough, 1995b, pp. 38–39). Compared to print, television allows for more human senses (e.g., audiovisual capability) to be involved in receiving messages, it enables information to travel much faster and relatively without much difficulty, and it allows for a much easier coding and decoding practices (Meyrowitz, 1985). While reading a written text requires one to be literate in a particular language and versed in the genre of the printed material, watching and following a television program requires no or very little skill. This is agreed upon by both proponents of medium theory (Meyrowitz, 1985) and its opponents (Williams, 1974). Although Williams does not share medium theory's proposition that media technologies can create social change apart from social, political, and economic forces, he still believes that "[i]f we can watch and listen to people in our immediate circle, we can watch and listen to television" (pp. 131–132).

Similar to satellite television, the Internet has also been among the ideal media for distributing texts that contribute to identity construction and reproduction at a transnational and cross-border level. One of the greatest features of the Internet is that it combines many features of the previous communication technologies in one single mass medium (Bargh & McKenna, 2004). It is interactive like the telephone (e.g., online messaging), it can be used for person-to-person communication like telegraph and letter writing (e.g., email), it is a mass medium and can reach millions of people simultaneously like radio and television, it can be a convenient place for publishing like the printing press, it can store and distribute texts and images like a great library, and finally, similar to satellite television, it is the medium that has the least respect for national-political borders. Thus, the Internet has proven to be a truly multimodal medium unlike any other in the human history, and that makes it ideal for distributing images and symbols of national identity (see also Poster, 1999; Erikson, 2007; Mills, 2002).

Sociocultural Practices

The second dimension of macroanalysis is analysis at the sociocultural, political, and historical level. At this level of analysis, the focus is on the social, political, and historical contexts to which the communicative event belongs. The role of texts in social practices cannot be understood by linguistic or semiotic analysis of the text alone. Textual analysis must be accompanied by analyses of context. With respect to television discourse, Hall (1980) says that

> though the production structures of television originate the television discourse, they do not constitute a closed system. They draw topics, treatments, agendas, events, personnel, images of the audiences, 'definitions of the situation' from other sources and other discursive formations within the wider socio-cultural and political structure of which they are a differentiated part. (p. 129)

Whereas analysis at the text level is devoted to describing the multimodal components of the text, and analysis at the discourse practices level is concerned with interpreting the description of the text, analysis at the sociocultural level attempts to explain what social, cultural, and political motives could have been behind the ways in which texts are produced, distributed, and consumed.

Politics and economics of the media are two major parts of the context that ought to be analyzed, along with textual/semiotic analysis. For example, studying the use of location in Scottish newspapers to illustrate the political use of discourses in the construction of national identity, Higgins (2004) observes that "various newspapers engage in particular textual strategies of articulating nation and politics, based upon a politically charged distinction between Scotland and Britain" (p. 469). Luther (2002), in his comparison of the representations of American and Japanese national identities in the American press, finds that there is an "interplay of national identities and political economic conditions on the formations of images of nations" (p. 78). Therefore, it is important to ask who has access to media production and distribution and, thus, dissemination of ideas, or in the case of this study, discourses of national identity construction. According to Guibernau (1996):

> Access to the tremendous power of the media depends on the resources available to each nationalist organization. The uneven use of the media by nationalist groups reflects the various degrees of power they enjoy and has significant repercussions upon the public image they are able to display both to the national community and the international audience. (p. 148)

In Kurdistan-Iraq, it is clear that only those organizations that have political power and also economic means have access to satellite television. They are the ones that set the agenda in Kurdistan, for example regarding what Kurdishness is and what a Kurdish identity is believed to be or should be.

The political aspect of media is closely related to their economy. According to Fairclough (1995b, p. 42), "the economics of an institution is an important determinant of its practices and its texts." An analyst needs to question the ownership aspect of media. Whereas the private mainstream media are under the influence of commercial and advertising pressures or of the state, public broadcasting could be more in the control of the citizens in a democratic society, or it could be in the hands of the state in totalitarian environments.

Finally, in analyzing discourse critically, one needs to situate discursive events not only politically and economically but also historically (Wodak, 2006a; 2006b). According to Wodak and Ludwig (1999), discourse "is always historical" (12). This means that discourse "is connected synchronically and diachronically with other communicative events which are happening at the same time or which have happened before" (Wodak & Ludwig, 1999). Consideration of the historical context of discourse is particularly important in studying discourses of national identity. This is because discursive practices of sharing memories, even though they are fictitious, myths and narratives of the origins of the nation are the building blocks of national identities.

CDA posits that discursive practices are simultaneously constituted by and constitutive of social structures, relations, and identities (Fairclough & Wodak, 1997). Put differently, what is happening socially, culturally, or politically is also happening discursively and vice versa. It follows that the construction of national identities, like other social constructs, is partially discursive. A CDA approach also assumes that language use and discursive practices are ideological (Eggins, 2004), and ideologies (such as nationalism) belong to social agents (e.g., nationalist elites and movements) who engage, consciously or unconsciously, in meaningful and consequential discursive practices (e.g., of identity formation) in their pursuit of certain interests (e.g., preservation of culture, or mobilization of the masses). Therefore, studying the discursive practices of identity construction with a CDA approach should reveal how and out of what identities are constructed, who constructs them and why.[14]

CHAPTER 3

Kurdish Identity

In this chapter, I present a critical account of Kurdish identity. Since nationalist discourses tend to historicize the nation, I find it appropriate to start with a brief overview of the history of the Kurds and Kurdistan. Then I submit that a Kurdish national identity emerged around the beginning of the twentieth century, bearing strong ethnic roots. In line with this conception of national identity, a Kurdish national identity is defined by a shared culture, language, territory, set of symbols, memory and experience, and future political aspirations. I will show, however, that most of these components of Kurdish national identity are deeply fragmented, due to both internal and external factors.[1] Fragmented components of Kurdish identity, along with external oppression of the four states (i.e., Turkey, Iraq, Iran, and Syria) have prevented Kurdish nationalists from achieving national emancipation, whether in the form of an independent Kurdistan or several autonomous smaller Kurdistans within the political boundaries of different states. In other words, the lack of a strong pan-Kurdish sentiment and cross-border identity has been one of the greatest obstacles to Kurdish national emancipation. A pan-Kurdish or cross-border Kurdish identity here is understood as a collective identity to which most Kurds, regardless of what nation-state they live in, have or could have a sense of belonging. The absence of a strong pan-Kurdish identity has resulted in the Kurdish parochial movements becoming pawns in the hands of the host states and being used against each other.[2] It has also continued to weaken regional and autonomist movements and to deepen cultural and political fragmentation in Kurdistan. I will end this chapter by exploring the suggestion that since the beginning of the 1980s, and more importantly since the mid-1990s, the Kurdish situation has changed profoundly; a cross-border or trans-state Kurdish identity has started to strengthen.

Kurds and Kurdistan: A Brief History

Myths of Kurdish Origins

Like all nationalist discourses, accounts of the origins of the Kurds have relied on myth-making. McDowall (2004) summarizes some of these myths as follows:

> The myths that the Kurds are descended from children hidden in the mountains to escape Zahhak, a child-eating giant, links them mystically with 'the mountain' and also implies, since the myth refers to children rather than one couple, that they may not all be of one origin. A similar story suggests that they are descended from the children of slave girls of King Solomon, sired by a demon named Jasad, and driven by the angry king into the mountains. Another myth claims that Prophet Abraham's wife Sarah was a Kurd, a native of Harran, and thus validates Kurdish identity within the mainstream of monotheism. (p. 4)

Although one might easily dismiss such accounts of the origins of Kurds as unfounded, doing so may not be constructive in understanding nationalist discourses. As McDowall asserts, these myths "are valuable tools in nation building, however dubious historically, because they offer a common mystical identity, exclusive to the Kurdish people" (p. 4).[3] Another account, yet controversial, traces the origins of the Kurds back to the first millennium B.C., to an ancient people, the Medes, who established the Median Empire (728–550 B.C.) in the present areas of western Iran, northern Iraq, and southeastern Turkey (Hassanpour 1992; Kreyenbroek & Sperl, 1992).[4] To nationalist Kurds, the fall of the Median Empire marked the end of their most ancient glory.

Pre-Modern History

Following the fall of the Median Empire, the areas inhibited by the Kurds made up parts of many other empires and powers ruling over the region, such as the Achaemenid (sixth to fourth centuries, B.C.) and Sassanian (third to seventh centuries, A.D.) empires, Arab Caliphate (seventh to thirteenth centuries, A.D.), and the Mongols (thirteenth to sixteenth centuries, A.D.). During the tenth and eleventh centuries, while part of the Arab Caliphate, a number of Kurdish dynasties took control over local matters (McDowall, 2004, p. 21). Many of these dynasties, however, were wiped out by the invasions of the Seljuk Turks (eleventh to twelfth centuries, A.D.) and the

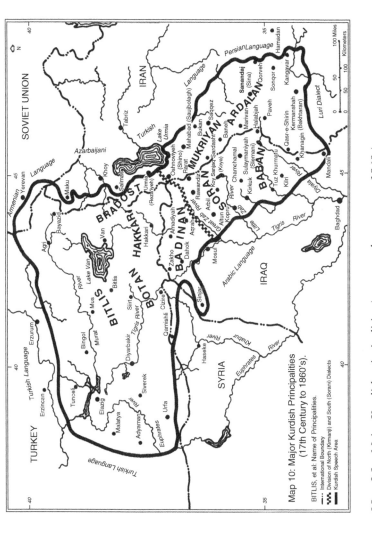

Map 10: Major Kurdish Principalities
(17th Century to 1860's).

BITLIS, et al: Name of Principalities.

···· International Boundary

〰〰 Division of North (Kirmanji) and South (Sorani) Dialects

▬▬ Kurdish Speech Area

Map 3.1 Major Kurdish principalities (seventeenth century to 1860s)

Source: Hassanpour, 1992, p. 51.

Mongols (thirteenth century, A.D.) (Hassanpour, 1992). From the fifteenth to the seventeenth centuries, most parts of Kurdistan again came under the rule of local governments (*hukumats*), under the central rule of the Ottomans and Safavids (Persia) (McDowall, 2004, pp. 27–29) (See map 3.1). The local governments enjoyed a considerable autonomy. Local self-rule, however, never turned into the formation of a unified Kurdistan under the rule of a Kurdish king, even though the idea was not alien to some members of the Kurdish literati at the time (Hassanpour, 2003b).[5]

In fact, being situated between the two powerful and hostile empires, the Ottomans and Safavids brought misery, devastation, and rivalry among the Kurdish principalities (McDowall, 2004; Hassanpour, 1992).[6] In the late seventeenth century, Ahmad Khani (or *EhmedêXanî*, d. 1706/7), a Kurdish *Mullah*, in his poetic epic *Mem û Zîn* (*Mam and Zin*) wrote:

> Whenever the Ottoman Sea [Ottomans] and the Tajik Sea [Persians]
> Flow out and agitate,
> The Kurds get soaked in blood
> Separating them [the Ottomans and Persians] like an isthmus (cc 220–25).
> (as cited in Hassanpour, 2003b, p. 119)

Kurdistan, along with Armenia and Azerbaijan, often were the battlefields for the constant wars between the Ottomans and the Safavids. In addition, the Safavids wanted to replace Kurdish princes and rulers, except for the House of the Ardalan (*Emaret-i Erdelan*),[7] with administrators and governors appointed by the center. The intentions of the Persian Empire faced fierce opposition among the Kurdish principalities, as a result of which thousands of Kurds in those principalities were massacred or deported to other parts of the empire (Hassanpour, 1992).[8] The Safavids' mistreatment of the populations in Kurdistan motivated many Kurdish princes and chiefs to ally with the Ottomans and, thus, played an important role in the defeat of the Safavids in the infamous Chaldiran War in 1514. In return, the Ottoman Sultan Salim respected the autonomy of more than a dozen Kurdish principalities.

First Division of Kurdistan

In 1639, a treaty between the Ottomans and Safavids resulted in drawing the first official border line between the two empires. It ran through Kurdistan and separated what is known today as Iranian

Kurdistan from the rest of Kurdistan, which today is made up of parts of Turkey, Iraq, and Syria. Not seeing the threat of invasion by each other as imminent any longer, the two empires started centralizing their powers and, one by one, eliminated local governments, including those in Kurdistan. After more than a century of revolt by the Kurdish principalities against the central powers, by the mid-nineteenth century all of the principalities were overthrown through military actions (Hassanpour, 1992).

Second Division of Kurdistan

In the aftermath of the Second World War, most of the Ottoman territories fell into the hands of the Europeans. The Treaty of Sévres signed in 1920 between the Allies and the Ottomans called for the establishment of two states, one Armenian and one Kurdish, in today's southeast Turkey or north Kurdistan. The Treaty of Lausanne in 1923, however, modified the agreement, and instead the Ottoman part of Kurdistan was divided between four countries (the new Republic of Turkey, Iraq and Syria, and the Soviet Union). The Iranian part remained intact. This political and geographical division has separated Kurds from each other for almost a century. Being part of or dominated by different cultures and social and political systems have further divided the Kurds culturally, linguistically, territorially, and politically.

KURDISH IDENTITY AND ITS FRAGMENTATIONS: SCHOLARLY DEBATES

Kurdish nationalists who adhere to the primordialist approach to nation and nationalism believe that the Kurds have existed since time immemorial as one nation, and they have always lived in their homeland, Kurdistan. They also believe that, due to external factors such as being invaded by other dominant nations, and also internal factors, such as disunity among the Kurds, their land has been divided and occupied, and, consequently, Kurdish identity has been violently and unjustly fragmented. Despite this, the dominant Kurdish nationalist discourses hold the view that Kurds are a homogenous group of people who are unified ethnically, territorially, linguistically, culturally, and politically—in the sense of having common aspirations and the long-term goal of establishing a unified and independent Kurdistan.

A prime example of a primordialist conceptualization of Kurdish identity and nationalism can be found in the literature of the pan-Kurdist society *Kajîk* (Kazhik).[9] *Kajîk* literature, primarily resting on pan-Kurdish ideas of the Kurdish linguist Jamal Nabaz, asserts that the "*Kurdayetî* [Kurdish nationalism] movement, as we see it, is not the construction of any class or group or any particular point in history… *Kurdayetî* is a natural, dynamic, and everlasting movement. It has been present since the emergence of the Kurdish nation" (*Edebîyatî Kajîk*, pp. 73–74, my translation).[10] Nabaz firmly believes that "the Kurdish nation is comprised of one ethnic unit, and has one history, one language, and one geography. But it lacks a political structure. Kurds' land has been forcefully divided among Turkey, Iran, Iraq, Syria, and the Soviet Union" (Nabaz, 1985, p. 16, My translation). For Nabaz, since Kurds everywhere have always comprised one nation, it is all logical and natural that they "re-establish" their glorious past in the form of an independent, unified, and homogenous Greater Kurdistan.

Hassanpour (2003b), while rejecting a primordial and essentialist approach to nation and nationalism, believes that the formation of Kurdish identities began in the seventeenth century. The acute awareness that the Kurds were different from their neighbors was reflected in the writing of Ahmad Khani (1651–1706), who wrote the poetic romance *Memû Zîn* based on a popular ballad. Khani was highly aware that his culture was different from that of the dominating Ottoman Turks and Safavid Persians, as he wrote, "I am a Kurmanj (Kurd), from the mountains and distant lands" (Hassanpour, p. 126). Khani was equally aware that an important factor that identified Kurds was their language. At the time, the most prestigious literary language throughout the Ottoman Empire was Persian, as it was also in India and Iran, but Khani chose to write his *Mem û Zîn* in Kurdish to make the language equal with Persian (see Hassanpour, 1992, p. 86). As van Bruinessen (2003) notes, Khani knew that he would have had a much wider audience had he written his work in Persian, but "he deliberately opted for the Kurdish language in order to raise the standing of Kurdish culture in the eyes of the Kurds' neighbours" (p. 42; see also Hassanpour, 1996).

According to Hassanpour (2003b), although Khani, as a Kurd, came from and wrote in the context of a feudal society, "his ideas and literary effort resemble, on the surface, the beginnings of the linguistic and literary movement that is often referred to as 'linguistic nationalism'" (pp. 126-127). Hassanpour, however, is quick to note that Khani did not advocate the ideas of modernity that are intertwined with western nationalism such as "bourgeois democracy or popular sovereignty" (p. 132; see also Vali, 2003). Khani did not envision a Kurdish nation that would be marked by what Anderson (1991) has called "horizontal comradeship." Instead, Khani wished for a king that would unite the Kurdish princes to elevate the status of the Kurds in the eyes of the dominating empires of Ottoman and Safavid, and would even attempt to subjugate the Turks and Persians (van Bruinessen, 2003, p. 45).[11] Van Bruinessen (2003) believes that at the time of Khani, the term "Kurd" only referred to "the Kurdish tribes and a part of the urban aristocratic elites, but not to the non-tribal peasantry" (p. 44). Furthermore, van Bruinessen doubts if Khani's readers at the time inferred the same political messages from *Mem û Zin* as Kurdish intelligentsia and nationalists did a few centuries later (p. 46).

For van Bruinessen (2000a), the formation of Kurds as a nation and the emergence of Kurdish nationalism are modern and relatively recent phenomena, going back to the beginning of the last century. He believes that a sense of belonging to one people has existed for a long time among the Kurds, but that is not the same as saying Kurds were always a nation in the modern sense. Writing in the late 1990s, he suggests that, "what unites [the Kurds] is not any set of objective, economic, political or cultural characteristics, but only the awareness among many of them that they constitute one people" (p. 45). He contends that "this awareness ['that they constitute one people'] is a result of a series of historical developments, the most important of which was the rise of Kurdish nationalism" (p. 45), which occurred at the beginning of the twentieth century (Vali, 2003; Smith, 1996). According to van Bruinessen (2000a), the emergence of Kurdish nationalism had two main causes. First, it was a reaction to Turkish, Persian, and Arab nationalisms, which were aiming at the assimilation of the Kurds and other ethnic groups in Turkey, Iran, Iraq, and Syria (see also Vali, 2003, 1998). Second, it was inspired by the European nation-building success.[12]

Vali (2003, 1998), who like Hassanpour and van Bruinessen is among the few scholars who have contributed to the theorization of Kurdish identity, also believes that "Kurdish national identity is unmistakably modern" (p. 104). Vali finds the primordialist view of Kurdish national identity essentialist and historicist. Vali (2003, p. 59, 66) characterizes Hassanpour's position as "ethnicist" and van Bruinessen's as constructivist, and contends that, "while the ethnicist approach derives national identity from a uniform ethnic origin given to and ever-present in history, the constructivist conception reduces it to a mythical origin constructed by capitalism and modernity" (p. 66).[13] Vali calls for a total separation between a modern national identity and an ethnic identity, a discourse of identity and a discourse of origins. This is very much akin to Gellner's (1983, 1997) modernist position, which reserved no space for ethnicity in the life of a nation (see also Smith, 1998). Vali contends that "nationalist discourse is not a discourse of origin, given or constructed. Rather, it is primarily a discourse of identity in which the popular claim to sovereignty is posed" (p. 68). For Vali, whereas ethnic identity is inscribed in discourses of origins and historicization, national identity is expressed and articulated in discourses of rights and citizenship and claims to popular sovereignty. For Vali, the Kurds are not a nation, because in a juridical-political sense they are not, although he may not deny that Kurds are a nation in a cultural and historical sense. One could argue that Vali essentializes the nation as popular sovereignty, which in the long run reduces the nation to juridical (Hassanpour, 2003b).[14] Furthermore, not all nationalisms are political: some are cultural, and some are both (Hutchinson, 1999; Smith, 1998; Kennedy, 2004; Sutherland, 2005). Since nationalisms create all nations (Gellner, 1983) one could suggest that some of these nations could be political from the beginning (i.e., state-nation),[15] some others could be cultural at first (e.g., nation), and then become both political and cultural (nation-state).

To Vali, all identities, individual or collective, are always relational (see also Billig, 1995; Hall, 2006; Heller, 1999; Wodak et al., 2009). National identities are defined in terms of differences and are inscribed in "otherness" (Vali, 1998, p. 83). Kurdish identity, Vali contends, emerged as a reaction to the affirmation of official national identities in Turkey, Iran, Iraq, and Syria because they hinged on "the denial of Kurdish ethnicity and ethnic and national identities" (1998, p. 82; also see Vali, 2003).[16] Vali defines Kurdish identity entirely in terms of "otherness" and leaves no room for historical and ethnic roots of national identity. However, as Smith (1999, 1991) has demonstrated time after time, we hardly know of any nation or national identity that has not been conceptualized around ethnic cores, at least at its inception.

To sum up, Kurdish national identity is not entirely modern, but Kurdish nationalism is. Kurdish national identity, similar to all national identities, has historical and ethnic roots, even if such roots happen to be constructed or fictive. In the beginning of the twentieth century, at the time when Turkish, Persian, and Arab nationalisms started to affirm themselves partially by denying the ethnic identities of the Kurds, Kurdish nationalism emerged to engineer a Kurdish national identity. The construction of a modern Kurdish national identity has depended on the appropriation of ethnic and historical origins such as language, culture, and territory, coupled with newly created nationalist symbols, and finally by political claims to modern values such as sovereignty and the right to self-determination. In addition to these characteristics, which aim at in-group solidarity, Kurdish identity has also born differences from other identities. However, a strong collective Kurdish national identity is yet to form. The majority of scholars of Kurds and Kurdistan, despite their differences on many historical, political, and theoretical issues, agree at least on one point: Kurdish identity is deeply fragmented. Notwithstanding the oppression imposed by the states, it has been suggested that the formation of a strong collective Kurdish identity has for the most part suffered from internal fragmentations: territorial, cultural, linguistic, and political.

Territorial Fragmentation

"Kurdistan" can be literally translated as the land/homeland of the Kurds, and it is divided by the internationally recognized borders of the four nation-states of Iraq, Iran, Turkey, and Syria. As Ciment (1996) notes, "Kurdistan has been virtually wiped from the map in the twentieth century" (p. 75). The only exception is the province of *Kordestan* (Kurdistan) in Iran, encompassing about one-third of the total area inhabited by the Kurds in Iran.[17] Most Kurds and Kurdish sympathizers refer to Turkish Kurdistan as northern Kurdistan or Kurdistan north, Iraqi Kurdistan as southern Kurdistan or Kurdistan south, Iranian Kurdistan as eastern Kurdistan or Kurdistan east, and Syrian Kurdistan as western Kurdistan or Kurdistan west. However, except for today's Iraq, the other states where most Kurds live refer to parts of Kurdistan as southeast Turkey, northern Iraq, and in Iran and Syria various names of provinces and regions are used. Kurdistan as conceptualized by the vast majority of Kurds and scholars of Kurdish studies is non-existent for those states.

Kurdistan's mountainous make-up, especially where the four nation-states of Turkey, Iraq, Iran, and Syria meet, is deemed very important to the host states. According to McDowall (2004), "the mountains certainly provide Iran and Iraq with a defensible strategic frontier; to move the boundary either west or east of Kurdistan would not make strategic sense to either states" (p. 7). As McDowall observes, the four states have proven that they are committed to keeping these borders, which run through Kurdistan, intact at all costs. Turkey has perhaps demonstrated the highest degree of antipathy towards not only the concept of a distinct territory as Kurdistan but also the very word describing it. For example, numerous researchers and ordinary people, Kurdish or non-Kurdish, traveling to Iraqi Kurdistan through Turkey have reported that their documents and laptops have been searched by Turkish border guards for the word *Kurdistan*. They have been asked to delete instances of the word from their documents and equipment (O'Leary & Salih, 2005); in other cases, documents, print materials, and pictures containing the word have been destroyed altogether. According to McDowall, Turkey "has an emotional and ideological view that its frontiers (except with Iraq) cannot be changed without threatening the foundations of the republic...The loss of Kurdistan, despite its great poverty, would be perceived as a grievous blow to the spatial identity of Turkey" (O'Leary & Salih, 2005). The same can be said about the other three states.

The rugged, mountainous, and harsh terrain of Kurdistan, while being important for the four nation-states, has been both a blessing and a curse for the Kurds themselves. These rugged mountains have been a blessing to many because, as O'Shea (2004) observes, "to most Kurds, even urbanites or dwellers of the plains, Kurdistan is defined by its mountainous topography. A common theme in Kurdish culture is the mountains as allies in the many Kurdish military struggles" (p. 162). The phrase "the only friends of the Kurds are the mountains," which is believed to be a Kurdish saying (O'Leary, McGarry & Salih, 2005, p. xix; see also Izady, 1992, p. 188), became the title of a book in 1992, *No Friends But the Mountains* (Bulloch & Morris, 1992). Mountains have become a national symbol and one of the most salient markers of Kurdish identity.

Kurdistan's rugged landscape has also been a curse on the unity of the Kurds because it has isolated communities of Kurds for centuries, especially since the final division of Kurdistan in 1923. According to Izady (1992):

> Just as the mountains create autonomy for the Kurds, they often prohibit easy communication between them...The mountains have broken down the language of the Kurds to a babble of dialects, their religions to a case study in diversity, and their art and costumes to a zoo of colourful variety. (p. 188)

In a similar vein, Yavuz (2005) suggests that Kurdistan's "rugged geographic conditions have been a major impediment to the formation of Kurdish unity" (p. 232). Physical barriers such as mountains have been among the biggest obstacles in the way of easy communication among the Kurds. Until very recently, most communication between the Kurds of different parts was between and through a small population of interrelated tribes living on the borders, as well as through smugglers, rebels of different parts, and a handful of the intelligentsia who were aware of each other, mostly through clandestine short-wave radio stations and literary or political pamphlets.[18] The absence of easy communication among the Kurds living in different states gradually deepened cultural, linguistic, and political differences.

Cultural Fragmentation

Van Bruinessen (2000a), contends that "Kurds were (and are) certainly not a culturally homogeneous group" (p. 45). For van Bruinessen, cultural differences among the Kurds are so great that he hesitates to call them an ethnic group. Van Bruinessen observes that "judging by objective criteria, one would be inclined to consider the Kurds as conglomerates of different ethnic groups rather than as a single one" (p. 9). In light of this critical observation, I submit that when referring to Kurds in general, the appropriate terms would be nation or people.

Cultural differences in Kurdistan are not due to internal and ethnic fragmentations alone. They also bear the traces of the different dominant cultures of the states in which Kurds have lived (van Bruinessen, 2000a).[19] Vali's (1998) observations are particularly insightful here. He suggests that the dynamics and patterns of Kurdish identity formation have been determined not only by its own internal factors but also by nation-building policies and practices of the "other," the national identities that have been imposed by the states ruling over Kurdistan. Since each state has adhered to different practices of nation-building with different cultures and languages and, thus, identity formation, Kurdish identity within each state has taken a different shape:

> [T]he emergent national states in [Turkey, Iran, Iraq, Syria], and the official nationalist discourses which were constructed to legitimize their authoritarian rule and hegemonist political culture, varied substantially in form and character ... Kurdish identity has borne the mark of this political and cultural diversity of the "other"; it has been deeply fragmented since its inception. (p. 82)

Cultural differences among the Kurds relate to music (Izady, 1992), clothing and costume, food and religion (Kreyenbroek & Allison, 1996), marriage, and many other cultural traits and attitudes. The cultural diversity is indeed remarkable; for example, there have been (and are) different religions and sects in Kurdistan. Although the majority of Kurds are Sunni Muslims, there are also Shi'ite, Ahl-e Hagh, Alavi,

Yazidi, Christian, and Jewish Kurds (Kreyenbroek, 1996; O'Shea, 2004, pp. 28–33). Religious differences seem to be a disadvantage for the Kurdish movement and quest for identity recognition. Van Bruinessen (2000a) observes that the vast majority of Shi'ite Kurds of Iran (residing in the provinces of Kirmashan and Ilam) have refrained from joining the Kurdish movement and, instead, have sided with the central government in Iran, where a particular brand of Shi'ism is the official religion of the country. On the other hand, because the government in Baghdad until 2003 was dominated by Sunni Muslims, Kurdish Shi'ites in Iraq have been actively participating in the Kurdish national movement in Iraq (p. 26). Since the vast majority of Kurds are Muslims, as are the vast majority of the neighboring nationalities and ethnic groups, religion has not been a major factor distinguishing the Kurds from the dominant national and ethnic groups; it has not been a key factor in defining Kurdishness.[20] In addition to religion, many cultural traits of the Kurds have become similar to those of the Turks, Persians, and Arabs as a result of being dominated by these cultures for about a century. Language, however, has remained as one of the most salient defining elements of Kurdish identity.

Linguistic fragmentation

[A language] is a flash of the human spirit, the vehicle by which the soul of each particular culture comes into the material world. Every language is an old-growth forest of the mind, a watershed of thought, an ecosystem of spiritual possibilities. (Davis, 2009, p. 3)

Language has been considered as one of the main indices of Kurdish identity (Vali, 2003; McDowall, 2004; Kreyenbroek & Allison, 1996). Hassanpour (1992) believes that language is like the air for the Kurdish nationalist struggle because it is the most obvious characteristic that differentiates the Kurds from the neighboring nationalities. Both Kurdish nationalists and the states where Kurds reside have realized the importance of language in defining Kurdish identity.

Unmistakably influenced by the nation-state ideology,[21] which holds that an ideal nation has no room for more than one language, Kurdish nationalists have contested any suggestion that Kurds speak more than one language, a proposition that has been put forward by some linguists (e.g., Kreyenbroek, 1992). Seeing Kurdish language as a decisive factor defining Kurdish distinct identity, the host states "have sought to 'assimilate' the Kurds by attempting to suppress Kurdish altogether,

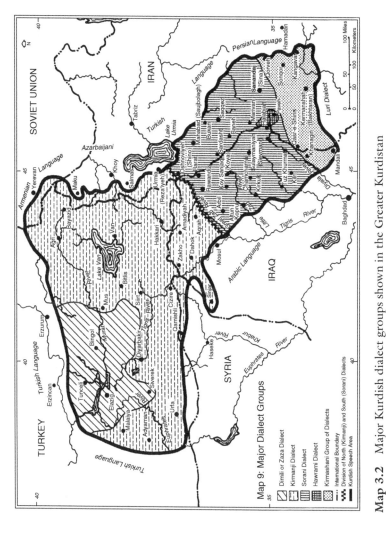

Map 3.2 Major Kurdish dialect groups shown in the Greater Kurdistan

Source: Hassanpour, 1992, p. 22.

or to discourage its development" (Kreyenbroek, 1992, p. 68). The official repression along with the linguistic differences among Kurdish varieties has left the Kurdish language deeply fragmented. The fragmentation of Kurdish language is twofold: different speech varieties, and different written scripts. In addition to many local dialects (e.g., Mukri, Sorani, Ardalani, Suleimani, Harki, Jalali, and so forth),[22] there are four major speech variety groups spoken by Kurds: Kurmanji (also called Northern Kurmanji or Northern Kurdish), Sorani (also called Southern Kurmanji or Central Kurdish), Zazaki/ Dimli and Hawrami/Gorani, and Kirmashani (Southern Kurdish) (Hassanpour, 1992) (See map 3.2).[23] These varieties are not mutually intelligible in most contexts (van Bruinessen, 1992). Kurmanji is spoken by about 60–65 percent of all Kurds, most of whom live in Turkey. Kurmanji speakers also combine about 20–25 percent of Iraqi Kurds, Syrian Kurds (about 1–1.5 million), and Kurds living in Armenia and other republics of central Asia, and a small number of Kurds living to the north of the city of Urumiye (*Wirmê* in Kurdish) in Iran. Sorani is spoken by about 25–30 percent of all Kurdish speakers, all of whom reside in Iraq and Iran. Zazaki is spoken by about one million people living in northern Kurdistan (or southeast Turkey, to use the state's official discourse) in the triangle between Diyarbakir, Sivas, and Erzurum (Kreyenbroek, 1992, p. 68). Hawrami or Gorani, considered by Kurds as the oldest Kurdish variety (Hassanpour, 1992), has fewer speakers living in the southern parts of Iranian and Iraqi Kurdistan. Finally, Kirmashani is spoken by the vast majority of Kurdish speakers in the southern part of Iranian Kurdistan (e.g., in and around the cities of Kirmaşan/Kermanshah and Kamyaran) and in and around the city of Khanaghin (*Xaneqîn* in Kurdish) in Iraqi Kurdistan. Of these varieties, Kurmanji and Sorani, as the two varieties with the majority of speakers, are for the most part standardized. They are used in Kurdish media, in all parts of Kurdistan and diasporas, and also for education and administration in Kurdistan-Iraq.[24]

Kreyenbroek (1992) finds Kurmanji and Sorani as different as English and German (p. 71) particularly with respect to phonology and morphology, but not vocabulary.[25] These differences have compelled some scholars to call Kurdish varieties "languages" (p. 71). In fact some researchers have even exaggerated the diversity of Kurdish varieties and reported that there are more than a dozen Kurdish "languages" (Jenkins, 2001). In contrast, almost all Kurdish nationalists and a great number of researchers (e.g., Hassanpour, 1992; McDowall, 2004; van Bruinessen, 2000a) prefer the word "dialect." I have opted for the term Kurdish varieties because I find the terms language and dialect politically loaded.[26] The crucial point of all this, especially for this study, is that Sorani and Kurmanji are not mutually intelligible. While referring to Sorani and Kurmanji as Kurdish "dialects," Hassanpour (1992) confirms that "until they have had considerable previous contact, the speakers of Kurmanji and Sorani are not able to communicate effectively *in all contexts*" (Hassanpour, 1992, p. 24, emphasis in original; see also van Bruinessen, 2000a, p. 27).[27]

The gulf between Kurdish speech varieties is further widened by the fact that they are written in different scripts. While Sorani speakers use a modified Arabic alphabet system, the Kurmanji speakers use both the Arabic modified (Kurds from Iraq) and a Roman script based on the modern Turkish alphabet (all Kurds from Turkey and Syria and some from Iraq). Kurds from central Asia (Armenia, Azerbaijan, Kazakhstan), however, use Cyrillic.[28] Although there have been some attempts (e.g., Nabaz, 1976) to unify the two major Kurdish varieties, Kurmanji and Sorani, grammatical differences between the two varieties, the absence of a unified state in Kurdistan, and the official repression against the language have made the efforts unsuccessful. The influence of the dominant languages on Kurdish is not only evident in different writing systems of Kurdish but also in very important aspects of the language such as vocabulary, phonetics, grammar, and style. The internal diversification of Kurdish language has been intensified by the state repression of the language.

From its birth, the new republic of Turkey saw no place for non-Turkish peoples and languages. The Kurds were called "mountain Turks" (Kreyenbroek, 1992, p. 73) and their language was officially banned in 1938 in all public domains. Kurmanji survived in homes and villages and it started to be written and standardized by Kurdish intellectuals in diasporic communities, first in Syria (1942–1945), when Syria was still under French Mandate, and then in the West.[29] In fact, it is safe to suggest that today's Kurmanji Kurdish was mainly developed, codified, and flourished in the West, notably in Germany and Sweden. As of 1991, more was published in Turkey than in diasporas, to the extent that many diasporic journals either migrated to Turkey or ceased publishing.

Although the use of Kurdish was legalized in Turkey in May 1991 (Olson, 2009), Skutnabb-Kangas and Fernandes (2008) report that the status of Kurdish in Turkey has not changed that much:

> Kurdish-medium schools are not allowed in Turkey. Neither do Kurdish children have the right to study their mother tongue as a subject in schools. In theory, courses in the Kurdish language can be taught to

teenagers and adults but in practice the obstacles and conditions have been so many and so bureaucratically and legally demanding that there are next to no courses at the time of writing this article. (p. 2)

The authors provide numerous examples of court cases in Turkey (during the time period of 2002–2006) in which "the Kurdish language and expressions in support of Kurdish culture/language are either overtly prohibited, or prohibited on the basis of being labeled "terrorist activities," which fall under the vague definition of terrorism in various articles in the Turkish Penal Code" (Skutnabb-Kangas & Fernandes, 2008, p. 3).[30] Since the mid-1990s, private Kurdish lessons have been offered in major urban centers such as Istanbul and Diyarbakir. However, these classes are usually short-lived, mainly because they are not supported by the government, and, as a result, pupils find them too expensive to attend or those who run the courses cannot secure sufficient financial support to run them.

The language policy of Iran has not changed since the first constitution of 1906 (Hassanpour, Skutnabb-Kangas & Chyet, 1996, p. 369; Sheyholislami, forthcoming), in which Persian or Farsi was declared as the official language of Iran. The local languages, such as Kurdish, have been allowed theoretically to be used in the mass media in limited and restricted ways.[31] Broadcasting, however, has always been a monopoly of the state. Thus, broadcasting in Kurdish has tended to be a propaganda vehicle for the central government. Currently, and much more than in the Shah's time, Kurdish books and magazines are published in Iran, but permission needs to be granted by the government for each publication. Also, heavy censorship is often at work, and many Kurdish periodicals that emerged in the mid 1990s, after the reformists took power in Iran, have been closed down. Kurdish does not have any official status in Iran and it is not taught in schools let alone being the medium of instruction. In recent years, especially during the presidency of Khatami, Kurdish student societies have managed to run a few courses devoted to Kurdish language and literature in a few universities (e.g., Shahid Beheshti University in Tehran, and the University of Kurdistan in Sanandaj). However, these courses and programs, similar to Kurdish periodicals, are short-lived. In addition, in a number of Kurdish cities, privately run Kurdish courses are offered. For example, in the city of Mahabad, Bokan, and other towns, Kurdish lessons are offered by Soma, *Komełey Ferhengî u Férkarî Soma—Férgey Zimanî Kurdî* (The Cultural and Training Society of Soma-Kurdish Language School). Not many people can afford the cost of private lessons, especially to learn how to read and write a language only for intrinsic reasons and not for gaining external rewards such as a job or passing grades in the formal school system. Instructors teach on volunteer basis and students' tuitions can hardly cover expenses for materials and the rent, to the extent that Soma apparently has been carrying a deficit in the amount of thousands of dollars for the past few years. Despite several attempts, Soma has not been able to obtain support, including financial, from the Iranian authorities. Above all, Soma reportedly has been under close surveillance to make sure that its activities do not cross any red lines set by the Iranian authorities when the initial license to open the school was granted. It is remarkable that, in spite of all the difficulties, both teachers and students have continued to teach and learn their mother tongue (see Sheyholislami, forthcoming).

In Syria, Kurdish is not recognized as an official language and it is not taught in schools, public or private (Amnesty International, 2005). From 1920–1937, under the French Mandate, Kurds in Syria could publish in Kurdish and use it in broadcasting, until the French authorities realized that Kurds were supporting the Syrian movement for independence. In 1941, publication and broadcasting in Kurdish, mostly for war propaganda purposes, were resumed and continued beyond Syria's independence in 1948. However, Syria's treatment of Kurdish from 1955 onward has been characterized as linguicide (Hassanpour et al., 1996). According to these Kurdish specialists, "[b]eginning in the mid-1950s...the [Syrian] government seized and destroyed Kurdish publications. Schools built in Kurdish communities banned language instruction in any language other than Arabic, which is still true today" (Hassanpour et al., 1996, p. 370).

Whereas Kurmanji Kurdish has been prohibited in Turkey, it has been the language of schooling, media, and public institutions in Kurdistan-Iraq since 1991, especially in the predominantly Kurmanji-populated province of Duhok. Prior to 1991, however, only Sorani Kurdish had an official status. From the early 1920s, under the British Mandate, Kurds in Iraq were entitled to use their language in primary education and administration. Kurdish was recognized as a "local language" in Iraq and the "official" language in the Kurdish region (Hassanpour et al., 1996, p. 369). The Iraqi state, however, showed no serious interest in promoting Kurdish until the aftermath of the coup of General Qasim in 1958, which turned Iraq from a kingdom to a republic. Significant developments at that time with respect to Kurdish language included the establishment of a Chair of Kurdish Studies in the University of Baghdad in 1959, devoting a special Kurdish department in the Ministry of Education, and the publication of many periodicals and books and radio broadcasting in Kurdish.

The Ba'thist coup in 1968 restricted publishing in Kurdish for several months. In 1970, however, after a mutual agreement between the Kurdish movement leadership and the Iraqi central government was reached, Sorani Kurdish was recognized as the second official language of Iraq. Sorani was further developed to a full-fledged standard language, and used in education, media, and the public institutions in most of the Kurdish region of Iraq.[32] In 1974, however, the war between the central government and Kurds of Iraq resumed, and the status of the Kurdish language started to decline. Despite this, Kurdish, especially the Sorani variety, has never been banned from public or private domains in Iraqi Kurdistan. Even under the rule of Saddam Hussein, Kurdish continued to be a language of instruction along with Arabic in publicly run education, and it continued to be used in broadcasting and publishing. However, secret documents obtained after the fall of Saddam Hussein in Iraq indicate that his regime was planning to put an end to the use of Kurdish as a language of instruction in Kurdistan-Iraq (Taha, 2006).

In the aftermath of the first Gulf War (1991), the Kurds in Iraq started to enjoy a de facto autonomy within which Kurdish (the variety is not explicitly stated, but it appears to mean Sorani Kurdish) has been the official language. In the new Iraqi constitution, Kurdish is recognized as one of the official languages of Iraq since 2005, Arabic being the other. Currently, in Kurdistan-Iraq, Kurdish is the language of public institutions, all levels of education, and the dominant language of publications, radio, and television programs. It is worth noting, however, that the dominant variety in that part of Kurdistan is Sorani or Central Kurdish. Kurmanji is only used in the province of Duhok. Furthermore, since 2006 there has been a continuous debate between the speakers of the two varieties as to whether Sorani alone or both Sorani and Kurmanji should be assigned the official status in the Kurdistan Regional Government (Sheyholislami, 2009b).

As for many other shortcomings in the Kurdish societies, Kurdish nationalists have blamed the central governments of the four states for the absence of a "unified Kurdish language" or a "Kurdistan national language." What have the Kurds done about their language during their self-rule in Iraqi Kurdistan since 1992? The media provide an excellent context for investigating this and other questions with respect to language; for example, how has Kurdish with all its varieties been used to define Kurdishness?

Political Fragmentations

Political rivalry among the Kurds goes back to pre-modern times. For example, the Kurdish poet Ahmad Khani (1605–1706) protested the lack of unity among Kurdish principalities and their inability to unite under the rule of one king or emperor (Hassanpour, 2003b). Kurdish disunity has persisted in modern times. In 1933, Kurds had their best opportunity to gain political autonomy under the British mandate in Iraq. When Iraq became a member of the United Nations, it was required to honor Kurdish autonomy in the northern part of the country (Kurdistan). Iraq backed off from the agreement without much trouble because of the lack of unity among the Kurds: "the absence of an effective and united Kurdish leadership capable of mustering internal and international support made it easy for the Iraqi government to drag its feet and eventually renege on the agreement" (Vali, 2003, p. 100). Internal conflicts within the Kurdistan Democratic Party of Iraq (KDP) that started in the mid-1960s led to the formation of the Patriotic Union of Kurdistan (PUK) in June 1975. Dreadful hostilities between the PUK and KDP continued during 1970s and 1990s (see McDowall, 2004, pp. 343–352).

More recently, from 1982 to 1986, the two most prominent Kurdish organizations in Iranian Kurdistan, the Kurdistan Democratic Party of Iran (KDPI) and Komala fought each other, while both continued their animosity towards KDP of Iraqi Kurdistan. Similarly, the fierce fighting between the two Kurdish Iraqi organizations, KDP and PUK, from 1994 to 1997, resulted in enormous casualties from both sides and a major setback in the Iraqi Kurds' first opportunity to establish their own democratic institutions in their region. In the late 1990s, PUK and *Partî Kirêkaranî Kurdistan*—PKK (Kurdistan Workers' Party) of Turkey clashed with KDP forces. Then, in 2000, however, fighting between PUK and PKK broke out. As Ignatieff (1993) says, "Kurds themselves admit that, for all the shared talk about a common homeland, they have actually fought each other more often than they have fought side by side" (p. 181). Why has factionalism persisted in Kurdistan?

Conflicts often occur among those who cannot or do not want to share belonging to similar values, interests, goals, and ideologies. Many factors have contributed to disunities among the Kurds, including tribalism, regional differences, factionalism within the same region, class struggle, and religious and ideological differences among Kurdish organizations. External factors such as pressures from the host states and international stakeholders have also played roles. None of these factors, however, may have been as powerful as the lack of a pan-Kurdish sentiment. The absence of this sentiment has not only prevented the emergence of a strong and durable pan-Kurdistani movement (Izady, 1992), but it has crippled movements in each part of Kurdistan (Romano, 2006). Writing in 1992, Izady contends that "in the past, and some may argue even today, the Kurds have never achieved sufficient unity to produce even the prototype of an organized pan-Kurdish political movement for independence" (Izady, 1992, p. 188). The first Kurdish movements and nationalist organizations, at the end of the ninetieth and the beginning of the twentieth centuries, aimed at independence for the Greater Kurdistan (Olson, 1991). However, the vast majority of Kurdish movements, more than 20 of them in the last century (Romano, 2006), have been led by regional and autonomist organizations.

Vali calls Kurdish autonomous movements "Kurdish nationalists without Kurdish nationalism" (1998, p. 84). They are without nationalism because they are not sovereignist. For Vali, akin to Gellner's (1983) view, nationalism is first and foremost a political principle that pursues sovereignty and citizenship rights for a nationality. Vali (1998) believes that the only Kurdish movement that has qualified as a nationalist movement was the Kurdish movement in Turkey, led by the PKK in the 1980s, because it bore the characteristics of a modern nationalist movement; it was secessionist (1998). The PKK, however, started to abandon its pan-Kurdish ambitions in the early 1990s (van Bruinessen, 2000a). In fact, by the mid-1990s, the PKK was willing to negotiate with the Turkish authorities as long as the Turks were willing to show some sort of "concession to Kurdish cultural demands" (van Bruinessen, 2000a). Vali finds Kurdish movements, particularly in recent decades, parochial and ineffective because they have been driven by regional interests instead of striving for popular sovereignty for Kurdistan. He contends that these regional and autonomous movements have effectively intensified Kurdish divisions.

However, many have found secessionism and quest for sovereignty whether of one part of Kurdistan or four parts altogether not the option for now or years to come. According to Romano (2006):

> [A] Kurdish project for statehood at this time seems both plagued with incredible obstacles as well as ill-advised. Turkey, Syria, and Iran could all be expected to continue collaborating in order to prevent such a development, and the chances of other states coming to the aid of repressed Kurds in Turkey, Iraq, or Iran appear extremely small. (p. 259)

International powers have not been in favor of the formation of any independent Kurdish state, either. They have not approved of the idea even for Iraqi Kurds who have been considered one of the most important allies of the U.S.-and Britain-led invasion of Iraq in 2003. This is despite the fact that the partition of Iraq, as a result of which the Iraqi Kurds would have a state of their own, has been entertained seriously by western diplomats and academics as one of the ways out of the difficulty and confusion that Americans have found themselves in, in Iraq (see O'Leary & Salih, 2005; Galbraith, 2005). In fact, the Iraqi Kurds are worried that the neighboring countries with sizable Kurdish populations, such as Turkey, may even interfere with the implementation of federalism in Iraq, which has been enshrined in the first draft of the Iraqi new constitution (O'Leary, 2002).

Whereas Kurdish secession anywhere has been considered impractical and "ill-advised" (Romano, 2006), the idea of establishing a greater Kurdistan state has been called a "dream" (O'Leary & Salih, 2005, p. 15). The creation of a greater Kurdistan could only be formed out of parts of four nation-states in the Middle East—Turkey, Iran, Iraq, and Syria. Horowitz (1992) calls this hypothetical formation "irredentism" as opposed to "secessionism" (p. 119).[33] Whereas secessionism upsets one state, irredentism would mean instability for four states and major reconstruction of borders and states in the region, something that no major world power has been willing to tolerate. Thus, for all practical purposes, Kurdish political parties and many Kurdish intellectuals have erased explicit references to their desire for creating a greater Kurdistan. The idea and dream, however, has been nurtured in Kurdish literature, poetry, music, and arts for more than a century and it will continue to be so, perhaps as long as Kurds in different states find their ethnic identities and human rights denied.[34]

In contrast to Vali (1998), Romano (2006) believes that the greatest obstacle to Kurdish emancipation is not so much that Kurdish movements are autonomist, as opposed to being secessionist. He contends that a pan-Kurdish sentiment, or what can also be called a Kurdish collective identity, is not present among the Kurds. He believes that as long as a pan-Kurdish sentiment is absent, the host states continue to make the political parties of different parts of Kurdistan their pawns and use them against each other. Romano contends that:

> Ankara, Tehran, Damascus, and non-Kurdish Iraqis are of course increasingly weary of growing pan-Kurdish sentiment, which accounts for their hostility to any Kurdish state in the region. While many Kurds

would like to see pan-Kurdish sentiment produce a situation wherein their leaders refuse to be made the pawns of these powers and played off against each other...all the states of the region are determined to keep the Kurds divided. (p. 251)

In other words, the formation of a pan-Kurdish identity may never lead to the formation of a greater Kurdistan. However, the existence of such a sentiment might motivate Kurdish populations not to allow regional organizations to turn against each other. In effect, a strong cross-border Kurdish identity might be helpful for achieving autonomy and cultural rights within different states.

STRENGTHENING OF A PAN-KURDISH IDENTITY

As discussed in the introductory chapter, there have been suggestions that a strong Kurdish cross-border identity has begun to emerge since the mid-1990s (Bird, 2004; van Bruinessen, 2000a; Romano, 2006). Until the mid-1990s, communication among different parts and regions of Kurdistan was limited. In 1992, Izady suggested that "the western Kurds [i.e., Kurds from Turkey and Syria] are novelties to the other Kurds and vice versa" (p. 208). Major political, social, or cultural events occurring in one region of Kurdistan had few consequences, if any, in other Kurdish regions. A prime example is the chemical bombardment of the town of Halabja in Iraqi Kurdistan in March 1988, during which about 5,000 Iraqi Kurds were killed after the town was hit by Iraqi planes (Black, 1993; Randal, 1997). The event generated no or very little immediate reaction in other parts of Kurdistan. On the one hand, the Kurds of other regions were not immediately aware of the atrocities that had taken place in Halabja. On the other hand, they became aware of the incident through non-Kurdish media, mainly the Iranian media.[35] Informed this way, the majority of Kurds seemed unable to experience the suffering of the Iraqi Kurds. Specifically, simultaneous awareness of the Iraqi Kurds' predicament by other Kurds through a Kurdish channel that Kurds could trust and relate to was absent.

One of the first signs of the recent rise of a pan-Kurdish sentiment surfaced in February 1999, following the kidnapping of Abdullah Öcalan, the leader of the largest Kurdish political organization in Turkey, PKK. In a matter of hours, simultaneous demonstrations took place in diasporic communities (Romano, 2002). These were followed by demonstrations of the Kurds in Iraq, Iran, and Syria in a matter of days (p. 146), even in cities where Kurdish nationalism never had a significant prominence, such as Kirmashan in Iran (*BBC*, 1999). In more recent years, nearly all major events in Kurdistan-Iraq, where the region has gone through some unprecedented changes (see further down) since the first Gulf War in 1991, have generated reactions among Kurds living elsewhere. For example, on May 16, 2005, the *Agence France Presse* reported that rioting erupted in the Kurdish city of Mahabad in Iran after MasoudBarzani, the Iraqi Kurdish leader, was sworn in as "the president of Iraqi Kurdistan" (*AFP*, 2005). According to a bulletin from the Institute Kurde de Paris, signs of welcoming the news and expressions of joy were demonstrated also in Turkey, Syria, and Kurdish diasporic communities (InstitutKurde de Paris, 2005). In March 2004, after the recognition of the Kurdistan of Iraq in the Transitional Administrative Law of Iraq, "the Kurds of Syria showed surprising cohesion and coordination in Qamishli [,Syria]" (O'Leary & Salih, 2005, p. 15).

Why this strengthening of a pan-Kurdish sentiment in recent years? In other words, what could have caused these changes among the Kurds? I submit that there are at least three reasons: political developments in Kurdistan in the past two decades, the emergence and expansion of Kurdish diasporic communities during almost the same years, and the use of new communication technologies such as satellite television and the Internet in the last decade or so.

Political Changes in Kurdistan

In the mid-1990s, van Bruinessen wrote:

> The political developments of the past decade have strengthened contact between the Kurds of Turkey, Iran and Iraq; there is now a stronger awareness of belonging together than there was in the past. The wish for a separate state, uniting the various parts of Kurdistan, has also become stronger. (2000a, p. 62)

This is a plausible observation, to which I would add two points. First, Syrian Kurds have also been affected by recent political developments in the region. Second, these changes have continued in the 2000s, but have taken different forms.

One of the major political changes, which can be traced back to the 1960s, is the spread of war between the central governments and the Kurdish armed organizations (i.e., Iraq: intermittently from 1960–2003, 1975–1988 being the worst; Iran: intermittently from 1980–present, 1980–1988 being the worst; Turkey: intermittently from 1984–present) (Hassanpour & Mojab, 2005). As a result of these wars, tens of thousands of people have lost their lives, the mental and physical well-being of more people have been compromised, and tens of thousands of civilian Kurds have been displaced and their villages and towns have been destroyed. The Iraq-Iran war and periodic conflicts among Kurdish rivals have added to the devastation. These wars have engendered a constant movement of Kurdish populations throughout Kurdistan, bringing Kurds of various regions into contact with each other sometimes for the first time. Despite their possible linguistic, cultural, and political differences, Kurds have managed to share experiences of struggle, displacement, and homelessness. In what follows, I will take a brief look at how political events in Turkey, Iran, Syria, and Iraq have shaped the experiences and aspirations of Kurds in each of the four parts. I will particularly focus on some positive developments.

Turkey

Under pressure from Kurds' continuous struggle to achieve their rights and from the European Union, the government of Turkey started to show some flexibility towards Kurdish language and culture in the early 1990s. Now, Turkish citizens can use the term "Kurd" (but not Kurdistan[36]) without the fear of outright persecution; as well, private institutions of Kurdish teaching have been established, Kurdish can be published, including a daily newspaper *Azadiya Welat* (The Freedom of Country/Homeland), and civil organizations and pro-Kurdish political parties have managed to introduce a dialogue on the Kurdish issue to Turkey's public sphere.

However, Turkey's war with Kurdish rebels belonging to the PKK continues. On the pretext of fighting these rebels, who are said to be stationed in the Ghandil (*Qendîl* in Kurdish) mountains of Iraqi Kurdistan, the Turkish military has conducted several incursions into that region. Turkey has also been concerned about the fate of the oil-rich city of Kirkuk in northern Iraq. Kurds make up the largest ethnic group of the city, but the city is not a part of the Kurdistan Regional Government's (KRG) jurisdiction. According to Iraq's interim constitution, the Kurds' long-time claim to that city is to be tested through a referendum. Turkey has expressed its displeasure with the possibility of Kirkuk's annexation to the jurisdiction of KRG. Although the city has a sizable Turcoman population about whom Turkey claims to be concerned, the majority of observers believe that Turkey is fearful of a strong Kurdish autonomous region in Iraq, because it may inspire the Kurds of Turkey to demand the same status within Turkey (O'Leary & Salih, 2005; Fraser, 2007).

Iran

In Iran, the election of the reformist Mohammad Khatami as the Iranian president gave some hope to the Kurds in 1997 (Koohi-Kamali, 2003; Entessar, 2007). However, the Kurds, along with the rest of the Iranian population, were ultimately disappointed in the reformists' inability to deliver on their promises made during the presidential elections, to advance Kurdish cultural, political, and economic demands through legal channels. While the reformists were in power, the Kurds in Iran managed to revive some aspects of their culture and language. In the late 1990s, about 20 Kurdish periodicals were being published in Iran, and in some places, such as the Kurdish-populated town of Mahabad, privately owned classes for teaching the Kurdish language were in operation. It became easier for some Iranian Kurds to legally visit Iraqi Kurdistan. Many Kurds who were outside Iran for several years and decades managed to return and visit family members and relatives.

The reformists officially lost power when Mahmoud Ahmadinejad won the Iranian presidential election in June 24, 2005. Since then, Kurdish cultural activities have decreased considerably.[37] Finally, it is important to note that since the mid-1990s, most of the Iranian Kurdish organizations have abandoned armed struggle. Their rebels and cadres have either immigrated to the West or remained in Iraqi Kurdistan under the condition (set by the Kurdish administration in Iraqi Kurdistan) that they will not engage in any cross-border armed activities against the Iranian state.[38]

Syria

The Kurdish reawakening in Syria started in 1999 when the Kurds began their campaign to gain linguistic and cultural rights in that country. In March 2004, during a soccer match in the predominantly Kurdish-populated town of Qamishli, fighting broke out between Kurdish and Arab fans. According to Amnesty International, more than 30 people from Kurdish communities were killed, hundreds were injured, and about 2,000 people were arrested by Syrian security forces. At the beginning of 2005, there were still 200 detainees in Syrian jails. Amnesty International (2005) paints a gloomy picture of the status of Kurds in Syria:

> Kurds in Syria have been subjected to serious human rights violations, as other Syrians, but as a group they also suffer from identity-based discrimination, including restrictions placed upon the use of the Kurdish language and culture. In addition, a large proportion of

the Syrian Kurds are effectively stateless and, as such, they are denied the full provision of education, employment, health and other rights enjoyed by Syrian nationals, as well as being denied the right to have a nationality and passport. (para. 6)

More recently, some flexibility with respect to publishing in Kurdish has been shown by the Syrian government. Diasporic communities, the Internet, and satellite television remain the most reliable and secure communicative spaces for the Kurds from Syria to continue their struggle to gain their rights.

Iraq

Compared to other parts, Iraqi Kurdistan has witnessed and experienced the most profound change in recent years. From the aftermath of the first Gulf War and under the protection of the United States and its allies, the Kurds in Iraq have been governing themselves since 1992; there is a quasi-independent Kurdish state in Iraqi Kurdistan. It is often referred to as the "free Kurdistan" or "little Kurdistan" (O'Leary & Salih, 2005). Although the "existing free Kurdistan is no paradise," it cannot be denied that it has become a source of hope for all Kurds that one day other parts of Kurdistan will enjoy similar freedom in the form of autonomy or independence (O'leary & Salih, 2005). Non-Iraqi Kurds observe events unfolding in Kurdistan-Iraq with interest, and they do this mostly with the help of the media. In addition, many Kurds originally from other parts of Kurdistan live, work, and study in the Iraqi part. The establishment of two airports in Hawler and Suleimania has made it possible for Iraqi and other Kurds to depend less on Turkey for travelling to and from Iraqi Kurdistan and connecting with the rest of the world.

Kurdish Diasporas

As discussed earlier, Kurds in general and Kurdish armed movements in particular have admired mountains as their only friends for decades (Bulloch & Morris, 1992). More recently, however, diasporas have become arguably the best friends of the Kurds. Kurdish diasporas reproduce the fragmentations of Kurdish identity but they have also become places of convergence, cultural and political revival, and collective identity formation. Diasporas have become pan-Kurdish communicative spaces. The dispersion of Kurds can be traced back to the pre-modern times (Hassanpour & Mojab, 2005, p. 215).[39] However, in this study, by Kurdish diasporas or Kurdish diasporic communities,

I mainly refer to Kurdish communities and settlements located in the West and not to all Kurds who live outside the Kurdistan proper (e.g., Kurds living in Khurasan, Istanbul, Baghdad, Tehran, Damascus, Armenia, etc.).

In Europe, the first Kurds, albeit in small numbers, arrived at the end of the nineteenth century (Hassanpour & Mojab, 2005). The first notable Kurdish diasporic organization was the Kurdish Studies Society in Europe, established in 1956. It consisted of Kurds from all parts of Kurdistan and campaigned for Kurdish self-rule (Hassanpour & Mojab, 2005). The second notable wave of immigrants to the West was comprised of economic immigrants from Turkey who settled in Germany and other neighboring countries in the 1960s. However, the most significant wave of Kurdish immigrants to Europe, North America, and Australia occurred around 1980, due to three important changes in Iran, Iraq, and Turkey: (1) The Iranian revolution in 1979 and the war over Iranian Kurdistan starting in 1980; (2) the Iraq-Iran war (1980–1988) and Kurdish armed resistance in Iraqi Kurdistan; and (3) the military coup in Turkey in 1980 (van Bruinessen, 1999, 2000a; van Den Bos & Nell, 2006). The size of Kurdish diasporas in the early 2000s has been estimated at more than 1,300,000: about 900,000 in Europe (Germany alone is home to about 500,000 Kurds), about 200,000 in central Asia (e.g., Turkmenistan, Kazakhstan, etc.), about 130,000 in Caucasia (i.e., Armenia, Azerbaijan, and Georgia), about 85,000 in Lebanon, and about 28,000 in North America and Oceania (Hassanpour & Mojab, 2005).

Kurdish diasporas are diverse because they are influenced by different factors, such as the sociocultural dimensions of immigration in different host countries,[40] the diasporans relations with the countries of origin (e.g., the four states), and Kurdish nationalism and the politics of the homeland, Kurdistan. Kurdish nationalism and the politics of Kurdistan, in particular, reproduce Kurdish fragmentations and at the same time strengthen a collective Kurdish identity. Wahlbeck (1999) observes that Kurdish nationalism "commits many Kurdish refugees to the restoration of their homeland" (p. 180). However, because the movement is divided in Kurdistan, it continues "to divide diasporans, especially in their first generation" (Hassanpour & Mojab, 2005). The relationship between Kurdish political parties often directly affects the relationship between Kurdish diasporans who are affiliated with political parties within Kurdistan. Regarding the effect of country of origin, Wahlbeck (1999) also observes that, depending on where Kurds come from, they identify themselves differently. For example, whereas most of the Iraqi Kurds in the U.K.

and Finland identify themselves as Kurds only, Kurds from Turkey see themselves as part of both Kurdish and Turkish communities (Wahlbeck, 1999).

Kurdish diasporas conveniently exemplify what Anderson (1992) has called "long-distance nationalism" (see also Wahlbeck, 1992, p. 228). Alinia (2004), studying Kurdish diasporic communities in Sweden, observes that all these shape and reinforce a complex collective Kurdish identity in that particular diasporic context:

> The Kurdish identity was formed in opposition to imposed national identities in the countries of origin. Further, in conditions of exile and exclusion the Kurdish identity is mobilized as a resource in order to resist the imposed immigrant identity and survive exclusion and exile. Inwardly, it is constructed through contradictory interactions between Kurdish individuals and groups with different standpoints within the movement. (p. 321)

Furthermore, Alinia observes that, in the face of "racism" and "exclusion" that the Kurdish communities in Sweden feel and experience, they see their diasporic communities as their "home" and a "location" where they can reaffirm a sense of belonging to a "we-identity" and an "imagined community that exceeds many national boundaries" (p. 328).

Although several scholars suggest, with reason, that the fragmentations of Kurdish identity in Kurdistan are reproduced among Kurdish diasporans, they have also advanced the argument that Kurdish diasporas have contributed to the reproduction and articulation of a collective and trans-state Kurdish identity (Alinia, 2004; Hassanpour & Mojab, 2005; Wahlbeck, 1999; van Bruinessen 2000b, 1999). For example, Wahlbeck observes that, despite the differences between Kurdish diasporans in Finland and England, both communities share the wish to return to the homeland Kurdistan, and they both create and maintain Kurdish "transnational social networks" that exceed several continents.

Van Bruinessen (2000b) also observes that diasporas have played a decisive role in shaping and reproducing Kurdish nationalism:

> The experience of exile has been part and parcel of the history of Kurdish nationalism...The awareness of Kurdistan as a homeland, and of the Kurds as a distinct people, has often been strongest in those Kurds who lived elsewhere, among people of different languages and cultures. The first Kurdish associations were established in Istanbul

and more distant places of exile, by Kurds who had studied in other languages and had been exposed to modern ideas. It was exile that brought educated Kurds of different regional backgrounds together and thereby helped them to imagine Kurdistan as their common fatherland. It was exile that transformed Kurdistan from a vaguely defined geographical entity into a political ideal. (para. 11)

According to McDowall (2004), "early advances of national ideas took place largely outside Kurdistan" (p. 455). From the late 1950s onward, Kurdish diasporans started to take advantage of freedom of assembly in Europe and embark on "pan-Kurdish activism," for example through the Kurdish Students Society (1956–1975), with the agenda of Kurdish self-rule (Hassanpour & Mojab, 2005, p. 219).

With the strongest wave of Kurdish immigration to Europe and North America in the 1980s, diasporas became locations where many Kurds of one part met Kurds of other parts of Kurdistan for the first time. Cultural occasions, such as the celebration of *Newroz* (New Day), the Kurdish New Year, on March 21, which is attended by tens of thousands in some places (e.g., Germany), become an expression of belonging to a collective Kurdish identity, despite coming from different regions, communities, ages, and social groups. Promotion of Kurdish culture and literature has also been the agenda for several cultural institutes, libraries, and information centers established in Berlin, Brussels, London, Paris, Stockholm, New York, and Washington (Hassanpour & Mojab, 2005, p. 221). According to Alinia (2004), Kurds from Turkey living in diasporas managed to publish 77 Kurdish periodicals between 1975 and 2003. Since the 1980s, Sweden has become a safe haven for Kurdish exilic writers, poets, and artists. Swedish governments have contributed generously to the maintenance and flourishing of Kurdish language and literature by providing grants to Kurdish writers and artists and supporting them with the publishing and production of their work (see also McDowall, 2004).

Kurdish diasporic communities have also been catalysts in the creation and operation of Kurdish media. The first Kurdish periodical, *Kurdistan*, was published in Cairo in 1898, but it was soon published in European locations. The first Kurdish satellite television, MED-TV (1995–1999), was launched from Europe, and the first Kurdish online activities took place in Western Europe and North America. The next chapter is devoted to a more detailed discussion of Kurdish media and, thus, I shall refrain from repetition. At this juncture it suffices to say that, until the mid-1990s, social networks among Kurdish diasporic communities were more robust than not only networks linking diasporas and their homelands but also networks between the divided parts of the homeland. According to the historian David McDowall:

> With modern technology, the Kurds of Europe rapidly discovered they need not be wholly cut off from their fellows in Kurdistan. In the 1970s transistor radio and cassette tapes provided an important channel for political action and cultural communication. These developments, however, were as nothing compared with the information revolution of the 1990s. (2004, p. 459)

New Media Technologies

In addition to recent political developments and Kurdish diasporas, the new media technologies have strengthened a trans-state or pan-Kurdish identity. Communication technologies foster the creation and strengthening of Kurdish trans-state networks not just from Europe but also from one part of the homeland, Iraqi Kurdistan. Christiane Bird (2004), after traveling throughout Kurdistan in 2002, commented on the fragmentation of the Kurds and at the same time on how this fragmentation might be dealt with after the Kurds have had access to satellite television and the Internet:

> The Kurds remain a fractured people on many levels—torn between countries, regions, political parties, tribes, families, dialects, outlooks, the old and the new.
> And yet, and yet…Modern technology, coupled with oppression, has changed everything. Through satellite communications and the Internet, the Kurds have their own television shows, radio broadcasts, publications, and websites, all of which are theoretically available to every Kurd anywhere in the world…The Kurds may not have their own physical nation, but they do have an international cyberspace state, along with a quickening sense of national identity that, decades from now, may yet give rise to Pan-Kurds unification—perhaps in the form of a federated Kurdish nation-state. (p. 373)

Bird believes that one of the ways in which satellite TV could engender a pan-Kurdish identity is by making Kurdish language varieties mutually intelligible:

> Many Kurmanji speakers cannot understand Sorani speakers, and vice versa…However, this barrier is breaking down, largely because of

television [partly because of war and upheaval]...Perhaps two-thirds of Iraqi Kurds now have access to satellite dishes, as do many Kurds in Iran and Turkey. (p. 143)

Like Bird, many Kurds and some observers have seen satellite television in particular, but also the Internet, bringing Kurds from different regions and factions closer to each other and mobilizing them for staging a mass nationalist movement, with the hope of achieving national emancipation. When the first Kurdish satellite television, MED-TV, was launched in 1995, a Kurdish newspaper wrote that the step is "more important than all [Kurdish] armed revolutions" (as cited in Hassanpour, 1998, p. 44). MED-TV's director, HikmetTabak, has been quoted as saying that Kurds all over the world were excited about the station because "they think this is the first step on the last, long part of the road to the formation of a Kurdish state" (Ryan, 1997, p. 5).

In light of these propositions, one cannot help but ask: why is it that in the case of the Kurds, it is only recently that this strong connection has been made between a collective Kurdish identity and mass communication technologies? To be more specific, what are satellite television and the Internet capable of doing for the Kurds that other media have failed to do? I will explore answers to this question in the next chapter.

CHAPTER 4

Kurdish Media:
From Print to Facebook

In the previous chapter, I suggested that a cross-border or trans-state Kurdish identity has been strengthening in the past two decades or so primarily due to three factors: political developments in Kurdistan, the expansion of Kurdish diasporas, and the use of satellite television and the Internet among the Kurds. In this chapter, it is suggested that the latter is a catalyst in strengthening a cross-border Kurdish identity. Why is this? Previously, I illustrated that other forms of media such as newspapers and radio or cable television have played crucial roles in the formation and reproduction of national identities and nation-building projects, particularly in Europe. Why has this not been the case in Kurdistan? Have the Kurds not had access to these more traditional media forms prior to using satellite television and the Internet? If they have, why have they not been able to embark on constructing a strong pan-Kurdish identity until very recently?

It is my submission that since the mid-1990s, satellite television and the Internet have facilitated a dialogic communication among the Kurds, a development that possibly has contributed to the emergence of a strong and unprecedented cross-border collective Kurdish identity. To examine the plausibility of this hypothesis, I take a brief survey of the development of various Kurdish media from print to the Internet. Through a critical review of the literature on Kurdish media and identity construction, I suggest that research on Kurdish satellite television and the Internet is in short supply. Empirical research on the discourse practices of these media needs to be carried out to understand how and in what ways these media articulate Kurdish identities. The new electronic media provide rich contexts within which the dynamics of group identity constructions and reproductions can be studied.

PRINT

About two centuries ago, *Nalî* (d. 1855),[1] a Kurdish poet from the *Şarezûr* (Sharazoor) region of today's Iraqi Kurdistan, realized the power that one can access by writing in a language that was for the most part only spoken until then. Because he was writing in three languages (Persian, Kurdish, and Arabic), he likened his multilingual collection of poems to ruling over three territories:

> *Fars û Kurd û Erab her sêm be defter girtuwe*
> *Nalî emřo hakimî sê mulke, dîwanî heye*
> I have captured Persians, Kurds, and Arabs with my monograph,
> Nalî rules over three territories today, [for] he has a *dîwan* (book of poems)
> (Nalî, 1976, p. 577, my translation)

In 1890, *Hacî Qadir Koyî* (Haji Ghadir Koyi), another Kurdish poet and *mullah*, considered by most nationalists and a number of researchers as the first modern Kurdish nationalist (van Bruinessen, 2003; Hassanpour, 2003a), was vividly aware of the role of the press in nation-building as he wrote: "A hundred epistles and odes are not worth a penny [any more] / Newspapers and magazines have [now] become valuable and respected" (Qadir, 1986, as cited in Hassanpour, 1992, p. 221). Despite this realization of the importance of writing and print in the life of a nation by poets like Nali and Qadir Koyi, the first publication in Kurdish did not appear until the very end of the nineteenth century.

Hassanpour (1992) perceives the Kurdish press as "the organ of Kurdish nationalism" (p. 221). To put it differently, the emergence of journalism among the Kurds marks the beginning of their movements for national rights (Ahmadzadeh, 2003). The first Kurdish periodical, *Kurdistan*, was published in Ottoman Cairo in 1898, by the princely family of Badir Khan. It was a bilingual (Kurmanji Kurdish-Turkish) periodical that was committed to "[stirring up] feelings in support of the Kurdish people, led by its notables and shaykhs" (McDowall, 2004, p. 90). The paper was initiated in Cairo because it was not granted permission in Istanbul, the seat of the Ottoman Empire. However, the pressure from Istanbul forced the paper to move to Geneva, London, and, finally, to Folkstone, U.K. (Hassanpour, 1992; see also van Bruinessen, 2000b).[2]

From the printing of the first Kurdish newspaper until 1985, about 145 periodicals were published, mostly in Iraq using the Sorani

Kurdish variety (Hassanpour, 1992).[3] By 1985, private journalism had disappeared and 11 periodicals published in Iraq, Iran, and the USSR were state sponsored. However, since the mid-1990s several privately owned periodicals have appeared in Iran, Turkey and Syria, albeit under strict state censorship. Since 1991, with the formation of the Kurdistan Regional Government in Iraq, hundreds of periodicals, including two dailies[4] have been published in Iraqi Kurdistan. It is important to note again that the vast majority of these periodicals have used Sorani Kurdish, the dominant variety in Iraq and Iran. Nearly all the Kurmanji periodicals and books were printed in diasporic communities, particularly in Germany and Sweden, prior to 1991 when Kurmanji publications gained popularity in Iraq and limited printed materials appeared in Turkey. In 1997, about 150 Kurdish periodicals were published worldwide (*Newrozi*, n.d.).

The press was a catalyst in engendering the first modern nation-states in Europe and America (Anderson, 1991). In the case of Kurdistan, however, due to many obstacles, the Kurdish press has not been the mass medium capable of fostering a Kurdish-imagined community, despite the increase in the number of publications in the last two decades or so. The Kurdish press has faced major difficulties from the very beginning. The state of the Kurdish press up to the end of the 1980s is summarized as follows:

> The Kurdish press is characterized by the absence of enduring dailies, low circulation, poor distribution facilities, dependence on subscription and single copy sales, lack of or insignificant advertising revenue, poor printing facilities, shortage of newsprint, and limited professionalization and specialization. These features are characteristic of the press in developing societies...although their persistence and hindering impact on the Kurdish press has been reinforced by the division of the Kurdish speech community and political restrictions on the use of language. (Hassanpour, 1992, p. 276)

Reports as recent as 2005 from Iraqi Kurdistan indicate that Kurdish periodicals have not been able to secure wide audiences and attract advertising revenues, and overcome the linguistic divisions in Kurdistan (Murad, 2005). A more recent observation suggests that the most popular periodical in Iraqi Kurdistan may not circulate more than 10,000 copies (Salih, 2010). This low consumption of print materials is also true about Kurdish books. The population of Iraqi Kurdistan is more than 4 million, but the average run of books is just about 1,000.

Kutschera (2005) reports on the political restrictions that the Kurdish press in Iran faces:

> The Kurdish press is limited to half a dozen weeklies . . . Kurdish journalists acknowledge that self-censorship is a daily routine. "There are many 'red lines,' we cannot speak much about the Kurds, and still less about the Iranian Kurds," explains a journalist of [*Ashti* (Peace)], founded in February 2004, suspended during the summer and which has only recently managed to resume publication. "The authorities have asked us not to speak too much of federalism, but we do. We publish articles about countries where federalism is implemented, about the various types of federalism," says a journalist of [*Ashti*], whose first issue was published on 18 January 2004. "We cannot write directly about the problems of the Iranian Kurds, so we speak of the problems of the other Kurds." "The press law allows us to write roughly 20% of what we think," concludes a journalist of [Ashti], who describes himself as a "revolutionary." "We walk on the back of a scorpion." (para. 17)

It is interesting to note that in the same report, Kutschera talks to a group of Kurdish student activists from the Kurdish city of *Sine* (Sanandaj), who blame Iranian Kurdish opposition groups outside Iran for not launching a satellite television channel. They believe that a satellite television station can "keep Kurds in touch with each other" (Kutschera, 2005).

Obstacles to Kurdish publications are closely connected to the issue of illiteracy in Kurdistan where the majority of the population are illiterate especially in their mother tongue (Matras & Reerschemius, 1991). Hassanpour (1992) suggests that, around the time that the first Kurdish newspaper *Kurdistan* was published in 1898, about 97 percent of the Kurds were not able to read or write in any language. McDowall (2004) refers to the Kurds from Turkey as "a largely illiterate population" in Turkish and particularly in Kurdish (p. 447). Statistical data shows that in the early 1980s, the average illiteracy rate, in any language, among the urban Iranian Kurds adds up to around 66 percent (Koohi-Kamali, 2003).[5] One should expect a much greater rate of illiteracy among the rural Kurds where fewer people have had the opportunity to go to school in any language.

With respect to the level of literacy in Kurdish in Syria, Malmisanij (2006a) writes: "Although there are no definite numbers, Kurdish politicians and writers I have spoken to have stated that as Arabic is the official alphabet in Syria and is used at all levels of education, the number of Kurds who can read and write in the Latin alphabet is very small" (p. 26). Reporting on the Kurdish literacy situation in Turkey in 2005, Malmisanij (2006b) reports that "very few of the Kurds in Turkey can read and write in Kurdish, most having learned it on their own" (p. 39). Learning Kurdish on their own also applies to the vast majority of Iranian Kurds.

The Kurdish speakers of Iraq who live in areas under the control of the Kurdish administration have had most of their education in Kurdish since 1991, but the vast majority of Kurds in Iran, Turkey, and Syria have not been able to read the Kurdish press. Even within Iraq, until the early 1970s, education in Kurdish was neither extended to the Kurmanji-speaking regions (e.g., provinces of Mosul and Duhok) nor to those Sorani speakers who lived outside the two provinces of Suleimania and Hawler, such as Kirkuk and Khanaqin regions.

Thus, printing in Kurdish mostly has been by small groups of the intelligentsia for larger groups of the intelligentsia. Even for these small groups, access to Kurdish print materials was not easy until very recently. For example, conducting his research as recently as 2005, Malmisanij (2006b) writes that:

> In Turkey the Ministry of Culture and Tourism has 1453 libraries. 1224 of them are public ones. 209 of the public libraries are situated in the 22 provinces with predominantly Kurdish populations. There are no Kurdish books even in the libraries of these predominantly Kurdish provinces. (p. 40)

He also observes that almost all of the few owners and managers of book-publishing houses in Turkey have been persecuted and spent time in jail for putting out Kurdish materials. The situation has not been better in Iran (Hassanpour, 1992) or Syria (Malmisanij, 2006a). In other words, the vast majority of Kurds have not been trained to read and write in their mother tongue, and those who have learned the language on their own (almost all the Kurds from Iran, Turkey, and Syria) have not been able to access Kurdish materials easily. Therefore, it seems safe to suggest that the Kurdish press has never been the mass medium that would enable the Kurds to imagine themselves as one community. Despite this, it is safe to suggest that the press shaped the ideas and politics of the intellectuals and activists, who are the architect of nationalism.[6]

RADIO AND CABLE TELEVISION

With the exception of Kurdistan-Iraq since 1991, the states of Turkey, Iran, Iraq, and Syria have nearly always held a monopoly on broadcasting. The first radio broadcast started in the Soviet Union in the Kurdish autonomous region in Transcaucasia (1923–1929) (Hassanpour, 1996, p. 73; see also Zimmerman, 1994). The second Kurdish radio broadcasting took place in Iraq in 1939. In Iran, broadcasting in Kurdish started in 1946 when the Kurds and Azerbaijanis of Iran established their autonomous republics without the consent of the Iranian government but with the support of the Soviet Union. This broadcasting came to a halt with the fall of the Mahabad Republic 11 months after its establishment. Kurdish broadcasting resumed in Baku, Azerbaijan, in 1949. Assuming that Kurdish broadcasting was established for the purposes of the construction of Soviet socialism, on the recommendation of the United States, the Iranian government started broadcasting in Kurdish in January 1950 (Hassanpour, 1992, 1996). In Turkey, under the pressure of the E.U., broadcasting in Kurdish was legalized in 2002 on the conditions that it would be carried on state radio and television only, and for less than one hour per day (*Associated Press*, 2002).[7] In mid-2006, a privately owned terrestrial Kurdish television outlet, *Gün* TV,[8] and a radio station, *Gün* Radio, started their broadcasts with limited hours, choice of programming, and under severe restrictions.[9] A significant development in Kurdish broadcasting in Turkey took place on January 1, 2009, when for the first time TRT6, channel 6 of *Türkiye Radyo ve Televizyon Kurumu* (The Turkish Radio and Television Corporation) started airing programs in Kurdish (Olson, 2009).[10] Limited Kurdish television programming on state-owned television stations started in Iraq and Iran in the early 1970s. The situation remains relatively unchanged in Iran. Except for clandestine radio broadcasting, which has played an important role in the Kurdish nationalist movements, for the most part, radio and cable television have been monopolized by the states that have used their media as tools of assimilation.[11]

In Iraq, Kurdish audiences witnessed a dramatic expansion in publishing and broadcasting following the first Gulf War when the Kurds started to establish a de facto state in northern Iraq. There are currently more than 20 television stations and a dozen radio stations in Kurdistan-Iraq. McKiernan (2006) reports that in 2002 "nineteen Kurdish television stations were broadcasting in northern Iraq" (p. 178). The vast majority of these are owned by the two major political parties, the PUK and KDP. Although nearly all the other organizations, from the Communist Party of Iraqi Kurdistan to the Islamic Movement in Iraqi Kurdistan, own their local radio and television stations, only the PUK and KDP have managed to reach the widest audiences with their satellite television channels.

Satellite Television

Strengthening pan-Kurdish sentiments has co-occurred with the use of the new electronic mass media, specifically satellite television and the Internet, by the Kurdish organizations, intelligentsia, and the public at large. This co-occurrence is not a mere coincidence. A truly Kurdish mass medium seems to have emerged only with satellite television.

The first Kurdish satellite television MED-TV started broadcasting to south and central Asia, North Africa, and Europe in 1995 from Europe (Ryan, 1997). It was licensed in Britain and had studios in Belgium, Britain, and Sweden. Karim (2006) calls the establishing of MED-TV "one of the most fascinating uses of DBS technology in the Middle Eastern context" (p. 274). He continues, "This is a case of a diaspora within and without the divided homeland attempting to sustain itself and to counter forceful suppression with the use of communications technology" (Karim, 2006). Many observers saw MED-TV as a unique case also because it was possibly the first significant satellite TV channel owned by a stateless and oppressed people (Hearse, 1997). Ryan (1997) reported that the station was "set up to 'develop Kurdish culture and language and to provide communication for the Kurds'" (as cited in Karim, 1998, p. 10).

Because the station was alleged to be owned and operated by supporters of the PKK, the Kurdish organization from Turkey, the channel was harassed by Turkey from its inception (Hassanpour, 1998; Hearse, 1997; Price, 2001; White, 2000).[12] This was not unexpected given the impact of the station:

> MED-TV has disturbed Turkey's constitutional blueprint for a pure, sovereign Turkish presence in the 'southeast.' It has established relations with Kurdish viewers not as members of an audience but rather as citizens of a Kurdish state, and, by doing so, it is exercising deterritorialized sovereignty. Every day, viewers experience the citizenship of a state with its national flag, national anthem, national television and national news agency. Indeed, everyday MED-TV raised the Kurdish flag in about two million homes. (Hassanpour, 1998, p. 66)

The station was also widely watched in Iran, Iraq, and Syria (Ryan, 1997). MED-TV's license was revoked in April 1999 on the charges of "breaching regulations on impartiality" (Wahlbeck, 2002, p. 6). Wahlbeck, however, believes that the main reason for closing MED-TV was that it represented Kurdish identity: "The whole project enraged the Turkish government, which is perhaps not surprising bearing in mind the oppression imposed on the Kurds in Turkey and the Turkish authorities' discontent at any Kurdish cultural expression" (Wahlbeck, 2002, p. 6).

Within a few months, on July 31, 1999, Medya TV started broadcasting from Europe, with its main studios in a small town near Brussels. Medya TV, similar to MED-TV, was perceived as Kurdish and Kurds' own channel by the vast majority of Kurds. For example, Birch (2003) reported from Diarbakir, the largest Kurdish populated city in Turkey:

> anybody with enough money to buy a satellite dish and decoder has been able to watch Kurdish programming 24 hours a day, beamed in from the Brussels headquarters of Medya-TV. "Thanks to Medya, our only reason for watching Turkish TV now is to see how much it lies," says Muzaffer, a patron of the cafe. "Only Medya is objective, the eyes and ears of our people." (para. 2)

However, in January 2004, after its content was being examined for five years by French authorities, they refused to grant Medya TV a license. French authorities concluded that Medya TV was a continuation of MED-TV in that it was "making propaganda" for the PKK (*French court cancels*, 2004).

The current satellite TV that is managed by the Kurds from Turkey is Roj TV, which is licensed by a Danish registered firm. It went on the air on March 1, 2004. Turkey has been pressuring Denmark to revoke Roj TV's license because Turkish authorities accuse the station of having ties with the PKK (Schleifer, 2006). In January 2006, 54 mayors of Kurdish-populated towns in Turkey sent a letter to the Danish authorities and urged them to ignore the pressure from Turkey and keep the station. The mayors have been charged with supporting the PKK and may face imprisonment (*Dozens of DTP*, 2007). According to the *Turkish Daily News*, in May 2007, the Danish Radio and Television Council ruled that Turkey's complaints against Roj TV were unfounded and that it will continue to honor the station's license (*Danish council gives*, 2007). In addition to Roj TV, there is also MMC TV (Mesopotamya Music Channel), which airs Kurdish music-video clips 24 hours a day under the license of Mesoptamya broadcast in Denmark.[13]

Impressed by the impact of the satellite TV stations of the Kurds of Turkey and Iraq (further discussion will follow), three political organizations from Kurdistan-Iran started launching their satellite TV stations in early 2006, 11 years after MED-TV was launched.

In January 2004, in an online discussion forum set up by Abdullah Mohtadi, the general secretary of the Komala Party, he explained why Kurds from Iran lagged so much behind other Kurds in launching their satellite TV stations. He wrote that in his party they had been thinking about this for a long time and they had seriously considered it, but that due to financial constraints they had not been able to launch their channel (Mohtadi, 2005). The three TV channels are Komala TV, Rojhelat TV, and Tishk TV, owned by three major Iranian Kurdish political organizations: Komala, the Komala Party (Revolutionary Organization of the Toilers of Iranian Kurdistan), and the KDPI (Democratic Party of Iranian Kurdistan), respectively.[14] The three stations have their studios in Europe and broadcast to Europe and the Middle East, including Kurdistan. The Iranian Kurdish channels have fewer programs and a much shorter air time compared to Roj TV and the Iraqi Kurds' satellite stations such as Kurdistan TV. Finally, it is interesting to note that these television stations of the Kurds from Iran were launched at a time when the dispute over the proliferation of uranium between the West and Iran was escalating. In fact, there have been suggestions that the United States is funding the stations (Sina, 2006; 2007b). The spokespersons for at least two of the stations, Tishk TV and Rojhelat TV, have rejected the "accusation" (Sina, 2006, 2007b).

Iraqi Kurds launched their satellite TV channels (i.e., Kurdistan TV and KurdSat) before the Iranian Kurds. According to the London-based Arabic newspaper, *Al-Sharq Al-Awsat*, "The success of MED-TV propelled the two main Iraqi Kurdish parties to try to duplicate the experience" (Sheikhani, 2004). Two major Kurdish organizations, the Kurdistan Democratic Party (KDP) and the Patriotic Union of Kurdistan (PUK) launched their satellite television stations, Kurdistan TV in 1999, and KurdSat in 2000, respectively. According to White (2000), Turkey was very concerned about the political impact of MED-TV, and later Medya TV. Knowing that closing MED-TV did not stop Turkey's Kurds from launching other TV channels (i.e., Medya TV and Mesopotamia TV), Turkey helped the two Kurdish political parties in Iraq to establish their own satellite TV stations in the hope that they would attract Kurdish audiences from Turkey and prevent them from watching Turkish Kurds' stations (pp. 175–179; see also Romano, 2002). According to Romano, KDP officials have rejected the assertion and have maintained that KTV's "purpose is simply to give a voice to Iraqi Kurdistan, its people, its reality and its culture" (p. 143). One can expect a similar reply from KurdSat.

The director for KurdSat told *Al-Sharq Al-Awsat* that the first goal of the station was to address the "Arab street" and the world regarding the Kurdish issue, and the second goal was "to reach the Kurdish communities scattered all over the globe" (Sheikhani, 2004). However, according to the same source, the spokesperson for the other station, Kurdistan TV, assured *Al-Sharq Al-Awsat* that one of the station's objectives was to promote the integrity of Iraq. This way, both stations avoided making any explicit statement, in an Arabic newspaper, that would upset Arab nationalism, which does have a stake in Iraq.

Kurdistan TV (KTV), the subject of this study, claims that viewers can watch its programs throughout the world. Thus, theoretically, it reaches Kurdish audiences larger than that of most of the other Kurdish satellite TV stations. Except for the other Iraqi Kurdish satellite TV channel, KurdSat, none of the other Kurdish satellite TV stations (e.g., Roj TV, Mesopotamia TV, Tishk TV, Rojhelat TV, Komala TV, Zagros TV) can reach North America or Australia.[15] KTV can also be watched on the Internet through a live streaming service (www.kurdistantv.net). Kurdistan TV is also important because it is stationed in Kurdistan under Kurdish self-rule. It does not seem to be facing any obvious financial or political constraints. The head of the KDP and the owner of Kurdistan TV is Masoud Barzani, who is the president of Iraqi Kurdistan. This situation understandably adds to the importance of KTV; however, there is a negative side to that. O'Leary and Salih (2005) suggest that both KTV and KurdSat "are still too close to the two main parties," but at the same time report that the stations' "partisan tilt results from their own deference rather than the instructions of the respective party leaders" (p. 28).[16] This study will investigate the accuracy of this assertion, keeping in mind that such claims are often framed within the theoretical positions of the liberal paradigm, which posits a separation of media and state powers. This perspective, however, has been refuted with influential theories and compelling empirical evidence (e.g., Herman & Chomsky, 2002; Winter, 2007).

The unique position of Kurdistan-Iraq makes KTV very significant for both cultural and political reasons. Kurdistan-Iraq is the only Kurdish region that Kurds can refer to as the "free Kurdistan" (O'Leary & Salih, 2005, p. 24). The assertion that the host states have prevented Kurds from achieving freedom and prosperity is widely held among the Kurds, including the common people. Kurdish nationalists have blamed "others" for the division of Kurdistan, the absence of a state of their own, and the lack of a unified language, culture, and identity. But now the Kurds in Iraq have the freedom to articulate their national identity, plan for their language, cultivate their culture, and decide on their political fate, partly through satellite television stations. KTV is one of the most powerful means of cultural production, providing a rich context for studying the dynamics of identity formation in Kurdistan. KTV is important also because it is not confined to the Kurdistan-Iraq region. It is watched by Kurds from all parts of Kurdistan and diasporic communities (Firouzi, 2005). A look at the press and broadcasting from other parts of Kurdistan indicates that a great number of Kurds follow the news from Iraqi Kurdistan with great interest. KTV is one of the sources of this news. This could be one of the reasons that Kurdistan TV is not welcomed by the governments of Iran and Turkey. KTV has complained about its reporters being harassed in the two countries. Mehmet Eren, Kurdistan TV's Diyarbakir bureau Chief, has reported about the "[constant] pressure" that KTV correspondents endure in Turkey:

> Although we totally comply with the legal framework [in Turkey], we can't cover official events, can't get accreditation without a reason, face random and arbitrgry pressure such as identity checks etc...Our focus is on news related to the Kurdish issue in Turkey and such coverage results in increasing pressure and obstruction on us...Our houses and offices are surveilled by the police. We also received anonymous e-mail threats. (Un, 2007, para. 3)

According to *Voice of America* (2007), KTV correspondents have also been under pressure in Iran.[17] These examples seem to further indicate the significance of KTV for the Kurds not only in Iraq but also in the neighboring countries. However, despite its importance, to the best of my knowledge, no empirical study of Kurdistan TV has been carried out to investigate its discourse practices of Kurdish identity formation. The subsequent chapters will do just that.

INTERNET

Whereas satellite television stations are mostly owned by dominant Kurdish political organizations, the Internet provides alternative communicative spaces to smaller organizations, social groups, cultural societies, and individuals who play their parts in the processes of identity construction in Kurdistan.

Like satellite television, Internet use started among Kurdish diasporic communities in the mid-1990s. The usage at the beginning was limited and comprised of email use and newsgroup discussions. According to Romano (2002), prior to 1995, there were fewer than 20 Kurdish websites (See also Wahlbeck, 2002). Until the early 2000s, very few households had access to computers, let alone ISPs in Kurdistan.[18] Many Kurds from the diaspora were facing difficulties using the Internet for political or cultural activities, because Arabic-based Kurdish alphabet was not supported on the web. The vast majority of websites were in English and other European languages spoken by members of the Kurdish diaspora.

In the early 2000s, two major changes contributed to a great increase in the number of Kurdish web sites and then weblogs. First, Kurdistan started to be served by relatively sufficient ISP services, something that until then was in a meager state, especially in Iraq, Syria, and Iran. Second, Kurd IT Group,[19] a technical group of Kurdish volunteers, developed the first Unicode-based Kurdish fonts (e.g., Unikurd Web, Tahoma, and so on) and the Windows Kurdish Support program, which made Kurdish writing with computers and publishing on the Internet a great deal easier.

One of the first studies of the Internet in connection to the Kurds was presented in a conference paper (Bakker, 2001). In June 2001, using the search engine hotbot.com, Bakker conducted a search for websites with the word "Kurdistan" in their page title, and the search returned 1,800 items. I conducted the exact search on May 22, 2007, and it returned 658,500 hits, which indicates a dramatic growth of the presence of Kurdistan on the Internet since 2001. It is not clear, however, what percentage of these websites are Kurdish-owned or are for and visited by the Kurds. The website Koord, one of the most reliable Kurdish sources which indexes Kurdish websites, provides links to more than "2,000 websites" in May 2007.

Research on the use of Internet among the Kurds is scarce in any language.[20] Bakker (2001), who engages in some brief analysis of Kurdish websites, underscores the importance of the Internet for enhancing identity among the Kurds. He summarizes his findings as follows:

> in most cases it is just information (or to be more correct propaganda). But according to the amount of visitors, it is something that is enjoyed very much…these websites can be important for some groups or individuals, research points in the direction of strengthening identity. (p. 17)

Bakker, however, does not mention the fact that at the time of his research (1999), the vast majority of the Kurds living in the Middle

East did not have access to the Internet (Romano, 2002, p. 139), and that the majority of the websites, including those that he has investigated (e.g., www.akakurdistan.com), were published in English and other European languages.

Romano (2002) focuses on the ways in which the use of media technology has transferred Kurdish nationalist movement, especially among the Kurds of Turkey. Although he does not engage in detailed analyses of Kurdish Internet, either, Romano makes some interesting observations. He notes that Kurds, like many other ethnic groups, have used e-mail for "organizing nationalist projects" (p. 139).[21] He also draws attention to the importance of the Internet as "a forum for discussions and arguments on 'forbidden' subjects" (p. 139). Kurds of Turkey used the Internet from their various diasporic communities to make their banned publications available to Kurds inside Turkey. Romano (2002), however, makes no reference to the use of the Internet by Kurds from Iraq, Iran, and Syria.

Mills (2002) looks at the attempts made by the Tibetans, the Chiapas, and the Kurds "to use the Internet to further their identity construction or self-determination projects" (p. 70). In response to those who have viewed the Internet mostly as an internationalizing force, Mills contends that "it is far too soon to declare the end of nationalism and parochial identity" (p. 70). Based on his observation of several websites, mainly in English, and without getting into much substantial textual analyses, Mills concludes that the Kurds are using the Internet to maintain their "'logical state' or 'cybernation' known as Kurdistan…providing common points of contact and sources of instantaneous cultural and political information to its members around the world" (p. 82). The advent of the Internet, like that of other communication media, unleashed a host of optimisms, including the end of so many things. While it is not difficult to see Internet sources that advocate internationalism, they are apparently dwarfed by those that nurture nationalism.

The assertion that the Internet strengthens ethnic and national identities is also echoed in Erikson (2007), who partially focuses on the use of the Internet among the Kurds. Of the four varieties of Internet nationalism identified by Erikson, he places the Kurds' in the "pre-independent" category, and suggests that "it may actually be said that the Kurdish nation reaches its fullest, most consolidated form on transnational websites in the metropolitan languages English, German and French" (p. 9). He also makes a very interesting observation regarding the Kurds, contrary to many other observers who perceive the Kurds as already possessing a national, as opposed to an ethnic, identity. He states that "Kurdish national identity may be said to be in a formative stage" and underscores the "considerable factionalism" and fragmentations among them. He concludes that the "diaspora or virtual nationalism" is unlike the nation-state model of nationalism, in the sense that it is "unstable," because it is not bounded by territory and it is non-homogenous. This should not mean that non-virtual nations are homogenous or that territory guarantees homogeneity. Erikson's observation, however, is significant in that he believes that in order to understand the nation formation of people without a state, like the Kurds, we must abandon the classic notion of the nation as a homogenous entity and, instead, consider pluralism as a part of the equation (p. 16).

Erikson's study, like most of the studies discussed earlier, suffers from a methodological shortcoming. His findings are based on Kurdish Internet sources presented in English or languages other than Kurdish. Non-Kurdish language websites and resources are often aimed at non-Kurdish speakers, mostly Westerners, as the very website that Erikson has analyzed (kurdishmedia.com)[22] indicates in its mission statement (Erikson, 2007, p. 9). Although these websites may also target audiences who do not speak the Kurdish language but identify themselves as Kurds; for example, the Kurdish diasporas, whose first and foremost aim is to gain support for the Kurdish cause by presenting the Kurdish case to prospective audiences in the "international community," especially the elites in the West, who might somehow benefit the Kurds by influencing their countries' foreign policies. In any case, it is doubtful if the prime objective of the non-Kurdish websites is to invoke Kurdishness in their audiences, since the majority of them may not be Kurds in the first place. In the project of identity formation among a people which considers its language as one of the most important indicators of group identity, media content presented in the native language matters a great deal. Studying the Kurdish-language Internet has been neglected.

To sum up, the assertion that both satellite television and the Internet have enhanced identity production among the Kurds remains a plausible hypothesis at best. Much empirical research is needed to test this hypothesis. The hypothesis is based primarily on the assumption that, because the Kurds now have access to these electronic media, they have started to connect with each other more than ever, to rediscover each other, and to become a unified nation. The assumption ignores the question of language, media content, the dynamics of identity formation, and the historical and political realities of Kurds and Kurdistan. These assumptions ignore the fact that connections and becoming aware of others sometimes draw out differences instead of creating commonalities. For example, a Kurdish student from Iran who was studying in Iraqi Kurdistan expressed his disappointment and frustration at the cultural differences that existed between the two parts of Kurdistan. He claimed that he was "homesick" there because he found Iraqi Kurdistan more "traditional" and "tribal," and that the people there "dressed and ate differently, and it was much easier to date girls in Tehran than in Suleimania [, Iraq]" (Watson, 2005, my translation).

CHAPTER 5

Discourse Practices of Kurdistan TV (KTV)

This chapter and the next will look at the satellite television channel Kurdistan TV (henceforth, KTV) to investigate the ways in which this channel is used in the construction and articulation of Kurdish identity. I will specifically focus on discursive practices that are deemed essential in constructing a pan-Kurdish sentiment, by which I mean the creation of a sense of belonging to one people or nation, the Kurds, and their homeland, Kurdistan. Analyses will be carried out according to the CDA method for analyzing media discourse that I have introduced in previous chapters. The analysis takes place at three levels: discourse practices analysis (this chapter), textual analysis (the next chapter), and sociocultural analysis (conclusion chapter).

This chapter focuses on analyzing KTV's programming or what can be called discourse practices. I will first expand my description of KTV by presenting the channel's mission declared on its website. This is followed by describing the data on which my analysis of the station is based. Finally, KTV's discourse practice is analyzed, including its programs and language use, and the ways in which these discourse practices contribute to the construction of Kurdish identities.

On its website, KTV is described as follows:

KURDISTAN TV is a Kurdistani Satellite Channel, the first Satellite TV to transmit from the free land of Southern Kurdistan. First programs [*sic*] were aired on January 17th, 1999.

In addition Kurdish language [*sic*], KURDISTAN TV aired its programs in Arabic, English, Persian, Turkish, Syriac and Turcoman languages. Some of the language services have been stopped for the time being.

KURDISTAN TV has a public policy, message, [*sic*] that it tries to apply in all its programs and activities.

> KURDISTAN TV pays attention and encourages dialogue, the free expression of views and has become a fertile ground for the exchange of opposite views.
>
> Viewers all over the world can watch Kurdistan through the following satellites. (Kurdistan Television, 2006)[1]

This self-describing text from KTV's website identifies Iraqi Kurdistan as "Southern Kurdistan," implying that it is only one part, the southern part, of a greater land, Kurdistan. Furthermore, by characterizing "Southern Kurdistan" as "free," the website implies that other parts of Kurdistan (northern, eastern, and western) are not free. The assertion that there is a greater Kurdistan is an indispensable part of the pan-Kurdish nationalist discourse. As an institution owned by a regional Kurdish organization, KTV is not explicit about this pan-nationalistic sentiment, choosing instead to reinforce it in subtle ways. My interest lies in making these subtle ways of constructing a pan-Kurdish identity transparent. In order to do this, these questions are asked: What discursive strategies aiming at constructing national identities are employed on KTV? To what extent are these strategies directed at constructing a pan-Kurdish identity? To put it differently, what aspects of KTV programming serve the purpose of defining a collective identity for all people of Kurdistan? What linguistic and audio-visual tools and elements are used in constructing identities discursively? Finally, what possible explanations could be offered for KTV's discourse practices and discursive constructions pertinent to identity construction?

KTV PROGRAMS

Fisk and Hartley (2003) suggest that "the starting point of any study of television must be with what is actually there on the screen" (p. 8). I have been following KTV broadcasting since 2002. In order to systematically collect data from the station, I videotaped one week of KTV broadcasting, 168 hours, from August 6 to August 12, 2005. As discussed earlier, in choosing this week, one criterion in particular was considered: that the data represent KTV's regular programming, as opposed to weeks or time periods during which many shows are devoted to national holidays, such as *Newroz* (the New Year) or anniversaries and commemorations, such as the bombardment of Halabja on March 18, 1988.

KTV airs its programs 24 hours a day, seven days a week.[2] Its daily schedule runs from 8A.M. in the morning to midnight, local time

(Hawler/Erbil, Iraq).[3] From approximately midnight until around 8A.M., a selection of the same programs is re-aired. Since KTV viewers are located in very different time zones (e.g., Middle East, Europe, Australia, and North America), the reruns allow the majority of viewers to watch the same KTV programs. This flexibility in viewing KTV programs is expanded by the fact that even during the original broadcasting period (about 8:00–24:00), several shows are repeated, such as news, news in brief, weather, and the children's program. Based on their content, KTV programs can be classified into these categories: arts and entertainment, news, children's, current affairs, sociocultural, history and demography, shows in non-Kurdish languages, and, finally, other programs.

Arts and entertainment makes up the largest portion of programs aired on KTV (about 36 percent), news (about 15.2 percent), children's (about 9.4 percent), and current affairs concerning political issues of the day (about 9.2 percent) come next in rank. About 20 percent of these programs, mostly news and talk shows, are live. Programs in languages other than Kurdish (about 8.5 percent), sociocultural—for example, employment, women's issue, youth education, family relations—(4.5 percent), and history and demography of Kurdistan (2.7 percent) make up the next significant grouping. The rest (14.5 percent) of the air time is filled with advertising, community announcements, promotions for KTV programs, and special reports. As part of this grouping, locally produced dramas (usually one per year aired during the month of Ramadan), and films made by internationally acclaimed Kurdish directors such as Bahman Ghobadi[4] are offered, along with dubbed drama series, predominantly from South Korea.[5] The language of most of these programs is Kurdish, Sorani, Kurmanji/Badini, and Hawrami. About 8 percent of them are in languages other than Kurdish varieties, including Arabic, Turkomani, and Assyrian.

In addition to recording KTV broadcasting for one week, I recorded various shows throughout my active observation of KTV since 2005. For example, I recorded a show aired on January 7, 2007 (Talib, 2007), devoted to audience reaction to KTV's performance. These shows provide useful insights from KTV's personnel and audience, albeit selected viewers, about the aims and objectives of the station and the kind of identity they are committed to maintain or construct. In addition, I have collected published literature and information pertinent to KTV. This literature, along with a number of informal communications with Kurds in Kurdistan and diasporic communities about KTV, will be used for contextualizing the data so that a sufficient intertextual analysis will enrich interpretations of data analyses and final discussions.

KTV Programming and the Construction of a pan-Kurdish Identity

In what follows, five key questions are asked in order to illustrate the extent to which KTV programming contributes to the construction of a pan-Kurdish identity. These questions focus on whether KTV shows represent the history, geography, current issues, and culture of Iraqi Kurdistan alone or other parts, as well. The questions also aim at eliciting whether Kurds from all parts of Kurdistan participate in and contribute to the production of KTV shows.

1. Are there shows that are devoted to the history, demography, and geography of other parts of Kurdistan?
2. Does KTV address current issues related to all parts of Kurdistan, or to Iraqi Kurdistan only?
3. Whose culture, that of Iraqi Kurdistan alone or all Kurds, is reflected on KTV?
4. Do Kurds other than the Kurds of Iraq contribute to the production of TV programs (e.g., as hosts or hostesses, producers, and directors)?
5. Do non-Iraqi Kurds participate in shows and programs as guests, callers, or interviewees?

Are There Shows That Are Devoted to the History, Demography, and Geography of Other Parts of Kurdistan?

Close to 50 percent of the shows which are devoted to the history and demography of Kurdistan are about either the Greater Kurdistan or other individual parts of Kurdistan (i.e., other than Iraqi Kurdistan). The daily five-minute program, *Emřo le Mêjû da* (Today in History), which comes right after the main news broadcast, recounts Kurdistan and world events and historical figures that are deemed important. KTV also broadcasts documentaries on not only the history but also the current demography and geography of Kurdistan.[6] One significant aspect of these shows is that they are directed and hosted by Kurds from the same region covered in the program (e.g., Iranian Kurdistan). Greater Kurdistan is not only defined by Iraqi Kurds through the lenses of KTV but also by Kurds from other parts who in different ways participate in KTV's programs. Moreover, for many of the viewers, this might be the first time that they see their fellow Kurdistanis and are exposed to their language, dialect and pronunciation.

Does KTV Address Current Issues Related to All Parts of Kurdistan or Iraqi Kurdistan Only?

According to Bendix and Liebler (1999), some studies of the role of physical distance on news-media coverage have suggested that "events 'close to home' receive more news-media attention, and that coverage decreases with distance" (p. 658). Other studies have shown that news coverage is determined more by the newsworthiness of an event or where it occurs (p. 658). They conclude that both physical and social distance affect the amount of news-media coverage (p. 673).

The data reveal that about 20 percent of KTV news covers political and cultural developments that either take place in or are related to other parts of Kurdistan. Examples of these news items include reports on the armed conflict between the Turkish army and the Kurdish rebels from Turkey, social unrest in Iranian Kurdistan, and the Kurdish women activists from Syria visiting the Iraqi Kurdistan parliament. In contrast, other parts of Iraq, including Baghdad, are in the news only when the story is related to Kurdistan (e.g., the state of negotiations between the Kurds and Baghdad over drafting the Iraqi constitution in Baghdad) or when there is heavy fighting and explosions in the capital Baghdad or other parts of Iraq. Overall, KTV news is more concerned with other parts of Kurdistan than the non-Kurdish parts of Iraq.

Whereas all parts of Kurdistan enjoy a considerable representation in KTV news, they are less represented in programs dealing with current affairs. The majority of these programs deal with the current political and social issues of Iraqi Kurdistan. One of the notable programs that is specifically devoted to all parts of Kurdistan, especially Kurdistan of Turkey, is called *Roni*, which is a one-hour live talk show. For example, on August 8, 2005, this show had four guests, each representing one part of Kurdistan. Later, I will return to this show and analyze a few excerpts from the discourse of the participants as examples of discursive constructions of a pan-Kurdish identity.

Whose Culture, That of Iraqi Kurdistan Alone or All Kurds, Is Reflected on KTV?

Sharing a common culture is indispensable to the formation of a national identity (Spencer & Wollman, 2002, p. 69). In addition to reflecting and representing the history, demography, geography, news, and current affairs, KTV programming is devoted to the promotion of arts, particularly music and literature, from all parts of Kurdistan and the diaspora. Prominent Kurdish singers from Turkey (e.g., Shivan Perwer, Kurdistan[7] Perwer, Birader, Aynur, Xelîl Xemgîn), Iran (e.g., Kamkaran, Nasir Razzazi, Merziye Fariqi, Leila Fariqi, Ezîz Sharux, Mamlê Family), Syria (e.g., Said Gabarî, Bengîn, Narîn Feqê) are featured on KTV frequently. In an interview, Seyid Ehmed Rewandizî, the head of the music section of KTV, says: "I can say with pride that [KTV] is my second home, because through this precious channel we have been able to strengthen our connections with [singers, songwriters and musicians][8] from all four parts of Kurdistan" (Sami, 2006).

For a long time, music has been one of the most convenient means of connecting the Kurds and facilitating the expression of a shared sense of belonging. Due to the lack of access to modern communications technology, however, until recent years only a few Kurdish singers and musicians could cross linguistic and geographical boundaries that made communication among the Kurds difficult if not impossible. Radio broadcasting and audio, and later video cassettes, enabled more Kurdish singers to cross some of those boundaries. The major breakthrough at this front, however, has occurred with the introduction of satellite television in Kurdistan. The combination of audio and visual modes of television, freely crossing guarded borders between different parts of Kurdistan, has created a concert hall where tunes from different corners of Kurdistan and Kurdish diasporas have been amplified and then projected to viewers and listeners throughout Kurdistan and the diasporic Kurdish communities.

Besides broadcasting music video clips from all parts of Kurdistan, and in a wide range of Kurdish speech varieties, KTV's entertaining talk shows feature Kurdish artists who manage to travel to Iraqi Kurdistan. In May 2005, in an interview on KTV, Rasool Nadri, arguably the most famous folk and wedding singer from Iranian Kurdistan, said something along the following lines: Kurdish television has brought more respect for singers and musicians in Kurdistan. Before television, singers and musicians were so disrespected that most people were ashamed to sing, and if they did, they were called *çawesh*, a derogatory term used for wedding singers. Thanks to Kurdish television, the same people nowadays are called *hunermend* (artiste) a word that was reserved for well-known poets and painters.[9] The fact that Nadri was invited to a talk show to express his views on Kurdish music, his contributions, and personal life proves his point; that he is not just a wedding singer, but an artiste.

KTV has contributed to the cultivation and expansion of Kurdish music from all parts of Kurdistan and the diaspora not just by playing music-video clips and inviting the singers and musicians to appear on talk shows, but also by broadcasting their concerts. Many Kurdish music lovers in Turkey, Iraq, and Syria who might never be able to go to Iran or abroad, can see and hear Iranian Kurdish singers and musicians on KTV. For example, on August 8, 2005, KTV aired a 50-minute concert that was performed in Iraqi Kurdistan by Shahin Talabani, an Iranian Kurd residing in Britain. Given all this, one could credit satellite television in Kurdistan, including KTV, with an unprecedented increase in the number of singers and musicians. Later in this study, by analyzing a patriotic song, I will also illustrate how the content of some of these songs contributes to the construction and articulation of collective Kurdish identities. In addition to music, other art and cultural forms from all over Kurdistan can be viewed on KTV. These forms include, but are not limited to, dance, painting, architecture, sculpture, and poetry reading. For example, on August 9, 2005, one entire show, *Dîwan* (Collection of Poems), was devoted to a poet from Iranian Kurdistan who read from and talked about his collection of poems.

Do the Kurds Other Than the Kurds of Iraq Contribute to the Production of TV Programs (e.g. as Hosts or Hostesses, Producers and Directors)?

A number of the programs that represent other parts of Kurdistan are also directed or hosted by Kurds other than Iraqi Kurds. For example, on August 12, 2005, the weekly show *Şev Bêrî* (Zamdar, 2005) was hosted by a very popular Syrian Kurdish singer, Said Gabari, whose presence seemed to attract many Syrian Kurds calling from Europe and North America into the show. Another show, *Kazîwe* (Twilight), which was broadcast on August 10, 2005, was directed and hosted by Iranian Kurds (Makhoudi, 2005).

In August 2005, about 10–15 percent of children's shows were directed and presented by Iranian Kurds. One show was called *Karî Destî* (Artworks), which was seven minutes long (out of 45 minutes of children's show), and was aired on August 8 and August 9, 2005. The other show, an Iranian puppet show, which is dubbed into Kurdish by Iranian Kurds, was aired four times during the week, each time for ten minutes. In August 2007, there was an expansion of children shows directed and hosted by Kurds other than Iraqi Kurds. The program *Kamo* is hosted by a puppet speaking in an unmistakably Mukri dialect of Kurdish from Iran, and it is broadcast for 30 minutes every

Thursday. The program features plays, games, music, dance, and other activities carried out by children from various Kurdish towns in Iran.

In addition, there is a daily program called *Zimanê Kurdî* (Kurdish language) presented in the Kurmanji accent of Kurds from Turkey. For someone who is knowledgeable about Kurdish, it is relatively easy to distinguish accents of Kurmanji speakers from Iraq and Kurmanji speakers from Turkey. Whereas the former has been influenced by Arabic phonetics and pronunciation, the latter demonstrates obvious traces of Turkification. The influence of dominant languages on Kurdish in different countries are also evident in the grammar and, more so, in the vocabulary. Sorani speakers from Iraq and Iran can be similarly distinguished. More on the importance of language issue on KTV will follow. However, one important point should be stressed at this juncture. Kurdish literate adult, and mostly male, nationalists had a sense of pan-Kurdishness at least since the beginnings of the last century. However, satellite television channels, including KTV, have made it possible for Kurdish children all over the world to see and hear each other, and in a sense, as it were, discover each other. KTV has been a part of this change.

Do Non-Iraqi Kurds Participate in Shows and Programs as Guests, Callers, or Interviewees?

Audience participation in programs can be seen in different forms: people who are selected to appear as guests on talk-shows, people who are asked to express their opinions on current social and political issues (e.g., on the street or other public settings), and finally those who contact shows either through phone calls or sending messages by fax and email. Although a considerable number of politicians, artistes, and scholars from other parts of Kurdistan appear on various shows of KTV, the current data contains only one example of this, where political analysts from four parts of Kurdistan, one in person and three on the phone, were interviewed on the program *Ronî* (Nawî, 2005).

KTV broadcasts live programs of both entertaining and also political nature where people can call in and participate either to express opinions, ask questions, request music videos, or send regards to their loved ones. Some of the shows that I surveyed during the week of August 6, 2005, included: *Keval*, a light entertainment show (August 8), *Le Kurdistanewe* (From Kurdistan),[10] a political/current affairs show (August 9), *Jivana Stranan*, music-video request show (August 11), and, finally, *Şev Bêrî*, a traditional music show (August

12). One of the features of the live shows is that they provide at least two phone numbers, one for callers from Iraqi Kurdistan and the other for callers from elsewhere. My close observation of these live shows indicates that about 50 percent of the callers are from Iraqi Kurdistan and the other half from Europe, North America, and Australia. Judging by their accent, it is also evident that the vast majority of those who call from abroad are originally from Iraqi Kurdistan, who could be KDP sympathizers for the most part. Kurds from other parts of Kurdistan, whether residing in the four states or the West, usually call a program when that program is hosted by or has guests from the same region as the callers. For example, Syrian Kurds were calling into the show *Şev Bêrî* (Zamdar, 2005) because the host of the show was Said Gabari, a well-known vocalist and folk musician from Syria.

KTV and Language Use

What languages are used and how they are used in media are closely connected to the maintenance of language and also to questions of ethnic and national identity (Bulck & Poecke, 1996; Cormack & Hourigan, 2007; Hult, 2010; Kelly-Holmes & Moriarty, 2009). As I have discussed in previous chapters, next to territory, language has been one of the most significant emblems of Kurdish identity. Two important points should be reiterated. First, there is not a unified Kurdish language; there are Kurdish varieties, especially Sorani and Kurmanji. Second, there are languages other than Kurdish in Kurdistan. Shedding light on the linguistic aspect of broadcasting should be indicative of the kind of identity that is promoted and constructed by KTV. The kinds of language used on KTV could also indicate who is involved in the definition and articulation of Kurdish identity.

Guyot (2007) observes that "television tends to confer legitimacy on any linguistic cause" (p. 39), and that "television can revitalize the cultures and languages of minorities" (p. 39; see also Jones, 2007). Television may not be capable of revitalizing cultures or languages on its own, but it does "confer credibility and legitimacy on language," especially on threatened languages (Hassanpour, 1997, p. 924). The Kurdish language has been called a dialect of Persian in Iran, and in Turkey it was banned in all public domains until 1991. To this day, it has no official status in Turkey, Iran, and Syria. The fact that Kurdish is the prime language of a television station broadcasting 24 hours a day, seven days a week, legitimizes the status of Kurdish and assists the language to sustain its vitality.

Hassanpour (1998) has referred to MED-TV as a language academy. This can equally be said about KTV. In Turkey, Iran, and Syria, Kurdish is neither the medium of schooling nor is it taught as a subject in public schools. Although providing private lessons on Kurdish has been tolerated by governments of Turkey and Iran in recent years, Kurdish courses usually do not last long, due to the lack of support from the states (Skutnabb-Kangas & Fernandes, 2008). KTV provides lessons on the Kurdish alphabet and reading.[11] Furthermore, KTV airs Disney, Japanese, and Russian cartoons dubbed into Kurdish. It is important to note that KTV occasionally airs non-dubbed English cartoons, but cartoons in the dominant languages of the states where Kurds live, such as Persian, Turkish, and Arabic are absent on KTV. This can be seen as a strategy of constructing out-groups. KTV airs English cartoons because the English language, unlike Arabic, Turkish, and Persian, is not seen as a threat to Kurdish language. English is not only a prestigious and instrumental global language, but it is also the language of Britain and the United States, the two countries that the ruling Kurdish organizations, including KTV's owner, KDP, consider as friends and allies.[12]

KTV fosters mutual intelligibility among Kurdish speech varieties by implementing unique programming techniques. For example, the main newscast is presented by two people, each speaking one of the two major varieties of Kurdish. As a common practice, when the news item is presented by the Sorani speaker, the report accompanying that report is given by a Kurmanji speaker. In addition, there are numerous talk shows that have guests who speak a different Kurdish variety from the host's.[13] Kurds from various speech communities participate in KTV shows, either by calling in to shows or by being a part of the production or presentation teams. Finally, music clips by artistes from all regions of Kurdistan and the diaspora are aired on KTV daily. In an interview, Heval Ibrahim, a young artist from Iraqi Kurdistan, and a native speaker of Kurmanji, said: "Today, most of the youth in the Badinan region [whose native tongue is Kurmanji] can understand Sorani, thanks to Sorani singers like Zakaria, Eyub Ali, Adnan Karim, and many more who sing in both dialects" (Himmati, 2007). Continuous exposure to different Kurdish varieties on KTV and other satellite television stations have made Kurdish varieties much more mutually intelligible. After six months of occasional viewing of satellite TV channels of the Iraqi Kurds, including KTV, an Ottawa resident said that "before I could not understand Iraqi Kurds, but now I do" (S. A., personal communication, February 16, 2002). Her husband, a Sorani Kurdish speaker, went further and confirmed that after being exposed to Kurmanji Kurdish on satellite television for several months, he started to comprehend that Kurdish variety. Rebwar Fatah, the director of Kurdish Media (www.kurdmedia.com), in an interview with Roj TV, said that he did not understand Kurmanji prior to watching Kurdish satellite television stations, starting with MED-TV (Ghazi, 2007). Another Iranian Kurd living in Ottawa said that prior to watching KTV (and other Kurdish satellite stations such as KurdSat) he thought that talking about many subjects especially those in the areas of sciences "was only possible in Arabic, Persian, or Turkish." He said that he had acquired many new words and expressions from KTV and other Kurdish media.

KTV celebrates linguistic diversity. From the French Republic of the late eighteenth century to the Turkish Republic of the early twentieth century and Franco's Spain which lasted well into the mid-1970s, the vast majority of modern nation-building projects have been funnelled by the nation-state ideology, which says that an ideal nation has only one official and promoted language.[14] Building nations has often involved nation destroying (Connor, 1994). The Kurdish language has been a victim of this suppressive modernist policy and scheme of nation building. In contrast, KTV, as an agent of nation-building, promotes language diversity in Kurdistan. This is in line with the KRG's public education system that promotes schooling in the mother tongue for at least two Kurdish varieties (i.e., Sorani and Kurmanji) and non-Kurdish and minority languages in the region (Skutnabb-Kangas & Fernandes, 2008).[15] In addition to broadcasting in the two major Kurdish varieties of Kurmanji and Sorani, KTV also produces and airs a one-hour weekly show in the Kurdish variety of Hawrami. In addition to daily Arabic shows and news, KTV also airs weekly programs in Turkomani and Assyrian Neo-Aramaic as the languages of minorities other than Kurds living in Kurdistan. One could argue that this democratic and pluralistic approach to linguistic diversity in Kurdistan is an indication of the civic, as opposed to ethnic, nature of the national identity that is fostered by KTV.[16]

In addition to investigating what languages are used in the media and to what extent along with other signs (i.e., audiovisual), it is equally important to analyze and interpret how these semiosis are used to construct identities discursively. This textual analysis of KTV discourse is carried out in the next chapter.

CHAPTER 6

Textual Analysis of KTV

This chapter focuses on discursive constructions of Kurdish identities on KTV. Particular attention is paid to the construction of a cross-border Kurdish identity. I will carry out detailed textual analysis of texts from KTV programs, such as excerpts from KTV's news, history narratives, talk show discussions, and, finally, a weather forecast. Given the scope of this study and the kind of detailed analyses that are performed here, it is important to limit my data to a manageable body of texts and a limited set of analytical tools that I described in Chapter 2. The analyses are further informed by several studies of national identity that have used CDA approaches (e.g., Billig, 1995; Bishop & Jaworski, 2003; Chouliaraki, 1999; Higgins, 2004; Wodak et al., 1999). The objective of this chapter is to illustrate how various components of national identity discourse, or what Wodak et al. (1999) call "semantic-macro areas" of national identity discourse, are realized and materialized in different modes of communication, such as verbal and visual languages. (See Appendix 1 for a description of these tools.)

Discursive Construction of a Common History

The program *Emřo Le Mêjû da* (Today in History) is about seven minutes long and is aired twice everyday. It provides a brief description of historical events that KTV deems important. These are mostly events that are pertinent to KTV's owner KDP. Major historical events in the neighboring countries, especially when there is a connection with Kurdistan, and international events (e.g., the First and Second World Wars) are also covered. Aside from events that are directly related to KDP, only certain types of Kurdistani events are covered: those that either took place prior to the emergence of modern Kurdish organizations (e.g., the Sheikh Ubaidalla revolt against the Ottoman Empire in 1880), those that do not have any direct connections to the modern Kurdish organizations other than KDP (e.g., Halabja's chemical bombardment in March 1988), and events and personalities that might have connections to other organizations but have become significant symbols of Kurdish national identity (e.g., the establishment of the Kurdish republic of Mahabad in Iranian Kurdistan in 1946). In other words, in constructing a historical identity for Kurdistan, KTV is interested either in events and personalities that are connected to its owner, or those events and people that are believed to be parts of a pan-Kurdish nationalist discourse.

Through the program *Emřo le Mêjû da*, and other shows, KTV attempts to reconstruct that greater Kurdistan not only through covering pertinent events but also in the ways in which the event is retold and reconstructed discursively. I will briefly look at the reconstruction of one of these events, the Treaty of Sévres, broadcast on August 10, 2005, in the program *Emřo le Mêjû da*.

On August 10, 1920, in a day like today, the Treaty of Sévres was signed... The Treaty of Sévres was important for the Kurds and also the abolishment of the Ottoman state. But, the discovery of oil in Kurdistan became one of the main factors that prevented the ratification of the treaty, especially the articles that promised Kurdish independence. On July 24, 1923, the Treaty of Lausanne annulled the Treaty of Sévres, and prevented the Kurds from achieving their national rights, and the promises that were made to Kurds were scrapped for the sake of serving the interests of the powerful nations. Furthermore, the Kurds, themselves, were not able to influence the regional and international politics through diplomatic and political pressures to realize their objectives. Although the Treaty of Lausanne further reaffirmed the division of Kurdistan as a reality, with a series of revolutions the Kurdish nation refused to accept that reality.

The narrator of this text is at pains to discursively construct a shared history and destiny for all Kurds, albeit at the expense of presenting a true account on a very important international treaty, the Treaty of Sévres.[1] This narrator achieves this not only by what is said about the Treaty but also via what is omitted.

The narrator claims that the treaty promised the establishment of an independent state for all Kurds, because she does not specify which part of Kurdistan was included or excluded in the treaty. The KTV show aims at discursively constructing Kurds as one people that has shared the same history and destiny for a long time. The narrator does not reveal the fact that the Kurdish state that was promised did not include all the territories that Kurds inhabited at the time. The Kurdish state promised in the Treaty of Sévres was supposed to be established in Turkey's southeast, or *Kurdistan North*. It would have not included Iranian Kurdistan, Syrian Kurdistan, the Dersim region in today's Turkey, or the territory that is known today as Iraqi Kurdistan. Albeit, the treaty "allowed for the adhesion" of the latter to "such a future Kurdish state" because it was under the rule of the Ottomans (see McDowall, 2004, p. 137). KTV's show ignores this historical fact. Instead, throughout the text, the three words Kurds, Kurdish nation, and Kurdistan are used interchangeably to further construct a unified nation with a common territory, history, destiny, and ethnicity. This is an example of the pan-Kurdism that is fostered by KTV. The task is not accomplished so much through what is said, but more through what is forgotten, in the commentary. A collective memory appears to be an indispensible constituent of any nationalist discourse (Martin & Wodak, 2003). The past is often remembered to serve the present. However, an aspect of this remembering is to forget those parts of the past that may not serve the hegemonic discourse of the nation at the present time (Brewer, 2006; Wodak et al., 2009). It is the task of discourse analysts, however, to reveal the unsaid, because as van Dijk (1988) suggests, "what is not said may even be more important, from a critical point of view, than what is explicitly said or meant" (p. 17; see also Huckin, 2002).

DISCURSIVE CONSTRUCTION OF A COMMON PRESENT AND FUTURE

The nation is often the main focus of the news (Billig, 1995, p. 117). Through the news, we are told who belong and who do not belong to the nation (p. 117). In relation to KTV, I stated before that a considerable segment of its news concerns other parts of Kurdistan. KTV's *Deng û Bas* program (news) encourages its audiences to be concerned about the present conditions of all Kurds, regardless of where they live. In doing so, however, KTV uses two different languages, one that can be called the language of the autonomist/regionalist Kurdish national identity (e.g., KDP's, the owner of KTV), and the second the language of a cross-border Kurdish identity. Here is an example from *Deng û Bas* (The News) aired on August 12, 2005. It is a report about unrest in Iranian Kurdistan, in August 2005:

Following a series of demonstrations and sit-ins by Kurds in Iranian Kurdistan [*Kurdistanî Êran*]…in the city of *Wirmê*, after having a state of emergency for three days in the Islam Abad district, a demonstration was held by the citizens. In response, the Iranian security forces attacked the crowed, and as a result, several people were injured and several others were taken to prison. (my translation)

As with this and other examples of reporting about Kurdistan in Turkey or Syria, the news anchors are consistent with respect to their naming practices. They refer to parts of Kurdistan as being parts of the countries of Turkey, Iran, Iraq, and Syria: Iranian Kurdistan (*Kurdistanî Êran*), and Turkey/Turkish Kurdistan (*Kurdistanî Turkîye*), and Syrian Kurdistan (*Kurdistanî Sûrîye*). This is the language of Kurdish autonomist/regionalist movement (e.g., KDP), which demands autonomy within the states where Kurds reside. The language of pan-Kurdismis different in that it constructs Kurdistan as a unified territory and Kurds as one and homogenous nation. Accordingly, pan-Kurdish nationalism promotes the following naming practice: Eastern Kurdistan/Kurds or Kurdistan East, Northern Kurdistan/Kurds or Kurdistan North, and Western Kurdistan/ Kurds or Kurdistan North, respectively (Iraqi Kurdistan is referred to as Southern Kurdistan/Kurds or Kurdistan South, or simply as *Herêm*, meaning the Region).[2]

Whereas the language of pan-Kurdism is excluded from the news items presented in KTV's studios in Iraqi Kurdistan, it is included in the report accompanying the same news item, perhaps because the reporting is from diaspora. Kurdistan Hesen (Hassan), a KTV reporter from Stockholm, Sweden, reports on the reaction of Kurds in diaspora to the Kurdish unrest in Iran, as follows:

According to news sources, the Islamic Republic of Iran's violence against the Kurds of *the East* continues. For this reason, and for the second time, the *Joint Committee*, which consists of the majority of *Kurdish and Kurdistani organizations and parties*, the Federation of *Kurdistani* Communities in Sweden, and *Kurdish* Platform in Europe, staged a demonstration in . . . Stockholm. (my emphasis, my translation)

The language of this report is pan-Kurdist. This is evident in that the reporter refers to Iranian Kurdistan as basically the "East," which means East of Kurdistan, implying that the Iranian Kurds' condition and destiny is not separate from that of Iraqi, Turkish, or Syrian Kurds. Anything that happens to Kurds anywhere is a concern for all Kurdistan. This pan-Kurdish identity is further strengthencd by reporting that "the majority of Kurdish and Kurdistani organizations and parties" have all come together under the direction of a single "Joint Committee" to support their fellow Kurds in the "east" of Kurdistan. To the KTV news program, and also many Kurdish individuals and organizations, including those that are regional and politically autonomist, it is acceptable, common, and somewhat natural to have pan-Kurdish sentiments, and also act accordingly, in Kurdish diasporic communities. This could be due to two factors. Pursuing the idea of having a greater Kurdistan could be punishable in Kurdistan as a separatist act and treason; it does not lead to similar consequences for the members of diasporic communities (e.g., Europe, North America, and Australia). The second reason might be that it is only in the West that Kurds coming from different parts of Kurdistan are able to freely communicate and interact with each other. Kurdish long-distance or diaspora nationalism seems to be pan-Kurdish, secessionist, and separatist more than most nationalist movements in Kurdistan.

In addition to constructing a common present among the Kurds, KTV also facilitates the discursive construction of a common future for all Kurds, albeit such a future is to be championed by KDP (KTV's owner). To illustrate this, a few excerpts from the program *Roni* broadcast on August 8, 2005, will be analyzed. In that particular program, representatives from four parts of Kurdistan discussed "Kurdistan region and other parts of Kurdistan,"[3] as the title of the show indicated. The representative of Iraqi Kurdistan, Ihsan Amêdî, a KDP representative in Kurdistan parliament, states that other parts of Kurdistan follow the Iraqi Kurdish experience with the hope that one day they could achieve the same:

> When people from Kurdistan, south, north or east, visit Kurdistan, they see that Kurds are the masters of their own homes and land, and they have their own institutions and sovereignty...[Kurdish people of] Iranian Kurdistan, Turkish Kurdistan and of Syria...desire to achieve the same...this is a national struggle for [the recognition] of their national identity...people here [in Iraqi Kurdistan] are concerned about there, they would like to see [other Kurds] embrace the same development, and they would like to help them [to achieve this]. (My translation)

There are three messages in Amêdî's comment which are shared by the ruling Kurdish parties, especially KDP, in Iraqi Kurdistan: (1) Iraqi Kurdistan is free, autonomous, and prosperous; (2) Kurds from Turkey, Iran, and Syria desire the same; and (3) Iraqi Kurdistan is concerned about other Kurds and is willing to help them to fulfill their dreams for freedom and autonomy. Since Iraqi Kurdistan is other Kurds' best hope, it follows that it is in the interest of all Kurds if the Iraqi Kurdistan experience succeeds in the sense of remaining autonomous within a federal Iraq or even as an independent small Kurdistan. This way, the future of all Kurds has been constructed as being dependent on each other.

Iraqi Kurdish authorities, however, do not explicitly ask for the help of other Kurds, because this might come across as a sign of weakness, or it may create fear among Iraqi Kurds, or it may shatter the hope among other Kurds who are looking up to Iraqi Kurdistan. Equally significant are the concerns of neighboring states, as well as the government in Baghdad, and also the United States, which is equally concerned about Turkey. Appeal for support, however, is voiced through Kurds from other parts who are carefully selected by KTV.[4] For example, in the same show that I have been discussing, *Ronî*, Arif Zêrevan, a Kurdish journalist from Turkey, talking on the phone from Hawlêr (Erbil), Iraqi Kurdistan, makes the following statement:

> What has been achieved in South Kurdistan has boosted Kurds' morale in all parts of Kurdistan, the North, [Turkey Kurdistan], the West, Kurdistan of Syria, and the East, [Kurdistan] of Iran. In Turkey, Kurds started, gradually, not to be afraid of Turkish soldiers or the PKK guerrillas. Kurds have started to demand their rights openly. (My translation)

The Syrian Kurdish guest, Mihemed emîn Mihemed, also on the phone from Hawlêr, confirms that Iraqi Kurdistan has given Syrian Kurds confidence in their struggle to achieve their rights similar to Iraqi Kurds:

> Kurdish nation in Syria sees a great opportunity too, and it hopes that [its] oppression will end as it ended in another part of Kurdistan...Kurds from other three parts of Kurdistan are really willing to support their brothers in Iraqi Kurdistan...Kurds today, from other three parts of Kurdistan, Iran, Turkey and Syria, are ready to support and defend this experience of freedom [in Iraqi Kurdistan]. (My translation)

These excerpts reveal that KTV is committed to the discursive construction of a common present and future for all Kurds, albeit such a present and future, the destiny of all Kurds, is to be determined by KTV and its owner KDP.

KDP views itself as the true representative of all Kurds and Masoud Barzani, the KDP leader, as the leader of not just Iraqi Kurdistan but Kurdistan at large. Again, such propositions are expressed through well-known Kurds, such as artists, independent politicians, and writers from other parts of Kurdistan. The program *Kazîwe*, which is dedicated to cultural issues of Iranian Kurdistan (directed and hosted by Iranian Kurds), provides an example of this (Makhoudi, 2005). In the episode aired on August 10, 2005, Mehdiye Zandi, a well-known radio announcer and also the wife of one of the most famous Kurdish singers, Hassan Zirak, states the following: "God willing, Kurdistan will be triumphant…Long live Kurds and Kurdistan…[God save] the President, the leader of all Kurds, Mr. Masoud Barzani." There are numerous similar examples on KTV that represent not only Masoud Barzani but also the entire Barzani family as the leader of all Kurdistan. For example, the program *Deng û Bas* (The News) on August 6, 2005, contained the following news item:

> Birader, the famous artist from Kurdistan of Turkey, visited the tombs of the eternals[5] [referring to Masoud Barzani's late father and brother]. Birader said: "we can say that Barzani is the father of the Kurdish nation…If today, *we have a free Kurdistan, it is because of the path that the undying Barzani took*…I bow to his path. Long live Kurds and Kurdistan. (My translation; my emphasis)

These are also examples of how KTV discursively constructs a common past and present for all Kurds by tying the past and present of Kurdistan to one single family, Barzani, and by extension the party they lead, KDP, the owner of KTV. Since it is commonly believed that leaders lead groups of people forward and into the future, the discursive construction of a common past and present also contributes to the production of a common future for all Kurds.

Discursive Construction of a Common Kurdish Language

An essentialist view of the link between language and nationality is undesirable for many theorists (May, 2008), but almost all of the approaches to nation and nationalism such as modernism, primordialism, and ethnosymbolism believe that language plays a "central role…in the nationalist project" (Spencer & Wollman, 2002, p. 76; see also Joseph, 2004, 2006; Edwards, 2009). According to Anderson (1991), "one notes the primordialness of languages, even those known to be modern" (p. 144). As I will explain in more detail shortly, whereas primordialists believe that language is the most salient marker of identity, be it individual, ethnic, or national, proponents of the modernist view find language vital not because of being an index of ethnicity but because it is a decisive factor in the creation and maintenance of a unified nation-state. Language is also important from a social constructivist perspective because it is precisely through language that other cultural and national values are negotiated, constructed, and constantly modified and articulated (Billig, 1995; Wodak, 2006b).

There is not one Kurdish language. As I have discussed previously, whereas a number of scholars speak of Kurdish languages, others, Kurdish nationalists in particular, speak of Kurdish dialects and claim that there is one single Kurdish language. In this study, I have opted for a more neutral term, Kurdish varieties. In discussing the linguistic fragmentation of the Kurds, I have suggested that some of these varieties (e.g., Kurmanji and Sorani) are as distinct as German and English (Kreyenbroek, 1992).

KTV's language use seems paradoxical. On the one hand, different varieties of Kurdish are used and presented as though they are different languages targeting different audiences. On the other hand, Kurdish varieties are still called Kurdish, to reinforce the conservative nationalist discourse that posits all Kurds have only one language. For example, KTV airs various programs in the two main varieties of Kurmanji and Sorani, a one-hour weekly show in Hawrami, and music-video clips in smaller varieties such as Faili (Kirmashani) and Zazaki. Newscasts are often presented by two anchors sitting next to each other and taking turns reading news in Kurmanji and Sorani. The assumption here seems to be that KTV audiences speak different varieties that may not be mutually intelligible. By broadcasting in all the varieties, especially Kurmanji and Sorani, KTV wants to reach these diverse audiences.

On the other hand, there is an explicit attempt to downplay the differences between Kurdish speech varieties. To KTV, they are only dialects of Kurdish by the virtue of the fact that all the varieties are referred to as Kurdish. For example, whereas the Kurdish lessons in the children's show teach Kurmanji only, the show is simply called *Zimanî Kurdî* (Kurdish language), as opposed to Kurmanji or Kurmanji Kurdish, even though it does not teach Sorani Kurdish at all. This nationalist stance towards Kurdish language is reinforced on KTV's website. The website is multilingual. Kurmanji and Sorani are treated as two languages; each has its own navigation button and separate pages. Despite this, both of them are called Kurdish. Visitors can distinguish them by the fact that each "Kurdish" is written in a different alphabet system. The Sorani section is transcribed in the modified Arabic alphabet, and the Kurmanji section is marked by the word *Kurdî* (Kurdish), which is written in the Latin-based alphabet. Again, the difference between these two Kurdish varieties is acknowledged for a practical reason, which is the dissemination of information, but they are still named the same: Kurdish. Naming matters. Although KTV acknowledges language diversity in Kurdistan, it is still haunted by the powerful and positivist nation-state ideology that one nation has only one language (Gellner, 1983; 1997).

DISCURSIVE CONSTRUCTION OF COMMON NATIONAL SYMBOLS

National symbols strengthen the ties and bonds among the "like-minded people" of a community (Kuusisto, 2001, p. 63). From flags and maps to fairy tales and ways of behaving (Smith, 1991), national symbols contribute to the construction of the nation (Geisler, 2005). Several symbols that are continuously reproduced on KTV are common to and shared by the majority of the Kurds. Among them are the Kurdish flag, mountains, rural life, dance, and costume.

Among these, none is more significant than the flag in articulating the political aspirations of the Kurds and in defining their national identity. Reporting from Iraqi Kurdistan, Thomas (2007) quotes a man: "We wear this flag as a crown on our heads...This flag is sign that we are great nation [sic]." In the Kurdish national anthem, *Ey Reqîb*, the main verse, which is repeated several times throughout, says: "Let no one say Kurds are dead, Kurds are living, Kurds are living, and their flag will never fall." When Masoud Barzani was selected as the president of Iraqi Kurdistan, addressing the Kurdistan parliamentarians, he pointed to the Kurdish flag next to him, and said: "I was born under this flag, and I am ready to die under it any minute" (Kurdistan TV, special broadcast, June 12, 2005).[6] In May 2004, Karim Nazhadian, an Iranian Kurd, who travelled to Iraqi Kurdistan, reportedly died of excitement when he encountered the Kurdish flag for the first time in person (Alay Kurdistan, 2004). The Kurdish flag crosses the linguistic, cultural, organizational, and geographical boundaries that have fragmented the Kurds, and it has become a badge of pan-Kurdish identity.

Although the neighboring countries continue to have productive economic relations with Iraqi Kurdistan, independent from the Iraqi

central government, dealing with the Kurdish flag is no small matter for those states. When a delegation from the Kurdistan Regional
Government (KRG) visits Turkey, Iran, Syria, or even Baghdad, the
Kurdish flag is not displayed in the meetings (*Le dîdarî Barzanî*,
2007). Those states seem to believe that the recognition of the Kurdish
flag implies recognizing Kurdish demands for political rights, at least
in the form of regional autonomy. Some states have exercised their
influence to ban this flag even outside their own territory.[7]

The Kurdish flag is waved freely on KTV every day and almost
every hour. It is very rare to see a Kurdish politician or government
official from KRG being interviewed on KTV without having the
Kurdish flag displayed next to him or her. The flag is shown waving
outside KTV's studios' windows, and in the hands of people dancing,
whether at weddings or during picnicking. Judging by the discourse
of KTV, one gets the impression that the Kurdish flag is waved everywhere and in every hand.

In addition to being waved and displayed overtly, the Kurdish flag
is also reconstructed on KTV by images that solely or predominantly
are made up of the four colors of the Kurdish flag: red, white, green,
and yellow. As Kress and van Leeuwen (2002) note, "color 'means'"
(p. 343). The meaning-making potential of color, however, is generally culturally dependent. For example, when mourning, people in
most of Europe and the Middle East wear black, but in northern
Portugal, brides wear black on the wedding day (p. 343). Colors
which are known to people as being associated with specific concepts
and events can invoke emotions and reactions. The four colors of
the Kurdish flag are reinforced in, for example, the opening scene
of the children's program called *Pepûlekanî Kurdistan* (Butterflies
of Kurdistan), children's drawings, logos for some institutions, and
some of the logos of KTV.

In places like Turkey, sometimes any close resemblance to the
Kurdish flag has been problematic. In the late 1990s, the city officials
of Batman, a Kurdish-populated town in Turkey, changed the traffic
lights colors to red, yellow, and blue instead of green because green is
one of the main colors of the Kurdish flag (see Hassanpour, 1998). In
March 2007, eight students in Kurdistan-Turkey were dismissed from
school for three days because they used the colors of the Kurdish flag
in their artwork (*Be hoy bekarhênanî*, 2007). These colors, however,
are used on KTV to reinforce the image of the Kurdish flag. This
is significant for two reasons. First, it reinforces the image of the
Kurdish flag without having the actual image overused. Second, this
implicit reconstruction of the Kurdish flag expands the semantic field

of the Kurdish flag; many things in Kurdistan look like the Kurdish flag, or vice versa. This further naturalizes and, thus, nationalizes, the colors of the flag and the flag itself. A part of being a Kurd or Kurdistani is to associate with this flag.

The Kurdish flag is also constructed, reinforced, and legitimized through the rhetoric of "us" versus "them" (van Dijk, 1993). It is not only constructed discursively and popularized in the daily life of the Kurds by having a prominent presence on KTV but also legitimized by ways of not showing and, thus, de-legitimizing, the flag of the "other," the Iraqi flag. For instance, on May 8, 2005, KTV broadcast a half-hour program called *Alay Éraq* [Iraqi Flag] with an explicit and clear message: "we need to throw away the Iraqi flag...We need to believe that this flag was buried along with Saddam Hussein's regime."[8] In a similar vein, O'Leary and Salih (2005) have noted that the Iraqi flag symbolizes "pan-Arabism" and it is not "inclusive toward Kurds, Turcoman, Christians, or Jews" (p. 35). On KTV, the Iraqi flag appears as part of occasional news items about Baghdad, most of which are related to contested issues between Iraqi Kurdistan and the central government. The frequent display of the Iraqi flag in this particular show is an exception in which the flag of the "other" is constantly juxtaposed with scenes of the previous regimes' police and army abusing and persecuting Kurds. In sum, every nation has a flag, and in the absence of the Iraqi flag, the existence of the Kurdish flag becomes more legitimized and naturalized.

Mountainous landscapes, which are believed to be among the most distinct symbols of Kurdishness (Izady, 1992; O'Shea, 2004), are common images displayed on KTV. If prior to the emergence of the new electronic media the mountains were among the decisive factors contributing to the cultural fragmentation of the Kurds, today their images serve to construct a common and shared attachment to the same homeland and territory: Kurdistan. The hilly landscape and mountains define the rural life in Kurdistan, as shown on KTV. It should be noted that a large portion of towns and villages of Iraqi Kurdistan, from the capital Hewlêr (Erbil) to the oil-rich city of Kirkuk, are located on flat lands. However, on KTV, it is the mountains that almost always define Kurdish rural life. It seems that the images of rugged hills, hidden valleys, inaccessible caves, and defiant peaks symbolize Kurds' long history of struggle and resistance, most of which might have not happened without having the mountains as the strongholds of rebels. Mountainous landscapes connect like-minded Kurds.

Discursive Construction of a Common Territory and Homeland

Most scholars of nation and nationalism agree on the great importance of territory and homeland in relation to the formation and maintenance of national identities. According to Kaiser (2002), "whatever else it may be, nationalism is always a struggle for control of land" (p. 231). For Smith (1996) nations have ethnic roots, and the history of ethnic communities is in crucial ways defined by an ancestral homeland or territory. It is one of the most important "deep resources" of ethno-history; it is the setting where sufferings, happenings, and experiences of the community take place. It is where a community is formed.

The importance of territory and borders as defining political boundaries of nation-states hardly needs to be proven. But territory is also important for nations without states and minorities who are said to have reached national awakening or what some scholars prefer to identify as "ethnic consciousness."[9] As Guibernau suggests:

> For [nations without state], territory is becoming a quasi-sacred component of their identity. Territory is turned into a symbolic space containing memories of the communities' history, sacred shrines, holy places, battlefields, and specific geographical features endowed with a highly emotional charge. Furthermore, territory also contains a strong political dimension since the nation's territory defines the limits within which self-government is to be exercised. (1999, p. 157)

Territories and homeland are constantly reconstructed in maps. Maps do not just record what is real, for example, by marking the internationally recognized borders, but they also represent the nationalist imaginations of the homeland, of the historical sacred land, and of what that land should have been or ought to be. Nationalists have long recognized the power of maps and iconography, not only to show where home is but also where it should and could be and where power can be exercised.

Mass media are common places where maps of homelands are reproduced endlessly (Billig, 1995). Whereas many Kurdish symbols such as the flag, mountains, dance, costume, and various customs are explicitly displayed and glorified on KTV, the map or maps of the Greater Kurdistan is rarely shown,[10] partially because the map of the Greater Kurdistan on an Iraqi Kurdish TV screen could mean more than this; it could also signify separatist and secessionist ambitions of Iraqi Kurds, something that Kurdish leaders have continuously denied.[11] What the map represents could be the reason for not overtly displaying it on KTV. However, as I will illustrate, the map is reproduced and reinforced instead implicitly and subtly, in both verbal and visual languages. The weather forecast is an interesting site for this semiotic construction.

The weather forecast in the mass media deserves attention because it has become one of the indispensable parts of the news in all forms of news media; people often rely on the weather forecast in their daily lives. Discussing the significant place of the news weather in the British banal nationalist discourse, Billig states:

> "The weather" appears as an objective, physical category, yet it is contained within national boundaries. At the same time, it is known that the universe of weather is larger than the nation. There is "abroad"; there is "around the world." These are elsewheres beyond "our" elsewheres. The national homeland is set deictically in the central place, syntactically replicating the maps of the North Atlantic. All this is reproduced in the newspapers; and all this, in its small way, helps to reproduce the homeland as the place in which "we" are at home, "here" at the habitual center of "our" daily universe. (1995, p. 117)

Here, I will show that KTV, twice every day, reminds its viewers of their homeland by redrawing the national boundaries of a greater Kurdistan.

Deconstructing the Verbal Discourse

In 2005, when reporting the weather, KTV reports the weather of Kurdistan and the rest of the world by presenting alphabetical lists of cities, which consist of two sets. The first set encompasses major Kurdish populated cities, regardless of what nation-state they actually are located in (i.e., Turkey, Iran, Iraq, or Syria). The second set includes the rest of the world's capital cities, including Ankara, Baghdad, Damascus, and Tehran. The cities that KTV believes to be Kurdish are presented as belonging to the same category and entity: home. In contrast, the capital cities of the states where Kurds live (Baghdad, Ankara, Tehran, and Damascus) are constructed, in Billig's terms, as abroad and elsewhere, like the rest of the world, different from home.

The Greater Kurdistan is mentally constructed also through renaming Kurdish cities. The states where Kurds live have employed both physical and symbolic violence to assimilate the Kurds as part of their modern nation-building projects (Hassanpour, 2003b, p. 116). One of the symbolic violent actions has involved changing, banning, and regulating names of people, places, towns, villages, roads, and even plants and animals that have borne signs of Kurdishness. For example, according to a *BBC* report, (Turkey renames…, 2005), Turkey changed the name of three animals in its southeast (Kurdistan) because the authorities believed that names which made references to Kurdistan and Armenia were "divisive" and against Turkey's "unity." Motivated often by the same nationalist ideology, throughout Kurdistan, one occasionally comes across two names for some villages and towns: the name known to the locals and the name given by the officials of the host states. By choosing the local names of the towns that have two names, KTV reclaims their Kurdishness. Naming is a strategy to declare ownership. By renaming them, KTV informs its audiences that these towns and cities belong to the Greater Kurdistan.

In January 2006, the weather forecast on KTV became more visual and technically more sophisticated. A list of the cities was still used to report the weather of the world capitals. However, for Kurdistan and the region surrounding it, including the capital cities of the host states, more visuals and images started to be used. The construction of the map of the greater Kurdistan was still implicit, but, as it will be illustrated, it became more visual and more powerful.

Deconstructing the Visual Discourse

As shown in figure 6.1, the forecast for the region and Kurdistan is presented in three camera shots. Shot one primarily captures the Middle East, where the four host states are located. The shot also extends to parts of North Africa (down-left corner), Greece (upper-left corner), and the Southern Caucasus (top), Afghanistan and Pakistan (right margin). Three observations are significant here. First, the borderlines that separate the host states and which run through Kurdistan are invisible on this map. One reason for that could be the fact that once these lines are drawn, Kurdistan will be divided into four parts, something that would go against what this piece of discourse is trying to achieve: re-territorialisation of Kurdistan. Second, although the borderlines on this map are not visible, someone who is familiar with the region can imagine Kurdistan right in the center of this map. This underlines the importance and centrality of the homeland, a notion that visual representations of weather forecast in the media often reinforce (Billig, 1995). Third, in Shot I only capital cities of non-Kurdish states are listed, such as *Enqere* (Ankara), *Şam* (Damascus), Baxda (Baghdad), Tehran (Tehran), *Televîv* (Tel Aviv),

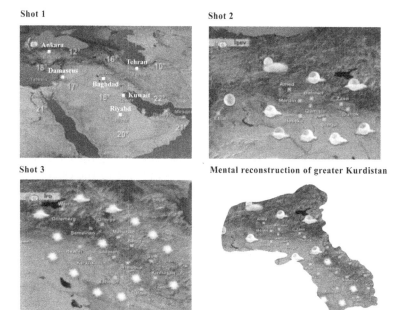

Figure 6.1 Screen shots of a KTV's weather forecast, on the Internet, fostering the imagination of a greater Kurdistan

Kuwait, *Riyaz* (Riyadh), and so forth. Although Hewlêr (Erbil) is also a capital city for the Kurds, it is not listed on this map. These are non-Kurdish or non-Kurdistani places. Again, in Billig's (1995) terms, these are "elsewheres" different from the homeland, which is represented in the second and third shots.

The second shot is a close-up of parts of northern and western Kurdistan, incorporating parts of predominantly Kurdish populated regions in Turkey, Syria, and Iraq. The third shot closely captures the southern and eastern parts of Kurdistan, which includes Kurdish cities located in Turkey, Iraq, and Iran. In doing this, KTV subtly, though never explicitly, redraws the map of the Greater Kurdistan. More than once each day, KTV assists its audiences to reconstruct a mental image of the Greater Kurdistan (see the bottom right corner of figure 6.1).

MICROANALYSIS OF A PATRIOTIC SONG'S MULTIMODAL DISCOURSE OF NATIONAL IDENTITY

In this section I analyze a patriotic song, or what is called *Sirûdî Nîshtimanî* (patriotic anthem) in Kurdish. I undertake a comprehensive multimodal analysis of the anthem to show in more detail the meaning-making potential of television discourse and the ways it contributes to the construction and reproduction of national identities.

Geisler (2005) observes that national anthems are "part and parcel of [the] myth of blood sacrifice typical of most nascent nationalist movements" (p. xxiv). The same can be said about patriotic and revolutionary songs, particularly in times of struggle for national emancipation. They, too, are used to reinforce the idea of blood sacrifice in the name of the nation. Patriotic songs are among the most emotionally charged national symbols that contribute to the creation of national identities and nations. As Anderson (1991) says, "nothing connects us all but imagined sound" (p. 145). When disseminated through a mass medium such as satellite television, popular patriotic songs can engender "an experience of simultaneity," in the sense that they enable members of a geographically dispersed community, whose members may never see each other face to face (p. 145), experience a shared sense of belonging to the same entity and at the same time.

The patriotic song *Kurdistan* has been one of the most frequently aired patriotic songs on KTV.[12] It has been aired in times of national crisis and other occasions when mobilizing Kurdish populations for action has been deemed necessary.[13] Kurdistan was one of the first patriotic Kurdish songs featured on the Internet, for example on YouTube with about 250,000 hits as of July 2010 (www.youtube. com/watch?v=kzWFLDfDjlY).[14] The lyrics of the song are by Ismail Khormali, a well-known contemporary Kurdish poet whose poems have been made into many songs by numerous Kurdish singers. The singer of this patriotic song, Zakaria Abdullah, who is commonly called by his first name, Zakaria, is a Swedish citizen who originally comes from Iraqi Kurdistan. He is one of the most, if not the most, popular Kurdish singers among the Kurdish youth in Iraq, Iran, Turkey, Syria, and the diaspora.

My objective in analyzing this song is to illustrate the ways in which it contributes to the discursive and symbolic construction of a pan-Kurdish sentiment. I carry out a multimodal analysis of the music-video clip Kurdistan at three levels: verbal language (linguistic terms and concepts), visual images, and audio. Furthermore, I will underscore the importance of language choice in the song. Although the analytical tools used here have already been discussed, I find it useful to repeat them. I will also use this part of the analysis to introduce most of the analytical tools that have been used in this study, in addition to showing the relations between different modes of discourse (verbal language and audio-visual). The transcription of translated lyrics and a description of images and music of the song are provided in table 6.1.

Verbal Language

Naming

Different names, titles, and labels given to people, objects, and concepts indicate the attitudes and beliefs of the speakers and writers towards them (Fowler et al., 1979). Names not only identify but they could also define things and people; they not only indicate the degree of intimacy with, but also distance from, people, places, and things. Studying the use of naming in the addresses to the nation in Poland, Galasiński and Skowronek (2001) observe that the practice did not just enable politicians and religious leaders to refer to places and persons; the speakers used specific naming also "to construct an ideologically preferred reality. Proper names were used to serve the political purpose of the day" (p. 63).

When it comes to the discourse of national identity, naming the nation and what are believed to be national characteristics and symbols are among the prime naming practices. Billig (1995) says, "Somehow, in ways difficult to articulate, the magic of 'our' name matters to 'us' deeply, whichever nationality 'we' are: it indicates who 'we' are, and, more basically, *that* 'we' are. In the secular age, the name of the nation is not to be taken in vain" (p. 73, emphasis in original; see also Shnirelman, 2006; Nicolaisen, 1990). For Bourdieu (1991), naming oneself is "the typically magical act through which the particular group—virtual, ignored, denied, or repressed—makes itself visible and manifests, for other groups and for itself, and attests to its existence as a group that is known and recognized" (p. 224). Clearly, naming practices have been indispensable parts of discourses of nationalism. Discussing naming practices in the nationalist discourses of the Québécois and Aboriginal peoples in Canada, Jenson (1993) states, "Nationalist movements are social movements involved in the definition of a collective identity; they make choices about names" (p. 337).

In the patriotic song, *Kurdistan*, naming is a significant discursive tool that contributes to the imagination of a collective Kurdish identity and the Greater Kurdistan. The most significant naming practice pertains to the word *Kurdistan*, which is literally translated as "the land of the Kurds." The states ruling over Kurdish territories do not recognize Kurdistan as a distinct territorial unit encompassing parts of

Table 6.1 Patriotic song "Kurdistan": Lyrics, images, and music descriptions

	Lyrics (Verbal) (mostly original subtitles)	Visual	Music
1	[No verbal language]	Opening scene: -a lake surrounded by mountains; a large crowd marching in the streets, shoulder to shoulder, waving Kurdish flags, throwing hands in the air, chanting slogans; a close-up shot of a youngster, with the Kurdish flag painted on his face, sitting on the shoulder of an adult	-Lines 1–9 -March music -Vocal: choir, with a strong, revolutionary and angry tune
2	Listen to the tombstone and grave of the martyrs that are calling	-A group of women in black are sitting around a coffin; Close-up of an elderly woman wiping her tears	
3	Listen to the heart and chest of your mountains that are calling	-Peshmarga climbing a hill	
4	Listen to the tombstone and grave of the martyrs that are calling	-A group of women in black dress crying, one throwing hands in the air; men behind them	
5	Listen to the heart and chest of your mountains that are calling	-Peshmarga on top of a mountain entrenching and firing guns	
6	We are all in the frontline trenches, oh Kurdistan!	-The crowd moving in solidarity, waving flags, throwing hands in the air, with the Kurdistan parliament in the background	
7	For your sake, we will remain in the frontlines, oh Kurdistan!	-different shots of the crowd, children in colourful clothes marching, constant close-ups of the Kurdish flag and people making V (victory) signs	
8	Our existence and yours are one and the same!	-brief shots of the crowed from various angles	
9	Your life and freedom are equal to our death, oh Kurdistan!	-crowds on the street marching; close-up shot of Kurdistan parliament; close-up shot of a Kurdish woman in police uniform; university of Hawler's entrance	
			Music changes
10	You will not surrender because your *Baban* and *Badinan* are with you	-close-up shots of the singer (Zakaria) juxtaposed with images of parts of a map, past Kurdish leaders and heroes (e.g. Shêx Mehmûd Hafîd), and towns and mountains fading in and out	Lines 10–13 -Slow rhythm, almost like a lullaby -Vocal: solo (singer)
11	Even the stones and trees of your *Germian* and *Hewlêr* are with you	-similar to the previous frame but with Hawler's ancient castle in the background	

Continued

Table 6.1 Continued

Lyrics (Verbal) (mostly original subtitles)	Visual	Music
12 You will not surrender since your *Afrin* and *Mehabad* are with you	-large crowed of people marching	
13 The people and tribes of your *Qamishli* and *Mardin* are with you, Kurdistan!	-the camera circles the singer sitting on a table and writing on a piece of paper; Mountains, a lose-up of a red tulip	
		Music changes
14 We swear by Nawroz, the uprising; we swear by your hundreds-year history	-Nawroz's bonfire surrounded by a large crowed; camera moving toward the entrance of a cave; a historical site	-Lines 14–19 -Music changes into a faster
15 We swear by the river of exodus and blood, and hundreds-year freedom	-close-up of the singer juxtaposed with a sparkling body of water	rhythm and a joyful tune -Vocal: Solo (singer)
16 We will never forget you Kurdistan, you are always in our hearts	-camera moves over green mountains surrounding a lake with a blue sky in the background	
17 Like breath in our lungs you're a part of our existence	- long shot of a city; the yard of a university/ school	
18 Do not worry, we will not allow them to burn down this spring of yours	-women and men in colourful clothes on picnic and dancing (Kurdish) -green mountains surrounding a pond	
19 We will not let them to hurt the anguished mothers of martyrs, again	-women in black crying -close-up of the singer (Zakaria) juxtaposed with scenes of Kurdistan's nature	
	Language changes from Sorani to Kurmanji Kurdish	**Music changes**
20 Don't you think you can stay [in this land]; in your dreams!	-Kurdish men beat up by [government] soldiers; Kurdish refugee women getting off a truck surrounded by armed soldiers; [repeat of lyrics] close-up of singer juxtaposed with the map of Kurdistan	-Lines 20–25 -Music : slower tune -Vocal: Solo (Zakaria)
21 No matter how many times you build on mount Gare, you will never rule over my homeland.	-close-up of red tulips on the foothills of a high mountain	

Continued

Table 6.1 Continued

Lyrics (Verbal) (mostly original subtitles)	Visual	Music
22 Many Alexander the Great(s) and Xenophons appeared here before you	-an ancient head sculpture [Alexander the great]; soldiers beating up and pushing Kurdish men; Pêshmerge with guns positioned at the top of a hill	
23 Our homeland turned into a fire for them, they all ran away	-Crowed waving Kurdish flags marching; close-up of a women in black holding a picture of a white dove	
24 I will inform the shepherds of all plots against us	-crowed marching on the streets holding placards; close-up of the singer juxtaposed with scenes of mountains	
25 The principles call upon us that you and I cannot get along	- close-up shots of the Kurdish flag; close-ups of marching crowds shouting slogans and waving Kurdish flags while the Kurdistan parliament is in the background	
	Language changes back to Kurdish Sorani	**Music changes**
26 Raise your head, oh Kurdistan! The storm of Kurdish sword has become known to the world	-Kurdish women soldiers marching during military training -Kurdish men soldiers marching during military training	-Lines 26-29 -Music: march music (similar to the opening of the song) -Vocal: Choir in a powerful, revolutionary and angry tune
27 Your children like eagles have crossed the world's last frontiers	-Kurdish soldiers marching; students in a classroom; close-up of a woman with headphones at the meeting	
28 Oh Kurdistan! How interference and occupation, then, can prevent you from living or your lips from smiling	-close-up of a mother with her child smiling; university students graduating ceremony; people dancing outdoors	
29 Your life and freedom are equal to our death, oh Kurdistan! Oh Kurdistan!	-waving flag crowd marching in the streets; long shot of Kurdistan parliament; Kurdish soldiers marching; close-up of tulips on the foothills of a high mountain	

Note: In describing the visuals, shots are separated by a semi-colon. Frames are described in rows (1–29). Each frame consists of a lyric segment (e.g., a verse), and could accompany several camera shots in addition to segments of music.

Turkey, Iraq, Iran, and Syria. In Turkey, for example, the use of the term "Kurdistan," regardless of what one might mean by it, is illegal and can be considered an act of separatism and, thus, punishable. Numerous researchers and ordinary people, Kurdish or non-Kurdish, travelling to

Iraqi Kurdistan through Turkey, have reported that their documents and laptops have been searched by Turkish border guards for the word "Kurdistan." They have been asked to delete instances of the word from their documents and equipment (O'Leary & Salih, 2005, pp. 3–4). In other cases, documents containing the word have been destroyed altogether.[15] It is also important to note that even some western officials and journalists refrain from uttering the word Kurdistan and tend to opt for Kurdish regions or Kurdish areas. For example, officials from the U.S. administration rarely, if ever, use the word Kurdistan when referring to Iraqi Kurdistan, despite the fact that the United States has had very close ties with Iraqi Kurds since the first Gulf War.

In this anthem, the word Kurdistan is at the focal position of the title of the song, which is aired on a TV channel called *Kurdistan TV*. Furthermore, throughout the anthem, which is about five minutes long, the word Kurdistan is repeated nine times. Thus, in addition to naming, repetition also plays an important role in expressing the writer's or singer's strong feeling and belief about his choice of the naming. But, does the word Kurdistan, in this song, only refer to Iraqi Kurdistan or the Greater Kurdistan, and how can we know this? We can infer from the lyrics and choices of naming that the Kurdistan imagined here is the Greater Kurdistan. The singer assures [Iraqi] Kurdistan that all the Kurdistan regions and towns are with her. Among these are cities and regions that are officially located in Iran, Syria, and Turkey. For example, *Baban, Badinan*(two regions) in line 10, and *Germian* and *Hewlêr* in line 11 from Iraq, *Afrîn* in line 12 and *Qamîshlî* in line 13 from Syria, *Mardîn* in line 14 from Turkey, and *Mehabad* in line 12 from Iran. At first glance, it seems that the lyrics are only saying that these cities and regions are in solidarity with the Iraqi Kurdistan. However, the use of the possessive pronoun "your"(e.g., see lines 10 and 14) leaves no doubt that these places are imagined as belonging to the same territory: the Greater Kurdistan. The identity that is constructed is a pan-Kurdish identity rather than a regional, Iraqi Kurdish one. This pan-Kurdish identity is not only constructed through unifying all the places that are believed to be Kurdistan, from a pan-Kurdish nationalist perspective, but also through separating these places from the states of which they are officially a part. Similar to all nationalist discourses, this song not only represents the discourse of in-group solidarity but also the discourse of out-group differentiation.

With respect to naming practices, it is also important to note that the word "Kurd/Kurds" is absent in this song. This is in a sharp contrast to the Kurdish national anthem, Ay Raghib or *Ey Reqîb*

(*O Enemy*), written in the late 1930s, which constantly repeats the word Kurd/Kurds but makes no mention of the word Kurdistan. This difference marks a discursive shift in the Kurdish nationalist discourse, particularly in Iraqi Kurdistan, where words like "Kurdistan," "Kurdistanis," and "the people of Kurdistan" have started to be used by the KRG officials and their media instead of the words Kurd or Kurds. This is especially evident in the speeches given by the Kurdish leaders, such as Masoud Barzani and some other officials of KDP, the owner of KTV.[16] This could have two important sociocultural implications. The word Kurd/Kurds identifies an ethnic group (Kurds), whereas Kurdistan identifies a territory with its entire people, which could be made up of more than one ethnic group. Thus, whereas the use of the word Kurd/Kurds could for the most part contribute to the reproduction of an ethnic group, the use of the word Kurdistan contributes to the construction of a territorial nation that combines more than one ethnic group who share the same land, Kurdistan. The two choices can also be interpreted as belonging to different kinds of nationalism, ethnic versus civic. There is a deliberate attempt to acknowledge the existence of other ethnic groups in Kurdistan.[17] One could also suggest that this discursive practice expresses KRG's ambition for more territorial and political autonomy.

Pronouns
As Fowler et al. (1979) suggest, "personal pronouns always deserve notice" (p. 201; see also Wodak et al., 2009; Higgins, 2004). Personal pronouns have proven very fruitful in analyzing discourses of national identity. Billig (1995) observes that "nationalism is, above all, an ideology of the first person plural. The crucial question relating to national identity is how the nation 'we' is construed and what is meant by such construction" (p. 70).

In the song *Kurdistan*, several pronouns are used: "we," "you," and "them." The "we" pronoun is inclusive, including the singer and the people of Kurdistan who are overtly presented in the visual images: the crowed on the street protesting, Peshmarga or *Peşmerge* ("Kurdish freedom fighters"), college students, newly trained Kurdistan military, and Kurdistan parliamentarians. There are 11 instances of "we" and seven instances of the corresponding possessive pronouns ("our," "ours"). Thus, the findings here are consistent with other studies that have identified "we" as the most prominent pronoun contributing to the construction of solidarity and unity in a nation (Billig, 1995; Wodak et al., 2009).

The use of "you," however, in this anthem, is not so straightforward. Fowler et al. (1979) tell us that " 'you' is, as might be expected, complementary in meaning and usage to 'I/we'; as every piece of language has an explicit or implicit source, so does it have an implicit or explicit addressee" (p. 203). The challenge in this anthem is that there are two addressees, Kurdistan and the "other" (e.g., 'tyrants'— enemies of Kurdistan). It appears that Fowler et al. (1979) have realized this complexity with the usage of "you" since they are quick to suggest that " 'you' needs to be discussed in the context of speech acts performed upon an addressee" (p. 203).

In the context of this anthem, "you" and its corresponding possessive "your" refer to Kurdistan (lines 7–14, 16–18, 25–28) and at other times refers to the "out-group" (e.g., "tyrants") (lines 22, 25). Why is the "other" not just referred to as "they" or "them," as is the case in line 18 and 19? One reason for that might be the fact that most of the anthem has a confrontational theme. As discussed earlier, there is a strong presupposition from the beginning of the anthem that Kurdistan had been treated badly previously and now it is under threat and, thus, it needs to be defended against "tyrants." The image of a strong Kurdistani people who are ready to stand up to the threat is built both linguistically and visually throughout the anthem. Thus, addressing the "other" as "you" instead of "them" or "they" in a few occasions could be intentional to illustrate that the Kurds are resolved and ready to confront the "tyrants." This comes out clearly through some of the lyrics (e.g., lines 19–28).

In addition to the confrontational "you," and direct naming choices such as "tyrants," the out-group is also referred to as "them," for example in lines 18 and 19. Whereas the inclusive "we" and the solidarity "you" (addressing the homeland) serves to construct a we-group, the confrontational "you" and 'them' pronouns construct a them-group. Nonetheless, they are all contributing to the construction of a distinct Kurdish identity.

Tense

Another central component of the modal function of language is tense. According to Fowler et al. (1979), different uses of tense are neither arbitrary nor neutral; they indicate different orientations toward the phenomena that are talked or written about. For example, present tense "signals certainty, unquestionableness, continuity, universality" (p. 207). Fairclough (2001), in a similar vein, suggests that the simple present tense form "is one terminal point of expressive modality, a categorical commitment of the producer to the truth of the propositions"

(p. 129). Dunmire (1997) cites Fleischman, asserting that "the greater the likelihood that a situation will be realized, i.e., the closer to 'reality' the speaker perceives it as being, the closer to 'now' (=present) will be the tense used to represent it" (p. 234). In contrast, the past tense will be used when things are desired to remain in the past and not to be of current concern. As Fowler et al. (1979) suggest, "Temporal 'distance' nearly always conveys modal 'distance'" (p. 207).

In the song *Kurdistan*, most of the utterances are structured either in the simple present tense or their verbs are accompanied by the modal auxiliary "will," which is indicative of the continuity of the nation into the future. In contrast, events of the past are often implied rather than presented in the past tense. For example, line 2 ("Listen to the tombstone and grave of the martyrs that are calling") refers to martyrs who are clearly gone, but interestingly enough, according to the lyrics, they are still alive, still defending Kurdistan, because their verbal action of "cry" is in the simple present tense. Mountains "cry" presently as well, as in line 3 ("Listen to the heart and chest of your mountains that are calling"). All parts of Kurdistan, located in four nation-states, "*are* with [the homeland]" presently (lines 10–13).

Next to the simple present tense, another primal grammatical element of modality that is used in this anthem is the modal auxiliary "will" (lines 7, 10, 12, 16, 18, 19, 21, 24). It can express certainty and self-assurance about both present and future situations and events. For example, in lines 10 and 12 (and by extension, through ellipses, in lines 11 and 13) it is an expression of self-assurance that Kurdistan "will not surrender," since other parts of Kurdistan (Iran, Turkey, Syria) are "with" the Iraqi Kurdistan. This way, the auxiliary "will" contributes to the imagination of a greater Kurdistan as a common goal for all Kurds, regardless of which state they live in. But, "will" can also signal willingness, with a high degree of probability, on the part of a speaker to embark on an action; it declares a serious promise (e.g., lines 6–9, 16, 18, 19). In these lines, the patriotic loyalty to the motherland is renewed by promising to Kurdistan that it will be protected against the "tyrants." In addition to a promise, "will" also seems to be a declaration of threat against the "tyrants." This way "will," on the one hand, contributes to the imagination of a common present and future among the in-group members, and on the other hand, it contributes to the construction of the out-group.

Metaphors

According to Lakoff and Johnson (1980), "the essence of metaphor is understanding and experiencing one kind of thing in terms of another" (p. 5, see also Fairclough, 2001). For example in the sentence, *he spends time with her family*, English speakers understand the importance of time in terms of their common understanding of the value of money which can also be spent, saved, or wasted. A crucial point to be raised here is that there is no apparent connection between time and money, but what brings them together is the perception, which is based on cultural assumptions, and also feelings that are mostly shared between humans from the same culture. On the importance of metaphor in our discursive practices, Lakoff and Johnson state that, "Since much of our social reality is understood in metaphorical terms, and since our conception of the physical world is partly metaphorical, metaphor plays a very significant role in determining what is real for us" (p. 146). In other words, we understand the world and conceptualize reality in part in terms of metaphors. As Wodak et al. (2009, p. 44) illustrate, metaphors play an important role in "the mental construction of nation" by implying in-group "sameness and equality" on the one hand, and out-group differences and inequality on the other. Finally, it is also important to note that metaphors are context and culture-sensitive. For example, the expression *time is money* might be quite alien to another culture where people are less preoccupied with time. The cultural and context sensitivity of metaphors have implications for the study of the discursive construction of national identity. Metaphors that contribute to the formation of imagined communities could be different from one context to the next.

There are different kinds of metaphors, one of which is personification. According to Wodak et al. (2009), "[p]ersonification attributes a human form to an abstract entity and thus constitutes a widely-used mean of realizing a constructive strategy, demanding, for example, identification with an anthropomorphized nation" (p. 43). Drawing on Billig (1995), Chouliaraki (1999) observes that "[p]ersonification and the concomitant attribution of intense human feelings to the nation metaphorize relations within the nation as relationships of kinship, of family, thus further forging a sense of imagined community among its members" (p. 49).[18]

In the song *Kurdistan,* one of the prominent personification metaphors employed is family, as in, "[y]our children like eagles have crossed the world's last frontiers [Kurdistan]" (line 27). In Kurdish, the homeland is female and a mother (Ahmadzadeh, 2003), and it is commonly referred to, particularly in patriotic poems and songs, as *Daykî Nîshtiman* or *Daykî Weten* (the motherland), as is the case in many other languages (Wodak et al., 2009). In some other languages, one can speak of the fatherland, but this is never the case in Kurdish. In this song, the homeland is personified as a mother who is dearly loved: "We will never forget you Kurdistan, you are always in our hearts" (line 16), "like breath in our lungs you're a part of our existence" (line 17). In order to show their love for their motherland, many of her children (martyrs) sacrificed themselves for her "freedom" (lines 2, 19), and now more children, according to the song, are willing to do the same (line 27). In order to convince the "children" to "sacrifice" their lives for the motherland, it is essential to make them believe in two things. First, that the motherland is like their mother, that they love her wholeheartedly, and that without her they will be orphans and homeless. And, second, that the existence of the homeland, the mother, is threatened. The motherland needs to be defended. The very suggestion that Kurdistan needs to be defended presupposes the existence of a continuous threat against Kurds and Kurdistan.

Presuppositions

A presupposition is "a proposition that is tacitly assumed to be true for another proposition to be meaningful" (van Dijk, 1993, p. 251). A presupposition is an assertion that is implied rather than explicitly and overtly stated. Consider this example from van Dijk (1993) which had originally appeared in a British paper: "We have to be more brisk in saying no, and showing the door to those who are not British citizens and would abuse *our hospitality* and *tolerance*" (my emphasis). In this example, it is presupposed that the British are "hospitable" and "tolerant," and therefore, claims of mistreatment that might be put forward by minorities become irrelevant and unfounded. In situations like this, presuppositions can be "manipulative" and ideological, although there are other times when they can be "sincere" (Fairclough, 2001, p. 154). In this example from van Dijk, and elsewhere, however, presuppositions can be ideological when "what they assume has the character of 'common sense in the service of power'" (p. 154). In addition to their ideological significance, presuppositions also deserve attention in discourse analysis because they are crucial features of the intertextuality of texts (Fairclough, 1995b). In other words, presuppositions are features of texts that have been constructed before, in other times and in other texts, but, nonetheless, they have become integrated parts of the meaning-making structure of the text in question.

In the song *Kurdistan*, there are several presuppositions that work towards crafting the Kurdish nationalist discourse. One that I have already alluded to is that Kurdistan is threatened today as it has always been: "Do not worry, we will not allow them to burn down this spring of yours" (line 18), "[w]e will not let them to hurt the anguished mothers of martyrs, again" (line 19). The presupposition that Kurdistan is threatened legitimates the song's proposition that it needs to be defended, it needs to be loved, and more lives should be sacrificed for its sake. The proposition that Kurdistan should be defended is also strengthened by two other presuppositions in lines 18 and 26, which I just quoted. That Kurdistan, which entails Iraqi Kurdistan here, is free, lives in its spring, and is "smiling." Given the long history of Kurdish oppression, it will be such a shame not to protect this "free Kurdistan."

The other presupposition is that Kurdistan is ancient and it has a proud past: "We swear by…your hundreds-year history" (line 14), and "hundreds-year freedom" (line 15). The presupposition that Kurdistan has existed for hundreds of years and that it has been free in the past works towards legitimating the proposition that Kurdistan deserves to exist not only now, and in the future, but also to be free, again. Side by side with this discursive construction of a free Kurdistan in the past, we can detect presuppositions that work around the construction of a not very distant past when Kurdistan was occupied, oppressed, disunited, and weak: "Don't you think you can stay [in this land]!" (line 20), "[n]o matter how many times you build on mount Gare," (line 21), and "[m]any Alexander the Great(s) and Xenophons appeared here before you" (line 22).

Over-lexicalization

Over-lexicalization (Fowler et al., 1979) or "over-wording" (Fairclough, 2001, p. 115), refers to a high level use of words and lexical items that are synonymous, near-synonymous, or semantically close enough to contribute to the construction of an idea, theme, and point of preoccupation. For a critical analysis of discourse it is important to consider over-lexicalization because this linguistic tool "points to areas of intense preoccupation in the experience and values of the group which generates it, allowing the linguist to identify peculiarities in the ideology of that group" (Fowler et al., 1979, p. 211–12).[19] Clustering the lexicon of this song into several categories that are often parts of nationalist discourses allows us to map out some important peculiarities of the Kurdish nationalist ideology that are represented in this song (see table 6.2).

As shown in table 6.2, using this analytical tool of over-lexicalization, we can tease out the lexical elements that effectively

Table 6.2 Analysis of over-lexicalization in the patriotic song *Kurdistan*

Common present & future	Common memory and history			Common territory	Common national characteristic			Invented traditions: Shared symbols	Solidarity and unity: Us	Difference: The "other"/them
	Ancient past	Glorious past	Sufferings of the past*		Love for the homeland	Unique Kurdish traits	Equating the nation and family			
Freedom	hundred-years long history	Glorious uprising	Exodus	Kurdistan	Existence	Martyrs [being at the] Front lines	Mothers	Mountains	We	Tyrants
Our existence	Xenophon	hundreds	Blood	Baban	forget	Vigilant	Children	Nawroz (Kurdish New Year)	Our	Xenophon
Your existence	Alexander the Great	of freedom	Martyrs	Badinan	Sacrifice	Sacrifice		Martyrs (there are many more expressed visually: flag, Peshmarga, landscapes)	With you	Alexander the Great built palaces failed
Smiling		years	Hurt	Hawler	Defend	"we'll never allow"			United	Conspiracy (the absence of being Iraqis)
Living		[defeating others]	Anguished mothers	Afrin	Heart	Defend				
Spring			Burn down	Mahabad	Breath	"never give in"				
Raise head				Qamishli		Strong				
				Mardin						

*Sufferings in the past could also qualify as a Kurdish trait. Kurdish poetry and oral literature is permeated with the notion that Kurds' land has been divided, their lives have been destroyed, their language has been prohibited, and their rights have been denied. Suffering is portrayed as an indispensable part of being a Kurd.

realize some of the core concepts of the Kurdish nationalist discourse. They are: common present and future, common memory and history (ancient history, glorious past, sufferings of the past), common territory, common national characteristics (love of the homeland, unique Kurdish traits, equating the nation with the family), invented traditions and shared symbols, solidarity and unity, and, finally, differences with others. Some of these invented traditions and symbols (e.g., flag and so on) are expressed more clearly and frequently in the visual images, which I will turn to shortly.

The verbal language in this text contributes to the construction of an imagined Kurdistan community that is ancient and has a glorious past, but then it was occupied, divided, and oppressed. The verbal language also aims at conveying the message that although the threat against Kurdistan continues, there is no worry because its loyal children are ready to defend it by risking their lives as they have done in the past. Kurdistan is stronger than ever, because its people are united now, they are proud of their recent freedom in Iraqi Kurdistan, and they are hopeful of enjoying a prosperous future. These lyrics, however, do not tell the whole narrative of Kurdish nationalism in Iraq. There is more to this narrative. For example, it heralds to the audiences that Kurdistan is enjoying its "spring" season, which is a metaphor for Kurdistan freedom and revival. Yet, we know that this is not the case; three parts of Kurdistan are not in the same situation as Iraqi Kurdistan. This is where images add important meaning to the content of the lyrics.

Visual Images

One of the first concerns in the area of multimodal analysis is: what kinds of relations exist between different modes of meaning-making or communication (i.e., verbal language, image, and sound)? For example, with respect to this song, we can ask: do images reinforce, summarize, expand, or negate what the lyrics say? Modes usually have two kinds of relations: *elaborative* or *extensive* (van Leeuwen, 2005). The relation is *elaborative* when messages and content in one mode are restated in another mode for the purpose of explaining the content, exemplifying, or summarizing it (van Leeuwen, 2005). The relation between different modes is *extensive* when the content expressed in one mode is expanded and added to by another mode.

Most of the images in this song are elaborations of the lyrics, as one might expect, because music-video clips are commonly made for songs that have already been recorded (Martinec, 2000).

For example, accompanying lyrics in line 2 are explained in images. The lyrics express a basic nationalistic message: Kurdish martyrs, who have sacrificed their lives for Kurdistan, are calling upon all the Kurds to do the same: to follow their path. The accompanying messages, in two shots, by showing women in black and crying around a coffin, elaborate the message of the lyrics: (1) those martyrs had mothers and families who have mourned the loss of their loved ones. They were just like us; (2) we hear the martyrs' call through the crying and wailing of the grief-stricken mothers. It is not easy to ignore them.

In addition to this kind of elaboration, which happens to be explanatory, there are other examples of elaboration that shed light on some of the ambiguities of the lyrics by exemplifying the content of the lyrics. For instance, in the lyric "your children are ready to defend you," it is not clear who the nation-defending children are. The images exemplify the children of the nation: Kurdish soldiers, school youth, and public servants. In combination with other images, the visual part of the song seems to convey the idea that, whereas in the past the Peshmarga were the main force fighting for Kurdistan, today everyone is.

In addition to elaboration, there are also images that are extensions of the lyrics, in the sense that they add new but related content to what is expressed in other modes (e.g., the verbal language). The lyrics make no explicit reference to Iraqi Kurdistan, and judging by the verbal language of the lyrics, one becomes convinced that the Kurdistan that is represented throughout this song is a Greater Kurdistan. However, images of the Iraqi Kurdistan parliament building (e.g., line 28), Kurdish police in uniform, and even images of Kurdish university students graduating, unmistakably identify Iraqi Kurdistan and not other parts. One could argue that the two modes, verbal and visual, betray each other because the lyrics construct a Greater Kurdistan, yet the images remind the viewer that the Kurdistan that is really talked about, at least partially, is Iraqi Kurdistan. However, there is another plausible explanation for this extensive relation between the two modes. Although it is Iraqi Kurdistan that is "free" and "smiling" and enjoying its "spring" season, the existence of this small Kurdistan depends on the support of other parts of Kurdistan. At the same time, the existence of this small "free Kurdistan" has given and will continue to give confidence and hope to all Kurdistan, and to even the Kurdish diasporic communities. This discursive practice with seemingly two different ideological objectives, one producing an Iraqi/smaller Kurdistan and the other producing a Greater Kurdistan, runs through most of

KTV's discourses. I will illustrate this later, when discussing excerpts from KTV's news and talk shows.

Music

In the music-video *Kurdistan*, the music elaborates the content expressed in both the lyrics and images. To illustrate this, the song can be divided into four stages, based on the changes and transitions of the music.

The video opens with marching music that possesses a powerful and angry tune, which is typical of Kurdish patriotic and revolutionary songs and anthems. The music and its tune are an elaboration of the lyrics "we will be in the front lines and defend you Kurdistan!" and images of Peshmarga, mountains, large crowds of people marching in the streets, waving Kurdish flags, and with hands thrown in the air as a sign of chanting slogans. In the second stage, when the lyrics encourage [Iraqi] Kurdistan not to succumb to threats because it is not alone and other parts of Kurdistan are with her, the music changes into a slower rhythm with a soft and melancholy tune, typical of Kurdish love songs.[20] The tune is an elaboration of the images, which exemplify other parts of Kurdistan. The music in the third stage falls into a joyful tune with a faster rhythm, a tune and rhythm that are commonly used in Kurdish dance music. This music elaborates the content of the lyrics and images that celebrate the free state of [Iraqi] Kurdistan and the people's renewal of allegiance and loyalty to the motherland. The fourth stage of the song is marked by yet another melody, which has a slow rhythm and a melancholy tune. It again elaborates the content of the lyrics and images, which recall the past oppressions of the Kurds and occupation of Kurdistan. In the final stage, the music changes back to the music of the opening scenes, a marching music with a revolutionary tune. This is an elaboration of the content of the lyrics and images that define and represent a Kurdistan that is proud of its free part (Iraq), and that Kurdistan, as a whole, is strong, united, and vigilant, and ready to defend itself.

A final note should be made regarding the language use in this song. The song is performed in the two major Kurdish varieties, Sorani and Kurmanji. Although the singer's mother tongue is Sorani, he performs the fourth stage of the song in Kurmanji. Singing in the two varieties has been a deliberate act by nationalist singers to alleviate the existing linguistic fragmentation in Kurdistan, and consequently construct the image of a unified Kurdish people and a

Greater Kurdistan. In the late 1980s, Nasser Razzazi, from Iranian Kurdistan, popularized singing in several Kurdish speech varieties, such as Sorani, Kurmanji, Hawrami, and Gorani and Kirmashani. Since then, especially among diasporic communities, many singers have joined the practice. Singing in two or more varieties, in the same song or anthem, as is the case in the song *Kurdistan*, however, is a recent phenomenon. This is another sign of Kurds becoming closer to each other and becoming more able to communicate their fears, affections, and dreams in each other's languages and voices rather than in isolated regional dialects alone.

CHAPTER 7

Discourse Practices of
Kurdish Internet

In the previous two chapters, I looked at Kurdistan TV's programs and analyzed the discursive construction of Kurdish identities that are enabled and disseminated by the channel. I illustrated that KTV's discourse of national identity to a large extent reflects its owner's interests and ideologies. Owned by a regional political organization, KTV mainly constructs a regional and Iraqi Kurdish identity, but at the same time, it engages in subtle and implicit discursive constructions of a cross-border Kurdish identity. Overall, the channel's discourse practices are carried out within the ideological framework and political interests of its owner, the Kurdistan Democratic Party (KDP).

The purpose of this chapter and the next is to investigate how Kurds use the Internet to present themselves and to construct, negotiate, and articulate their identities. The Kurdish Internet is important insofar as it gives voice to those who cannot afford to broadcast on satellite television channels, which are exclusively owned by dominant Kurdish political organizations. Thus, unless I find it useful for the purpose of contextualization, in this chapter and the next, I will not be concerned with online activities of the Kurdistan Regional Government in Iraq or the major Kurdish political parties. Instead, I will be focusing on smaller political organizations, societies, and individuals.

I assume that the Internet provides alternative communicative spaces for different discourse practices and discursive constructions of Kurdish identities. I also assume that, in contrast to KTV, Kurdish cyber activities are in significant ways devoted to explicit and overt construction and reproduction of a cross-border and pan-Kurdish identity. Finally, it is assumed that because online communication within a community in important ways depends on a shared language, Kurds might seem more fragmented than unified when judged by their online activities. To test the validity of these assumptions the following three questions are posed: (1) What are the main features or constituents of the Kurdish Internet? (2) What roles could these constituents play in the processes of negotiation and articulation of Kurdish identities? (3)Are the discourse practices fostered by the Kurdish online resources unifying or further fragmenting Kurdish identity? I will answer these questions after introducing my data.

The Internet data for this study were accumulated during my active observation of Kurdish online activities from 1998 to 2009. They consist of numerous screen shots, images, video clips, and textual content of the following Internet sources: Kurdish web directories, websites, chat rooms, weblogs, and forums. Most of the data have been collected through what can be termed guerrilla ethnography (Androutsopoulos, 2006; Yang, 2003). Parts of data, however, have been collected in more systematic ways. For example, the entire blogging activities of two Kurdish bloggers, starting in 2002, have been downloaded. Furthermore, the data also consist of a two-hour video recording of an online session of Kurdish bloggers on the Internet chat service Paltalk on April 14, 2004. In addition, my data encompass personal communications with webmasters, chat-room administrators (moderators), and webloggers (bloggers). Moreover, the data are accompanied by various media outlets' reports and interviews about Kurdish online activities. Finally, the data for this study are enriched by my personal involvement in online activities from 1998, which has enabled me to gain some useful inside knowledge about the affordances and also constraints of the Internet with respect to Kurdish online activities.[1]

In what follows, I will provide an overview of Kurdish cyber activities or the major constituents of Kurdish Internet. I am particularly interested in identifying alternative voices in platforms such as websites, chat rooms, weblogs and forums (discussion groups) that do not seem to be owned by the dominant Kurdish political organizations or the host states but rather by individuals, social activists and societies. To locate these internet sources, I have mainly relied on Kurdish web directories such as www.Koord.com, which in May 2007 indexed about 2,500 websites and 6,500 links to Kurdish Internet sources (B. N., personal communication, May 24, 2007).[2] In analysing Figure 7.1, I have divided these websites and online sources into the following categories: websites, chat-rooms, weblogs, and other constituents (Erikson, 2007). To avoid repetition, and in order not to take up too much space in the text, I will cite websites and Internet sources either

Figure 7.1 A screenshot of the Kurdish web directory www.koord.com

by their titles or authors. The URL and other details about these sources will be provided in the main References.

WEBSITES

According to its webmaster, the website Koord provides links to about 2,500 websites (B. N. personal communication, May 24, 2007). These websites range from personal to organizational and from entertainment-oriented to political. Approximately 10 percent of these websites are affiliated with the major Kurdish political organizations. The rest of the websites belong to smaller Kurdish organizations (i.e., those that do not own satellite television channels or other major media outlet, such as dailies), different individuals and groups of Kurdish intelligentsia (e.g., women activists, human rights groups), and ordinary individuals. These groups and individuals use the Internet either as a platform for advancing their political and social interests or expressing and articulating their cultural identity (i.e., Kurdishness), personal beliefs, anxieties and nostalgia for the homeland. As I will show shortly, websites are used as libraries, publishing houses, distribution systems of print materials, online news agencies, broadcasting facilities, and alternative and personal communicative spaces.

Websites as Libraries and Distribution Systems for Print Materials

As noted earlier in my discussion of Kurdish media, Kurdish publishing and journalism have suffered since their inception from the lack of adequate distribution systems (Hassanpour, 1996). The Internet has enabled Kurdish writers, publishers, distributors, and readers to overcome this obstacle in important ways. For example, there are several websites from which it is possible to download the newest books that are published both in Kurdistan and the diaspora. Some of the notable websites that provide free access to Kurdish books are www. nefel.com, www.amude.net, www.koord.com, and *Kitêbxaney Kurdî* (Kurdish library) (www.pertwk.com/ktebxane). It should be noted, however, that because the medium of the first and second websites is Kurmanji Kurdish, the books they carry are only in that Kurdish variety.[3] In contrast, most of the books that are available for downloading on *Kitêbxaney Kurdî* are in Sorani Kurdish. This is an example that indicates the fragmentation of Kurdish online activities across linguistic lines, a theme that I have encountered throughout my analysis. Nonetheless, it is important to point out that this fragmentation does not seem to be a product of the differences between the Kurdish varieties per se. Rather, it is the extra-linguistic factor that shapes Kurdish language use on the Internet. For example, theoretically any of these websites could carry books in a Kurdish variety other than their own without facing any technical difficulty.

The website that provides free access to the largest collection of Kurdish books is *Kitêbxaney Kurdî*. In June 2007, the website had 896 books available for download, mostly in PDF format, and free of charge. The number of books increased to about 1,100 by June 2008, and 1,300 by June 2010. The logo of the website, in the top left corner, reads: *"em kitêbxaneye hî hemû kesêke û hîçkesîş xawenî nîye"* (This library belongs to everyone, [but] no one owns it). According to the owner of the website, the books are made available with the permission of the copyright holders (B. H., personal communication, April 18, 2007). The webmaster of this site, Behroz Hasan, a university student residing in Denmark, in an interview with the *Kurdistan Post* reveals his purpose in hosting this website: "I believe that books make up an important part of any nation's culture; therefore, they deserve more attention" (Muhammad, 2006, p. 12). This indicates that Hasan's volunteer work to distribute Kurdish books is a conscious act of national identity construction. The vast majority of the books are published in Iraqi Kurdistan and they are all in Sorani Kurdish. On the impact of this website, Hasan says that more and more writers and publishers are willing to offer their books for free distribution on his website, but he also agonizes over the fact that the majority of people who visit the website are from the Kurdish diasporic communities, rather than from Kurdistan or Kurdish communities living in the Middle East. He believes that the main reason for this is the fact that people living in Kurdistan have limited access to the Internet (Muhammad, 2006, p. 12). In July 2010, however, the situation seems to be different. According to www.alexa.com, the audience distribution for the website *Kitêbxaney Kurdî* is as follows: Iraq (and Iraqi Kurdistan) 75 percent, Germany 6.2 percent, other places 18.7 percent. Although this may indicate a great improvement in Internet access in Iraqi Kurdistan, it may also be an indication of the lack of easy access to the Internet in Iranian Kurdistan, where the majority of the population speak the same Kurdish variety as the language of the books on that website.

Despite the limited access to the Internet within Kurdistan, it is difficult to underestimate the usefulness of a website like this and its place in the nation-building project. Only about a decade ago, many Kurdish readers were taking many risks to obtain one or two of these books, particularly in places like Iran, Syria, and Turkey, where the danger has not vanished. Until very recently, even members of Kurdish diasporic communities could not easily access Kurdish printed materials. On top of the costs associated with purchasing and shipping books, most of which were obtained from Iraqi Kurdistan, one had to wait months to receive them by mail. Many times, mailed books would never arrive at their intended destinations. Now the same readers have thousands of books at their fingertips, thanks to the Internet.

Websites as Periodicals and News Agencies

In addition to books and monographs, many Kurdish periodicals are distributed, redistributed, or reproduced on the Internet (e.g., magazine: Raman—www.raman-media.net; weekly broadsheet: Azadiya Welat—www.welat.org; daily newspaper: Xebat—www.xebat.net). In many instances, visitors to these sites not only access the online version of these periodicals, for example, in HyperText Markup Language (HTML) format, but they can also see what the print version looks like by downloading the Portable Document Format (PDF) of the publication. Nearly all these periodicals, including access to their archives, are open access and made available to all visitors freely.

The Internet has not only helped with the distribution of printed materials including Kurdish magazines and newspapers, it also has given rise to online news websites that have no print version, for example Avesta Kurd (www.avestakurd.net), Renesans (www.renesans.info)and Rizgarî Online (www.rizgari.com). The technology has also enabled a website such as Renesans to have its audiences react to news items and featured articles by leaving comments on the website. This has enabled readers from different diasporic Kurdish communities and different regions of Kurdistan to interact with the webmasters and, more importantly, with each other. Audiences can experience a sense of shared belonging, not only by being involved in the ritual of reading the same thing simultaneously, in Anderson's term (1991), but also by discussing and debating the same issues that concern them.

In addition to online dailies devoted to news and commentaries, there are also news agencies that did not exist prior to the emergence of the Internet. One of the most popular news agencies is Peyamner: *Ajansî Hewal u Bediwadachûnî Kurdistan* (Kurdistan News Agency) (PNA), which was established in 2005. As the Kurdish website with the most visitors (Sina, 2007b), the PNA operates from Iraqi Kurdistan, but provides news from throughout Kurdistan and diasporas, in several languages (Kurdish—Sorani and Kurmanji, Arabic, Persian, Turkish, and English). It covers a whole range of issues and news from current political affairs and news interest stories, to arts and entertainment. According to Alexa, the site is ranked 25 in Iraq and it is one of the rare Kurdish websites that attracts audiences from all the countries where Kurds reside, in the Middle East, Europe, and North America. One reason for that might be the fact that the site is multilingual.

Websites as Broadcasting Facilities

Except for the two satellite TV channels, Kurdistan TV and KurdSat, which are owned by the two dominant Kurdish political organizations in Iraqi Kurdistan, no other Kurdish radio or television station could have been received worldwide, if it were not for the Internet. Prior to 1991, no Kurdish broadcasting was permitted in Turkey or Syria, and in Iran and Iraq governments held monopolies on radio broadcasting.[4] Kurdish-owned radio stations belonging to Kurdish political organizations were operating clandestinely, usually from mountainous hideouts, and were received on short-wave receivers. The Internet has changed this. Now, most political organizations have either live or archived broadcasts available to their audiences worldwide (e.g., Dengê Mezopotamya). There are also privately owned radio stations broadcasting from Iraqi Kurdistan via the Internet, such as Radio Nawa. From diasporas, among popular radio stations one should mention Zayele, Swedish Radio International, Kurdish service, Radio Rojawa, and Radio Kurdland. In addition to the fact that everyone with access to the Internet can listen to live programs from these radio stations, in many cases, they can also go back and listen to archived radio shows. The availability of these shows in MP3 format[5] has also made it easy to download them, save them, or redistribute them via email.

In addition to a number of radio stations, most of the major Kurdish TV stations can be viewed on the Internet, as well. A number of these TV channels provide live streaming broadcast on the Internet (e.g., Roj TV), and in this way, they have managed to reach those audiences who may not have access to a satellite dish or those who live in some parts of the world where the signal of some channels cannot be received at all (e.g., Roj TV, Tishk TV, Komala TV, Aso Sat, Zagros TV, Newroz TV, etc., cannot be received by satellite in North America). Those TV stations that do not provide live streaming broadcast make a selection of their programs available for viewing and downloading on their websites. Having access to TV broadcasting on the Internet is important, especially for those who either cannot own satellite dishes or cannot freely use them, for example in Iranian and Turkish Kurdistan. McDowall (2004) observes that "in Kurdistan, Turkish security forces had for some years been smashing satellite dishes" (p. 460).

The Internet is also the easiest and most economical way of broadcasting audio-visual clips that can be created on personal computers. In addition to hundreds of Kurdish websites and weblogs that offer free download of audio and video files, ranging from songs to images of Kurdish rebels, the Kurds also take full advantage of audio-video sharing websites such as YouTube. The search query "Kurd or Kurdistan" on October 5, 2007, conducted on YouTube returned more than 60,000 hits. This is a considerable figure compared to the number of hits that on the same day were returned for the following queries: "Canada or Canadian," 155,000, "Iran and Iranian," 145,000, and "Palestine or Palestinian," 44,200. The same search query, "Kurd or Kurdistan," in July 2010 returned more than 90,000 hits, indicating a considerable growth in information sharing among the Kurds. Comments posted in response to popular video clips indicate that video sharing social networks such as YouTube are among the top media constituents, where exchange of ideas and information among the Kurds from different regions and linguistic communities occurs.

Websites as Alternative Communicative Spaces

One of the greatest features of the Internet is its capability to amplify alternative but otherwise marginal voices (Bargh & McKenna, 2004; Mautner, 2005). Andrew Shapiro has talked about "control revolution" to capture the idea that the Internet has enabled individuals and disenfranchised groups to communicate outside the realm of nation-states and major media corporations (Mills, 2002, p. 74). This is certainly true of the Kurdish Internet. On the one hand, Kurdish opposition groups have utilized the Internet, along with other media at their disposal, including satellite television. On the other hand, with the use of the Internet, voices different from the dominant political parties have been able to reach Kurdish audiences in unprecedented ways.

These alternative voices range from smaller political groups that have minimum presence in the daily political life in Kurdistan (e.g., *Yekyetî Nîshtimanî Demokratî Kurdistan,YNDK*—Democratic National Union of Kurdistan), social activists, and NGO members (e.g., *Nawendî CHAK*—The Center of Halabja against Anfalazation and Genocide of Kurds [sic.], and *Jin*—Kurdish Women Network), and individuals. Among these, there are websites that openly advocate pan-Kurdism and the idea of establishing a greater Kurdistan (detailed analysis will follow). Other alternative voices are ordinary individuals who often use their websites for personal use, cultural activities, and also political activism. A great number of these personal websites are very explicit about identifying themselves as pan-Kurdish. They often express patriotic emotions towards Kurds and Kurdistan by displaying the Kurdish flag and the map of Greater Kurdistan, and playing patriotic songs and video clips (I will provide more detail on these semiotic practices in the next chapter).

Finally, among the alternative Kurdish voices using the Internet, there are websites that appear to be very serious about the status of Kurds and Kurdistan and engage in related debates on political, social, and cultural issues daily (e.g., Kurdistan Net and Bo Rojhelat—For the East[6]). Many of these websites claim to be independent from Kurdish political parties. In fact, they direct a great portion of their writing and content against the dominant Kurdish political parties and criticize them for being parochial, non-Kurdistani, and corrupt. Addressing the current Iraqi president, Jalal Talabani, who is also the leader of one of the two most powerful Kurdish organizations in Iraq (PUK), the title of an article on Kurdistan Post, on July 07, 2007, reads: "Talabani! We are all tired of you because you are the implacable enemy of all of us [all Kurds]." This biting title is reinforced by images of Talabani crossed with a black marker as a strong sign of rejection. In another article titled "The Leader of All Kurdistan," published on September 23, 2007, Kurdistanpost accuses Masoud Barzani, the *Serok* (president) of Iraqi Kurdistan, of "xeyanet" (treason) and stealing Kurdistan's wealth.

Chat Rooms

The chat room is another significant feature of Kurdish Internet. While chat rooms are among the most popular sites where pan-Kurdism is constructed, they are indicative of Kurdish fragmentation.

Text-based chat rooms are the oldest forms of real-time online synchronous communication among a group (many-to-many). Most people associate this system with Internet Relay Chat (IRC). Throughout the world, IRC has been facing a fierce competition with voice and video chatting systems in recent years. Among the Kurds, however, IRC has never been popular. There are a number of text-only-based chat rooms devoted to chatting in Kurdish, but, visiting them in various times of the day and night, one finds the vast majority of them either empty or, at best, attracting only two dozen participants. Another feature of these text-only-based chat rooms is that they are predominantly used by youths for casual interaction and not for discussing social or political matters. Despite this, most chat rooms are very restrictive on what language can be used for chatting: Kurdish only. Most of the chat rooms are extremely nationalist.

Although being persistent about the use of Kurdish in their domain, it is not easy to chat in text in these chat rooms because most of them do not support the Kurdish Arabic-based script. The writing script is nonstandard and idiosyncratic, a mixture of the characters from the Kurdish Latin-based writing system and English. The majority of participants from Iraqi, Syrian, and Iranian Kurdistan cannot write in the Latin-based Kurdish properly and the Kurds from Turkey are much more comfortable writing in Turkish. As a result, most of them tend to write Kurdish in Roman characters and this makes communication difficult, at least for people who are not familiar with the writing conventions of a given chat room. If there were a unified Kurdish writing system, the situation might be very different. The absence of such a common writing system seems to be the main factor that has caused the Kurdish text-based chat rooms to lag considerably behind the voice- and video-activated chat rooms in popularity.

In contrast to the text-only-based chat rooms, real-time online voice and video chat rooms are popular among the Kurdish Internet users. Of the popular protocols Paltalk is the one that attracts the vast majority of Kurdish chat room users. As long as one does not mind banner ads at no cost, one can participate in chat rooms or even create a chat room of her own, assign a theme and create a set of rules for the room. On July 5, 2007, under the category "Ethnic Groups," there were 51 rooms listed under the sub-category "Kurdish," compared to 70 rooms under "African-American," 24 rooms under "Hispanics," and one room under "Native American." The number of participants in each room could vary from a few people to 250, the maximum capacity.[7] On February 3, 2007, more than 1,000 people were participating in Kurdish chat rooms.[8] Of these people, 649 were gathered in three rooms with the same title, Kurdistan United, because the maximum capacity for each room is only 250 participants.[9] With the help of several volunteers acting as moderators in different rooms, the rooms were connected by a network of computers in order to have all the 649 people participate simultaneously in the same discussion (A. A., personal communication, July 6, 2007).[10] Theoretically, all the people logged into a room can listen to others and they can also talk. However, in reality, many people never have a chance to talk because of time constraints.

However, not all the rooms administrated by Kurds are as popular as Kurdistan United, nor do all of them concern themselves with impassioned discussions on the history, culture, and politics of Kurdistan. There are rooms that are solely devoted to jokes, absurdity, and silliness. For example, the title of a room for several years has remained as Kurdistan ChaxanayTrrTss...(Kurdistan: Farting Café). Other rooms provide virtual spaces for political parties' sympathizers, young people who gather to spend time chatting and playing music, and finally those who either offer or need high-tech help. The same diversity of use and online activities can be found regarding websites, weblogs, and forums. This confirms findings by other researchers, for example, Bernal (2006), studying the Eritrean online activities, who writes: "The sensibilities of farce and the absurd coexist on Dehai [an Eritrean online forum], along with sincere patriotism and utopian yearnings for Eritrea's bright future" (p. 171).

Weblog (Blog)

A weblog or a blog is a personal webpage that is easy to use, at no cost, and it is supposed to be updated with new entries, called posts, frequently. A number of other characteristics set the blog apart from regular websites. First, blog entries, called posts, often are automatically date-stamped. Second, they are organized in reverse-chronological order so that the latest post comes first, at the top of the other posts. Third, readers can reply to posts by leaving comments. Finally, posts on a blog are automatically archived, again in a chronological order. Blogs can consist of plain texts, still pictures (photoblog), audio files, or videos (vblogs) (Somolu, 2007; Miller & Shepherd, 2004). One who blogs (verb) is a blogger (noun).The exponential growth of blogs has captured the attention of many researchers (Miller & Shepherd, 2004). The first blogs emerged between 1994 and 1998. With the release of several types of blogging software in 1999 (e.g., Pitas, Blogger), the number of blogs proliferated. From a few hundreds, the number of blogs reached more than 4 million in 2003 (Herring, Sheidt, Sabrina, & Wright, 2004b), about 50 million in 2005 (Riley, 2005), more than 70 million in 2007 (Somolu, 2007), and more than 80 million in 2009, according to www.technorati.com, a website devoted to monitoring blogging activities.

Perhaps the first blog written in Kurdish is *Gulagenim* (Wheat Flower), which was launched by a blogger with the same nickname on May 26, 2002 (www.gulagenim.blogspot.com). Within a few months after Gulagenim's first post, there were more than three dozen Kurdish weblogs.[11] The number of Kurdish blogs reached 100 by early 2004 and 150 by the middle of 2006 (Sina, 2007b). In October 2007, the website Koord had a list of 400 blogs managed by Kurds writing in Kurdish and also other languages, such as English.

However, the majority of blogs were short-lived (Ahmadi, 2004). Gulagenim, who also was instrumental in designing, modifying, and organizing the first Kurdish weblogs, identifies several reasons for the weblogs not becoming popular among the Kurds:

> laziness, the challenge of using this new medium which does take some effort, not knowing the mother tongue, and more important than all of this is the fear of being attacked at a personal level when you identify yourself as the author. Weblog is a medium without limits and when you reveal your identity [as the author of your writing] you will become the target of insults by those who do not like your ideas. And this discourages those who start writing. (Ahmadi, 2004, para. 4, my translation)

As a Kurdish woman, Gulagenim draws our attention to two crucial points with respect to Kurdish composition on weblogs. The first point relates to freedom of expression. The Internet has been commonly viewed as a space where communicative events can take place without many political, social, and cultural restrictions. For example, one can hide her or his true identity but still express her or his views on weblogs (Somolu, 2007). Also, the Internet has been praised for its ability to foster democratization by giving voice to marginalized people, on the one hand, and enabling interaction among the citizens and between writers and readers or producers and audiences on the other (Simone, 2006). However, Herring et al. (2004b) suggest that "a 'democratizing' technology does not automatically result in social equality, and points to the importance of social and cultural factors surrounding technology adoption and use" (para. 2). Kurdish writers have often faced persecution in their own homeland. Kurdish women have also suffered from the domination of the patriarchy in Kurdistan (Mojab, 2001). In the next chapter, I will show that blogging does provide a safe space where Kurdish women could amplify their voices, as groups of African women have done (Somolu, 2007), but at the theoretical level, it is also important to reiterate that having access to a medium alone does not automatically engender freedom of expression or "democratic" values.

In addition to the lack of individual freedom, which could discourage someone from writing publicly, Gulagenim, in her writing, reveals another obstacle that discourages Kurdish bloggers: their struggle with writing in the mother tongue. The vast majority of Kurds who have gone to school, especially those from Turkey, Iran, and Syria, have neither had Kurdish as the medium of instruction nor had it as a subject taught in the public school system. Their discomfort in writing in Kurdish might be the most important difficulty that Kurdish bloggers face. In her first entry on May 26, 2002, Gulagenim wrote: "Let's write in Kurdish. [This is] the first step in Kurdish blogging" (http://gulagenim.blogspot.com/2002/05/blog-post_26.html).

However, based on bloggers' writings, one can infer that writing in Kurdish is not easy, even for committed bloggers such as Gulagenim, who has learned reading and writing in her mother tongue on her own. Gulagenim writes that when for the first time she tried to write in Kurdish, she felt that she had difficulty finding words and realized that until then she had only known how to speak the language and not to write it. In the next chapter, I will analyze Gulagenim's writing and another Kurdish blog to elucidate their attitudes towards writing in their mother tongue.

Despite these obstacles to blogging in Kurdish, a sharp increase in the number of Kurdish blogs occurred at the end of 2006 and the beginning of 2007 when the website *Kurdblogger* was launched (www.kurdblogger.com). This new platform for the first time made it very easy to blog and write in Sorani Kurdish. Displaying the Kurdish flag and the current date according to the calendar exclusively used by pan-Kurdish nationalists, are clear indications that the first and only Kurdish blogging software is devoted to the construction of a cross-border Kurdish identity. These and more overt signs of Kurdishness seem to have been the motivators for hundreds of bloggers to sign up on Kurdblogger. In July 2007, there were more than 1,000 blogs on Kurdblogger and in July 2010 more than 10,000 blogs. This is in addition to blogs that are hosted by English, Persian, Turkish, or Arabic platforms. However, it is important to note that not all blogs are updated frequently or last for long or even have any life after they are launched.

Overall, blogging (especially written blogs as opposed to video blogs, audio blogs, or photo blogs), like other features of the Internet, have provided Kurds with means of writing in and promoting their language. But, at the same time, the difference in the writing systems of the two major Kurdish varieties is reinforced in blogging. Very few Kurds from Turkey blog, because most of them cannot read or write in Kurdish (Kurmanji Kurdish). Those who can may blog in isolation from Sorani Sorani Kurdishbloggers.

Other Features of the Kurdish Internet

On the Internet, Kurds also use forums, electronic mailing lists, email, and instant messaging services. Recently emerged social networking tools such as MySpace and Facebook have also started to be used by Kurdish individuals and groups. A survey of pro-Kurdish groups on Facebook in October 2007 showed that the group "Support an Independent Kurdistan" had 1,306 members. This is a relatively small number for a people with more than 20 million population worldwide.[12] In July 2010, the group Kurdistan had more than 5,000 members.[13]

Among these social networking tools, the forum seems to be the tool used interactively the most for the promotion of a Kurdish cross-border identity that I am concerned about here. Forums are web-based message and discussion boards to which original messages or replies to them can be posted. Most forums require registration and adhere to certain etiquettes of discussion and dialogue. The emergence of these forums among the Kurds is quite recent. Some forums are strictly devoted to the exchange of general information and entertainment, such as personal relationship, health, interest stories, music, computers (e.g., Malî Kurdan/Home 4 Kurd), but there are also forums that emphasize discussions on the political, cultural, and social issues of Kurdistan, for example, the forum Roj Bash Kurdistan (Good Day Kurdistan) (northerniraq.info/forums/index.php). The forum is organized in several categories that are listed in the left column of figure 7.1. The first category on the list, "Kurdistan," with 740 topics, has received 11,170 posts. It is important to note, however, that the vast majority of the posts on this forum are in English. According to Alexa (www.alexa.com), a web company which measures traffic for websites, except for some visitors from Turkey and yet fewer from Iran and Iraq, Kurds from the west, especially the U.K. and the Scandinavian countries, make up the majority of the forum's visitors. In contrast, the forum Kurdish Love, which uses Sorani Kurdish as its main medium, attracts more than 50 percent of its users and visitors from Iran and Iraq. Another forum, Baydigi, which uses Turkish and Kurmanji Kurdish as its main languages, has more than 80 percent of its visitors and users from Turkey (www.bydigi.net). Language is one of the main factors that determines the type and size of audiences that Internet sources attract. In the next chapter, and through textual analysis, I will further underline the significance of language in investigating online activities in general and in the practices of national identity construction, in particular.

CHAPTER 8

Textual Analysis of Kurdish Internet

In the previous chapter, I described the main constituents of the Kurdish Internet. Among them were websites, chat rooms, weblogs, and social networking services such as forums, YouTube, and Facebook. I showed that, in contrast to the traditional mainstream media—including television—the Internet has amplified marginalized voices that are excluded from the discursive domains of the dominant Kurdish political organizations. In this chapter, I carry out textual analysis of the verbal language and images of various Internet constituents (e.g., websites, chat rooms, weblogs, forums, and social networking services such as YouTube). My objective is to locate the discursive strategies that are used on the Internet to construct Kurdish identities. The focus of the investigation at this level is captured in this broad question: How do Kurdish online resources use language and images to define and present Kurdish identities?

To analyze the discourse of the Internet, I will continue using the analytical tools from my analysis of television discourse. For example, by focusing on naming practices, I will highlight the significance of words and labels in the URLs of websites and Internet sources. In addition, I will use analytical tools such as vector (definition will follow) in the composition of images and the visual organization of Internet sources. I will also utilize discourse analytical tools that are specific to the structure of the Internet, such as links or hyperlinks. I will explore the organization and distribution of hyperlinks on websites to show that the very structure of the Internet could contribute to discourses of national identity construction. The main components of national identity discourse are as follows: A common past and history, present and future, language(s), national symbols, and territory and homeland.[1] In the subsequent pages, I will present analyses of the discursive constructions that contribute to the articulation of these aspects of Kurdish national identities.

DISCURSIVE CONSTRUCTION OF A COMMON HISTORY

As Martin and Wodak (2003) note, "Identities need founding myths and certain pasts, which they can integrate easily and positively" (p. 11). Somehow, deeper roots in the past make peoples' claims to greatness at present more legitimate. On the Internet, the Kurds are often defined as an ancient nation that has inhabited the same homeland, Kurdistan, since time immemorial. As discussed earlier, a powerful myth that has become an indispensable part of the Kurdish nationalist discourse is the idea that today's Kurds are the descendants of the Medes, an ancient people who established the Median Empire (728–550 B.C.) (Hassanpour 1992; Kreyenbroek, 1992). This myth is reproduced over and over on the Internet in various forms and modes, for example in English, on the website Kurdistanica: The Encyclopaedia of Kurdistan (www.kurdistanica. com), and in Kurdish, on the website Kurdistan Parliament [Iraq] (www.kurdistan-parliament.org/default.aspx?page=sitecontents&c= Kurdistan-History). Individual Kurds also contribute to the reproduction of this myth, either on their personal websites or on public video sharing websites such as YouTube. For example, a video called "The Median Empire and Fall of Nineveh" (http://ca.YouTube.com/ watch?v=2Lf_W9ADw4A) available on YouTube, in which the opening image features a Kurdish flag providing the background for the phrase "Median History (Kurdish)."[2] The word "Kurdish" is put in brackets after the phrase "Median History." The history of Medes is taken to be the same as the history of the Kurds. It is presupposed that today's Kurds are descendants of the Medes.[3]

A primordial and glorious history of the Kurds and Kurdistan is also constructed in the images of ancient and historical sites and monuments, some of which, interestingly enough, Armenians, Turks, Assyrians, and other ethnic groups and nationalities claim as theirs. For example, out of the more than 100 videos on YouTube that are devoted to the history of Kurds and Kurdistan, "Kurdish history, Kurdistan history" is the most viewed video (www.youtube.com/ watch?v=3EgqqUDzkt0).[4] The video has upset some non-Kurdish viewers because, apparently, it has identified some Armenian and Turkish sites as Kurdish. This is apparent in the comments left by viewers of the video clip.[5] A poster, with the username kurdsaresuper-gay, writes: "The buildings shown in [this] video are mostly [in] turkey [, and] they are either turkish, armenian or arabic built [*sic*]. How can kurds [sic] build a church?" Another poster, "davidwhitman," writes: "many of the pictures in this film are of Armenian Churches and monuments, not Kurdish." In contrast to posts like these, almost all of the posts by the Kurds praise the video, which is indicative of the nationalist sentiment among Kurdish Internet users.

Disputes over archaeological artifacts or historical personalities to prove peoples' greatness have often been a part of nationalist discourses (Wodak et al., 2009). This is an example of what Rudolf Burger has called the "nationalist dilation of time" (Wodak et al., 2009). The strategy of historicizing the nation has inundated all nationalist discourses. It expands the nation "into a transhistorical, and thus eternal, entity" (Wodak et al., 2009). What is significant here in relation to the construction of Kurdish national identity is that the narrative identifies one single historical root for a fragmented people. Connecting the Kurds to one common past and common myth, such as the Median Empire, contributes to the construction of a single Kurdish identity, a pan- or cross-border identity. Furthermore, this discursive strategy of historicizing the nation suggests that since all Kurdistan was once ruled by one powerful empire, it should be ruled as one single nation-state today. As Fishman (1989) suggests, "[t]he heirs of past greatness deserve to be great again" (p. 276). The historicization of Kurdish identity and the glorification of a unified Kurdish nation in the past are calls for the establishment of Greater Kurdistan.

In addition to an ancient glorious past, a nation is also built on memories of common sufferings and sacrifices that its members have made as a people (Renan, 1990; Smith, 1999). One of these common sufferings in the Kurdish history is the division of Kurdistan. The idea that Kurds and Kurdistan have been unwillingly divided among at least four nation-states has been ingrained in the Kurdish nationalist discourse, so much so that the division of Kurdistan can be evoked simply by expressions like *çiwar parçe* (four pieces), *çiwar beş* (four parts), or even *çiwar* (four) alone in particular contexts.[6] For example, whether intentionally or not, the presence of the number four in the URL of the following web sources playfully evokes the image of a Kurdistan that is divided into four parts: home4kurd.com, it4kurd.com, chat4kurdistan.com, best4kurd.net, bamo4kurd.com, voice4kurd.com, links4kurd.tk, kurd4all.nl, kurd4voice.net. Of course, because of the way it is pronounced, the number 4 also denotes the preposition "for" in the context of URLs, for example in visas4america.com or canadahomes4sale.com. However, in the Kurdish context, "4" in a URL could mean more than a preposition because the number connotes the division of Kurdistan. Thus, it is plausible to suggest that 4 means both the preposition and number

4 in the URL of Kurdish websites.[7] In some URLs, however, for example in kurd4voice.net, 4 clearly does not mean the preposition "for"; it makes reference to the concept of Kurdistan being divided into four parts, and, as such, 4 is a salient discursive tool contributing to the construction of a cross-border Kurdish identity.

A common Kurdish experience of sacrifice and suffering is also reproduced in remembering a number of events that have occurred in modern times. Among these are major nationalist revolts such as Said Reza's revolt in 1925 in Turkey, the Kurdish Republic of Mahabad in 1946 in Iran, and the Barzani rebellion in Iraq from the late 1950s to 1975. In addition to the images and accounts of these events, which symbolize Kurdish heroism and sacrifice, images of being a victim of history is also strong in the Kurdish nationalist discourse. Among these are images of Halabja and the mass exodus (about two million) of the Iraqi Kurds in 1991.

The prevalent ancient history of Kurdistan constructed on the Internet is similar to the history constructed on KTV. For both, Kurds and Kurdistan have always existed. However, when it comes to modern history and more recent shared memories, there are some important differences. The discourse of the Internet is overtly pan-Kurdish and it is more inclusive. According to KTV's discourse, after the proliferation of Kurdish political parties during and after the Second World War, modern Kurdish history is synonymous with the history of the KDP (KTV's owner). Other political parties from all parts of Kurdistan are often excluded in KTV's narrative of Kurdish history. On the Internet, however, the history of Kurdistan includes most of the Kurdish nationalist parties and heroes, whether they are regional or pan.

For example, figure 8.1 shows a screenshot of a video on the history of Kurdistan posted on YouTube (www.YouTube.com/watch?v=PrMVwKsxZOw). It includes the leaders of various Kurdish political parties and rebellions from all parts of Kurdistan. These national heroes, some dead and some alive, along with some of the most powerful national symbols in this image (e.g., map of the Greater Kurdistan, mountains, and the Kurdish flag) make up the Kurdish modern history. This example indicates that pan-Kurdish identity is more prevalent and explicit on the Internet compared to KTV and perhaps other television stations that are owned by regional political organizations. As I illustrated in the previous chapters, Kurdish identity on KTV is constructed and represented within the overall ideological framework of the station, which is defined by its owner's main political goal: securing autonomy for

Figure 8.1 Kurdish leaders from all parts of Kurdistan and different eras are captured in a screenshot from a video clip on YouTube

the Kurdish region within the state of Iraq. In contrast, a video on YouTube can be posted by any individual or group who has access to the Internet. The Internet has enabled individuals and groups to sidestep the political constraints that have been imposed on the expressions of a cross-border Kurdish identity, by both the dominant Kurdish organizations and the four nation-states of Turkey, Iraq, Iran, and Syria. This is an example in point showing the amplification of Kurdish marginalized voices.

The presentation of the history of Kurds and Kurdistan on the Internet is also different from KTV's, in that the former is sometimes overtly racist. For example, the video "The Median Empire and the Fall of Nineveh," which I have already mentioned, visually reconstructed the conflicts between the Assyrian Empire and the Medes. In this video, the Assyrians are portrayed as invaders, ruthless and barbarous. At the same time, the Medes' invasion and burning of Nineveh and beheading of the Assyrian king is celebrated as a noble act, an example of the danger involved in the discourse practices of "othering," which is said to be a characteristic of nationalist discourses (Brubaker, 2004; Billig, 1995). It is this process of othering and the creation of differences between "us" and "them" that makes nationalist discourses hospitable to racist attitudes and ideologies. There is, however, a difference between how far this discourse of othering can be taken on the Internet versus a controlled medium such as KTV. Control over the content of the Internet has proven to be extremely difficult, if not impossible. In contrast, KTV's content is controlled by its owner, the KDP.[8]

Discursive Construction of a Common Present and Future

As Fishman (1989) suggests, "[the] heirs of triumphant unity in the past must themselves be united in the present and future" (p. 276). A nation is built not only on common memories rooted in the past but also on the existence of consent and the "will" among its members to live together at present and into the future (Renan, 1990, p. 19). Kurdish online activities represent and construct a common present and future for all Kurds.

Thanks to the Internet, more than a dozen daily news websites have emerged within the past several years. They inform Kurds throughout the world about the current events of Kurdistan. The first Kurdish news agency, *Peyamner*, which I talked about in the previous chapter, emerged over the Internet. As is evident in its description, the website is committed to the construction or reproduction of a cross-border Kurdish identity. The website's description says:

> This website is prepared and launched from the capital of Kurdistan. It strives to deliver the news as it happens to the people of Kurdistan and the world...We work around the clock to deliver the truth about Kurdistan to the readers from the three major cultures of Arab, Turk and Persian so that they become aware of the good intentions of the people of Kurdistan...[Peyamner] wants to be a strong and firm bridge for connecting readers from the four parts of the homeland...(*Peyamner News Agency*, 2005, my translation, my emphasis)

First, the statement recognizes Hawler, where Peyamner's office is based, as the capital of all Kurdistan and not Iraqi Kurdistan alone: "This website is prepared and launched from the capital of Kurdistan." Second, the website seeks to explain the Kurdish issue, not just to Arabs of Iraq but also to Arabs of Syria, Turks of Turkey, and Persians of Iran; it aims at representing all Kurds to all their "others." The text presupposes that the readers from the three dominant cultures have not been informed well about Kurdish demands and circumstances. Finally, the last sentence leaves no doubt that *Peyamner* is committed to the construction of a pan-Kurdish or cross-border Kurdish identity, because it "wants to be a strong and firm bridge for connecting readers from the four parts of the homeland." This is why it provides news in the two main Kurdish varieties, as well as English, Arabic, Turkish, and Persian. Informing non-Kurds about the Kurdish issue is seen as one of the Kurdish Internet's primary functions. Several English-only websites, for example, are operating with this objective (e.g., Kurdmedia.com, kurdistanobserver.com). Furthermore, it is important to note that there are a considerable number of news websites that cover cultural, social, and political events from all parts of Kurdistan (e.g., kurdistannet.org, rizgari.com, azadiyawelat.com, renesans.nu, rojhelat.se). These websites, similar to *Peyamner*, present themselves as voices for all Kurds, regardless of where they are located or who owns them.

The construction of a common present contributes to the formation of a common future among the Kurds. In other words, once it becomes a common belief that all Kurds share the same experience of oppression and denial, then they may think that they have a common fate and future. It seems natural for people with common problems to seek common solutions. Illustrations of what that common solution for Kurds might be are abundant on the Internet. Diri Shaswar, a poster on the forum Roj Bash Kurdistan: There is no Northern Iraq, envisions the future when the four parts of Kurdistan are reunited.[9] According to his redrawing of the map of the region, in 2007, Iraqi Kurdistan was going to become independent, in 2010 Syrian Kurdistan is going to join the independent small Kurdistan, in 2015 Iranian Kurdistan will be annexed to Kurdistan, and finally, in 2020 there is going to be an independent Greater Kurdistan. In addition to the map, the phrase under the maps, "United We Stand" is also significant. The two words "united" and "we" elaborate the solidarity and oneness image of Kurdistan constructed in the maps. Furthermore, the color of the three words (green, yellow, and red) invokes the image of the Kurdish flag. Regardless of how sophisticated or naïve this semiotic envisioning of the future of Kurdistan by a young Kurdish-Norwegian might be, it speaks to the pan-Kurdish ideology that Kurdish emancipation depends on the solidarity of at least four parts of Kurdistan.

Discursive Construction of a Common Kurdish Language

I have discussed in previous chapters that language is seen as a decisive symbol of national identity in the Kurdish nationalist discourse because, more than any other ethnic or national characteristic, it separates Kurds from the dominant ethnic groups of Turkish, Arab, and Persian (Vali, 2003; McDowall, 2004; Kreyenbroek & Allison, 1996). I have also discussed that what is often referred to as the Kurdish language encompasses a group of speech varieties, some of which (e.g., Kurmanji, Sorani, Hawrami and Zaza) are not mutually intelligible in many contexts (Kreyenbroek, 1992). The linguistic fragmentation is reinforced on the Internet (Warschauer, 2000). Some scholars find the Internet to be a savior of minority and endangered languages (Cormack & Hourigan, 2007), but others believe that the Internet fragments peoples and communities along linguistic lines (Schaap, 2004). This paradox is well exemplified in the case of Kurdish speech varieties.

The Internet has been used to maintain, promote, and teach Kurdish. Although Kurdish sources use many languages, Kurmanji and Sorani Kurdish are the primary languages of the Kurdish Internet. About a dozen websites effectively use the multimode feature of the Internet (i.e., text, animation, and sound) to teach Kurdish to both children and adults.[10] Interestingly, all these websites offer open access to their materials. There seems to be a genuine commitment to the maintenance and promotion of Kurdish language as a vital feature of Kurdish identity. For example, the website *Férbûnî Zimanî Kurdî* (Kurdish Language Learning) (kurdi.info) displays the following slogan: "Language is identity...Kurdish lessons are steps towards the fortification of Kurdish language." The website Nefel (www.nefel.com) displays this prominent message on its banner, in Kurmanji: "Kurdish is lightness for our eyes. Kurds! Preserve your language."[11] This indicates how important the Kurdish language is in defining Kurdishness.

Holding the mother tongue as a major part of national identity goes against Anderson's (1991) view that, though the nation is imagined in language, it matters very little what language may serve this function (p. 133). For Anderson, the nation was not imagined in any language per se, but in print language, and that print language could even be the language of the colonizer and the "other," for example, in the case of Ghana.[12] For many Kurds, however, Kurdishness is imagined in the Kurdish language.[13]

The idea that writing in Kurdish is an indispensable component of Kurdishness and that the Internet has facilitated writing in Kurdish comes through vividly on weblogs. The first Kurdish blogger, Gulagenim, in the first post on her blog with the same name/title writes: "Let's write in Kurdish. [This is] the first step in Kurdish blogging" (2002a, my translation). In another entry, Gulagenim writes passionately about her experience of writing in Kurdish:

> They never taught me [how to write in Kurdish]...For me, writing in Kurdish is still like a childhood dream that has not come true, and now as an adult I am approaching it with hesitation and trepidation; I am afraid that I might make too many mistakes, become a stranger with myself...with my language. (Gulagenim, 2002b, my translation)

Gulagenim uses her blog as a space for practicing writing in Kurdish and overcoming the fear of writing in her mother tongue. In a chat room session devoted to Kurdish blogging in 2004, Gulagenim admits that prior to blogging she did not know how to write in Kurdish and that the medium has encouraged her and enabled her to write and learn her first language.

Tewar, another Kurdish blogger, echoes Gulagenim's concern:

> I have been thinking about what Gulagenim has said that writing in the mother tongue comes with a unique sensation. I have been thinking about the uncertainty and nervousness that I experience every time I want to write in Kurdish. (Tewar, 2002, my translation)

Despite difficulties, the two bloggers have continued writing in Kurdish. In fact, they have become the veterans of Kurdish blogging and one wonders what keeps motivating them to write.[14] When admitting the fact that writing in Kurdish is so difficult that it pushes her to quit, Tewar writes:

> But, I cannot quit...Language is a part of me. Words are mirrors that reflect my ideas and feelings...Without [our] language we are nothing...A language is as important as a country, history and flag...Language is a part of our personality...Language is identity...To express your inner thoughts and feelings...you need the language of feelings and the soul; no language is closer to one's feelings and soul than the mother tongue...When writing we might make mistakes...We may not have a rich vocabulary...but, let's not quit; let's continue [writing]. (Tewar, 2002, my translation)

For Tewar, language is important as a national symbol in defining a people; it is also a decisive factor in defining a person. This idea that the mother tongue is a strong link between the individual and the nation has been advocated by prominent scholars of nationalism and language as well. Fishman (1989) states:

> The essence of a nationality is its spirit, its individuality, its soul. This soul is not only reflected and protected by the mother tongue but, in a sense, *the mother tongue is itself an aspect of the soul*, a part of the soul, if not the soul made manifest. (p. 276, emphasis in original)

Fishman has referred to the rediscovering of the mother tongue as an "intellectual rebirth" (p. 283). It seems that Tewar and Gulagenim have experienced just that by blogging in Kurdish. McLuhan (1960), discussing the impact of the printing press on writing in the mother tongue, writes: "Perhaps also the ability to *see* one's mother tongue in uniform and repeatable technological dress creates in the individual reader a feeling of unity and power that he shares with all other readers of that tongue" (McLuhan, 1960, p. 571, emphasis in original). In spite of the change in the medium, it seems it has the same dynamics as print. More examples to illustrate this will follow.

Along with writing, speaking Kurdish has also been enhanced by the Internet. Aram Ahmad, one of the moderators of the most popular Kurdish chat room, *Kurdistan United*, suggests that many of the people who are regular speakers in that chat room had difficulty discussing political and social issues in Kurdish at the beginning (A. A., personal communication, July 6, 2007).[15] This is especially true of the Kurds from Iran, Turkey, and Syria who are educated in languages other than their mother tongue. In most of the Kurdish chat rooms, including Kurdistan United, speaking in Kurdish is a must. Speaking in those chat rooms in any other language is considered non-Kurdish behavior and is not tolerated. At times like this, the chat-room moderator usually gives the non-Kurdish user a warning indicating that they cannot use languages other than Kurdish. Users who ignore the warning can either be suspended for a while, meaning they can still be in the room but they cannot send messages, or they can be bounced from the room for at least 24 hours.

The Internet has also fostered the maintenance and promotion of Kurdish speech varieties such as Hawrami and Zazaki, which have fewer speakers compared to Kurmanji and Sorani. There are several websites, for example Hawraman (www.hawraman.com), that actively use the Hawrami variety and promote its status. Other sites, such as *Dibistana Kurdî* (Kurdish School) (modersmal.skolutveckling.se/ nordkurdiska/zazaki/start.htm), use Dimli or Zazaki as their communication medium and they teach the language. There are sites that are entirely or predominantly in Zazaki (e.g.,www.zazaki.net). It is important to note that while these websites are very keen in presenting Hawrami or Zazaki as distinct languages, they do insist on their Kurdishness.[16]

The Internet provides the means by which Kurdish varieties are promoted but at the same time it seems to be reinforcing the differences between Kurdish language varieties. Previously, I suggested that by broadcasting in different Kurdish speech varieties, Kurdistan TV might gradually enable Kurdish viewers to understand varieties other than their own and this might make communication easier among such viewers. However, this is not the case with the Internet. Most Kurdish chat rooms are separated along linguistic lines. For example, very few Kurmanji speakers, who encompass about 60–65 percent of the Kurdish speakers in the world, participate in the most popular Kurdish chat room, Kurdistan United, dominated by Sorani speakers (A. A., personal communication, July 6, 2007). Kurmanji speakers, including those from Iraq, have their own separate chat rooms. Linguistic fragmentation, albeit of a different kind, is also evident in weblogs. Here the fragmentation is caused by different alphabet systems. For example, almost all the bloggers who have subscribed to Kurd Blogger, be they speakers of Sorani, Hawrami, or Kurmanji Kurdish, write in the Arabic modified alphabet. This practicality separates the Kurds of Turkey, who write in the Latin modified alphabet, from the Kurds of Iran and Iraq.

Discursive Construction of Common National Symbols

Whereas varieties of language can be a fragmenting factor, national symbols are among the most common homogenizing forces (Geisler, 2005). In this section, I use the concepts of given and new information (Goodman, 1996) and vectors to examine the visual location and presentation of images and links to national symbols (such as the flag, patriotic songs, folk and popular songs, and images of mountainous landscapes in Kurdistan) on Kurdish websites.

The most striking common national symbol on the homepage and banner of Kurdish websites, weblogs, forums, and chat rooms is the flag (e.g., see figure 7.1). On the top banner of the website koord the Kurdish flag is placed in the center, as is the case with many more sites such as http://www.kurdland.com. Placing the flag in the middle of the banner is only one way in which the flag is given prominence.

In addition to occupying the top-center position of many websites' homepage, the importance of the flag is also highlighted when it is placed more frequently on the right side of the banner rather than the left side. Why is this important? Generally, in English writing, the given information comes first, followed by the new information (Goodman, 1996). This principle is also applicable to websites. On English websites, the navigation menu is the given, common, and familiar information, and is placed on the left side of the homepage. Sorani Kurdish is written from right to left. Thus, what is placed on the right, for example, the flag, is the given, common, and familiar information (e.g., see www.zmziran.com/ku/news.php, kdp.se, kurdblogger.com/search?cat_id=4, mediapress.kurdblogger.com). A powerful presupposition is embedded here: the Kurdish flag is considered a common and familiar symbol of Kurdishness. Interestingly enough, the flag on a homepage in English (e.g.,northerniraq.info/forums/portal.php, www.kurd.org) is placed on the left, even when it has Kurdish content and is maintained by Kurds. The dynamics of print and the literary language influences the design of websites.

The significant of the flag is also underlined when it acts as a vector on homepages. According to Kress and van Leeuwen (1996), vectors are "lines which lead the eye" when looking at an image. They guide the viewer to look at the components of a visual composition in a particular sequence; they show the narrative pattern in an image. For example, in the banner of the website kdp.se the Kurdish flag, as a familiar symbol to Kurdish viewers, acts as a vector to lead the eyes to the title of the website in the center, and from there to the logo PdK in the left side of the banner. This may not be the direction to which the vector could take all audiences. It may also lead some audiences' gaze to the mountain range in the background and on which the flag rests. Here the flag is not only a national symbol, but it also leads audiences' online reading and viewing activities. The flag marks both the website and the discursive practices it fosters as Kurdish.

There is one more position in which the symbolic importance of the flag is indicated: in the address bar of websites. Many websites have the Kurdish flag as part of their URL; the image of the Kurdish flag is placed in the URL bar preceding the website's address (e.g., kurdistannet.org). In this case, the flag is placed on the left side of the homepage, or the URL address bar, because the address is written in a left to right script (i.e., English). In this case, too, the flag is again the given information and the familiar and common Kurdish national symbol. The flag is again leading the eyes.

Along with the flag, other national symbols, such as audio and video clips of patriotic anthems and folk and popular music, and images of national heroes, mountains, and rural Kurdistan, are prominent on Kurdish websites, weblogs, and forums. Sometimes, all these symbols are presented on the banner of a single website (see figure 7.1). The black and white picture placed at the far left side is linked to the music video of one of the most popular Kurdish patriotic songs, *Her Kurd Buyn u Her Kurd Debîn* (We Have Always Been Kurds, and We'll Remain Kurds), written and performed by Iraqi Kurds.[17] The next image, showing a girl dressed in red and standing in a typical Kurdish rural landscape, is linked to the music video, *Berîvan* (milkmaid), of Leila Fariqi, a female singer from Iranian Kurdistan and well-liked throughout Kurdistan. In the song, Fariqi sings in both main Kurdish varieties of Sorani and Kurmanji. Kurdish bilingual singing has become a deliberate expression of pan-Kurdishness, and it has been interpreted as a way of defying fragmentation among the Kurds. It is believed that singing in both major speech varieties brings the Kurmanji and Sorani closer to each other and makes communication among the speakers of the two varieties easier (Himmati, 2007).[18]

The hyperlink next to Fariqi's is labeled "Kurdish Radio & TV on Satellite," which leads to a comprehensive list of Kurdish radio and TV stations, with complete information on their frequency, and so forth. It is safe to suggest that hyperlinks to Kurdish satellite television channels are among the most common on Kurdish websites and weblogs, indicating the importance of satellite technology among the Kurds, as I argued in previous chapters.

The next image on the banner is hyperlinked to a cheerful song, *Şahjina Rojhelatê* (The Queen of the East), by Zakaria Abdullah. Although a native speaker of Sorani, Zakaria sings this song in Kurmanji. With both lyrics and images, Zakaria takes a virtual trip through most of the towns, cities and regions of the Greater Kurdistan and says of each stop: "lê rinde, lê rinde" (it is so beautiful, it is so beautiful). The rest of the images on the banner of the website Koord are linked to Kurdistan's landscapes, Kurdistan Encyclopedia, Kurdish calendar,[19] and Kurdish folk music. The last box on the right side of the banner is linked to a single artwork consisting of traditional Persian handwriting. Written artfully in both Persian and Kurdish, the artwork quotes Rene Descartes's famous saying: "I think, therefore I am." The connotation here seems to be that for Koord, cyber activities are acts of thinking and purposeful practices of identity representations and reproductions.

Discursive Construction of a Common Territory and Homeland

One of the most salient discursive means of constructing and reproducing the Kurdish homeland on the Internet is an extensive use of the word "Kurdistan," which is still prohibited in places like Turkey. A Google search for the word "Kurdistan" in the title of webpages, conducted on July 10, 2007, returned about 300,000 hits. This number is significant, considering the fact that the same search for the name of an independent nation-state like Tajikistan returned about 700 hits.[20] In July 2010, these numbers changed to more than 4,000,000 and about 900,000 respectively. "Kurdistan" also appears in the URL of thousands of websites (e.g., Kurdistanpress.com, kurdistannet.org, kurdistanpost.com, akakurdistan.com, kurdistan4news.com, kurdistanonline.com). This high usage of the word Kurdistan on the Internet represents and reproduces a cross-border Kurdish identity in that it invokes a common and shared territory for Kurds, a territory that encompasses lands from at least four nation-states (i.e., Turkey, Iraq, Iran, and Syria).

In my analysis of KTV, I reported that the map of a Greater Kurdistan and its discursive and semiotic reconstruction is subtle. On the Internet, however, the map of Greater Kurdistan is displayed again and again, and in different shapes, colors, and sizes.[21] Since the map is often presented visually on the Internet, it is important to see what prominence is given to it on websites. Looking at banners is particularly interesting because the banner is usually the most stable fixture of a webpage, and there are many webpages that they have the map placed at their focal position (e.g., www.rizgari.com, www.psk2006.org).

The reconstruction of the Greater Kurdistan is also embedded in the design of some Kurdish websites, for example in what is included in their list of links and how the list is organized. By examining the links or hyperlinks of websites and online sources, we can see who is included and who is excluded in the collective identity that is being expressed. Links lead viewers of one webpage to other pages on the same website or, more importantly, to other websites and web resources. According to Sorapure (2003), "links can be read as expressing meaningful connections or relations" (p. 14). In fact, it has been suggested that "an important component of critical literacy for Web readers is learning how to interpret [links]" (p. 14). Halavais (2000) has effectively demonstrated that "while nation borders seem to be less intrusive on the web than they are in earlier networked media, the resilience of cultural structures is demonstrated in the organization of this new medium" (p. 8).[22] Examining the hyperlinks of 4,000 websites from 16 countries, Halavais (2000) observes that the actual national borders had a direct effect on the distribution of hyperlinks and where they were linked; that is, for the most part, websites provided links to online resources that were from the same nation and located within the same physical national borders. Based on this connection between hyperlinks and the borders of the homeland, we can look at a website's hyperlinks to see how borders of the nation are drawn.[23]

Table 8.1 The organization of popular media links on www.koord.com on July 10, 2007

Belonging to Kurds from	Links on www.koord.com		Belonging to Kurds from
	Radio & TV	News	
IN	Komala TV	Amude	S & D
IN	KURD Channel	DIHA	T
D	Kurdplanet TV (Live)	Denge Xelikan	T
IQ	KurdSAT TV (Live)	Hetawi Kurdistan It Ku	IQ
IQ	Kurdistan TV Low High	Kerkuk Kurdistane	IQ
T	Mezopotamya TV (Live)	Kurdishmedia	D
T & D	Roj TV(Live)	Kurdistan Observer	D
S & D	Rojava TV & Radio	Kurdistan Online	IQ
IN & D	Rojhelat TV	Kurdistannet	IQ & D
IN & D	Tishk TV	Kurdistan Media	IN
?	Vin TV	Nasname	T & D
IQ	Zagros TV	Nawxo	IQ
NK	BBC (Ar) (Fa) (Tu)	NETKURD	T & D
T & D	Dengê Mezopotamya	Peyamnêr	IQ
IN & D	Dengi Komalah	PUK Media	IQ
IN	Radio Kurdistan	Rojhilat	IN
IQ	Radio Nawa	Rojname (RNN)	D
NK	Radio Zayele	Rizgari Online	T & D
NK	VOA(So) (Ku) (Audio)	Sibeiy	IQ
IN	Voice of Kurdistan		
	→ more	→ more	

Note: IN= Iran, IQ= Iraq, S = Syria, T = Turkey, NK = Not belonging to Kurds although it might be in Kurdish such as Voice of America-Kurdish Service, D = Diasporas (here attributed to websites or online sources that claim or appear to represent all Kurds and which are managed outside Kurdish regions). The vast majority of these websites and media outlets, however, are produced in and distributed from diasporas.

There are several web directories, for example www.kurdland.com, www.koord.com, that provide hyperlinks to thousands of websites and Kurdish online resources in different Kurdish speech varieties (i.e., Kurmanji, Sorani, Hawrami, Zazaki), English, or Swedish, belonging to Kurds from different parts of the world. The important thing is that the websites that are indexed on these directories not only carry content relating to Kurds and Kurdistan, but the vast majority of them are also pro-Kurdish in the sense of being sympathetic to calls for the cultural and political rights of the Kurds. The Kurdish websites and online sources that are connected reinforce each other's discursive constructions of a common Kurdish identity.

Table 8.1 shows two sets of links (the two columns in the middle) to the most popular online Kurdish news sources, and television and radio stations from the Kurdish web directory www.koord.com (see also figure 7.1). In the far left and right columns, I have indicated each link's affiliation with different Kurds (e.g., of Iran, Iraq, Syria, Turkey, and diasporas). The table shows that links are connected to news and entertainment sources that belong to and are managed by Kurds from different parts of Kurdistan, in addition to Kurds from diasporic communities. This shows that the very structure of the Internet (i.e., hyperlinks) has been utilized to symbolize expressions of a cross-border Kurdish identity, of the awareness that Kurdistan and Kurdish nation are divided, and of the desire to be more connected and to communicate more effectively. The image of a greater Kurdistan is reconstructed infinitely in the minds of those who visit one of the most reliable and commonly used Kurdish Internet directories.

CHAPTER 9

Discussion and Conclusion

As discussed earlier, the particular version of CDA that I have adopted in this study enables analysis of media discourse at three levels: discourse practices, text, and sociocultural context. The previous four chapters were devoted to the first and second levels of analysis. My analyses at these two levels have described and interpreted the communicative events and discursive constructions facilitated by KTV and the Internet. This has enabled me to show how and out of what Kurdish national identities are constructed, and who constructs them. In this chapter, I attend to the third level of analysis, the explanation of identity discursive constructs in light of the sociocultural and political contexts that bear upon these discourse formations. At this level of analysis, I attempt to explain why Kurdish identities are constructed the way they are and what the implications of these constructions might be. In addition to my sociocultural and political analysis of identity discursive constructs on KTV and the Internet, I will briefly discuss some research implications based on the findings of this study.

Socio-Cultural Aspects of KTV

Recapturing KTV's Background

KTV belongs to one of the oldest and largest political parties in Kurdistan-Iraq, the Kurdistan Democratic Party (KDP). The KDP's leader, Masoud Barzani, is the "president" of the Iraqi Kurdistan region. His nephew, Nechirawan Barzani, was the prime minister of the Kurdistan Regional Government (KRG) during most of the time that the KTV data was collected. In the KRG, the KDP shares power with the other, rival major organization, the Patriotic Union of Kurdistan (PUK), and a number of other smaller organizations, albeit in limited measure. The PUK's leader, Jalal Talabani, is the current Iraqi president. At the same time, since the fall of Saddam Hussein, high-ranking members of the KDP have been key players on the Iraqi political scene, both in the Iraqi National Assembly and the Iraqi cabinets.[1]

The KDP, as with all major Kurdish organizations, is a regional organization that seeks autonomy for the Kurds in its region, Iraq. It has not identified itself either as a separatist or a pan-Kurdish nationalist organization. In response to the occasional "separatist" charges it faces,[2] KDP leaders have continued to declare openly and officially that they have no ambition for the establishment of an independent "smaller" Kurdistan (Kurdistan-Iraq) or a Greater Kurdistan. In 2003, Masoud Barzani, in a statement originally published in the Arabic-language newspaper, *Al-Ta'akhi*, wrote: "We will make every effort to defend a united Iraq providing that it is a federal, parliamentary, and democratic Iraq" (Barzani, 2003; see also O'Leary, 2002).[3] The KDP's official stance on Iraq, Iraqi Kurds, and other Kurds is presented in the following excerpt from the KDP's self-descriptive text, which can be found on many websites of KDP:

> Preservation of unity and integrity of Iraq is an aim of the party... the rights of the Kurds in neighbouring countries can only be guaranteed through democratic and peaceful means within the boundaries of states in which the Kurds live. Furthermore, the KDP has always adopted the policy of non-intervention in the internal affairs of neighbours [sic]. (KDP, n.d.)

Contentions within the KTV/KDP Discourse

My analyses in this study show that the representation of Iraq beyond Iraqi Kurdistan is minimal on KTV. Most of KTV's discourse practices and discursive constructs represent Iraqi Kurdistan as a free, autonomous, and even independent, small Kurdistan. At the same time, a great number of KTV discourse practices aim at constructing and reproducing a cross-border Kurdish identity. In contrast, minimal space is given to the articulation of an Iraqi identity. How does one account for this paradox, which saturates KTV's discourse? This is an important and interesting question when we realize that the majority of observers, including Kurdish organizations, believe that establishing a Greater Kurdistan is not imminent, realistic, or practical (O'Leary & Salih, 2005). Furthermore, the states of Turkey, Iran, and Syria continue to refuse any kind of autonomy for the Kurds, because they believe that this will bring the Kurds one step closer to claiming an independent Greater Kurdistan (O'Leary & Salih, 2005). In other words, having any pan-Kurdish ambition could seriously damage regional movements and efforts to guarantee some political and cultural rights for the Kurds in countries other than Iraq as well.

Dialogic Analysis of Discourse

According to Steinberg (1999), from a positivist perspective, representation processes are perceived as competitions between actors with very separate discursive fields, and the process of meaning-making in language is straightforward, an "uncomplicated process of sending and receiving messages" (p. 739). From a CDA perspective, however, discourses are not only social, ideological, and embedded in situation, they are also dynamic, interactional, and multivocal (Fairclough, 1995b, pp. 54–55). Discourses are characterized by "textual heterogeneity," which "can be seen as a materialization of social and cultural contradictions and as important evidence of reinvestigating these contradictions and their evolution" (p. 60).

A discourse is often the site of struggle among actors who compete for hegemony and legitimation of their own ideologies. The competition for hegemony between two or more ideologies could take place within the same discursive field, often that of the dominant ideology. For example, studying British cotton spinners' contentious actions in the 1820s and 1830s, Steinberg (1999) observes that:

> Rather than deploying a distinct economic discourse against political economy, or employing an alternative such as cooperationism, the spinners struggled within this hegemonic genre to establish the legitimacy of their claims. Contention was thus not between predominantly two distinct discourses or frames, but rather within a discursive field largely not of their own choosing. (p. 769)

Subsequently, Steinberg calls for a kind of discourse analysis that focuses on the ways in which "challengers seek to legitimate hegemonic genres within a field while appropriating pieces to inflect it with their own subversive meanings" (p. 751). Discourses are heterogeneous, and they are inundated with tensions. Tensions within discourses of identity do not necessarily result in producing monolithic and separate identities; they may foster the construction and reproduction of multiple identities that are in a constant dialogue, albeit from very different power positions.

Politics of National Identity Construction on KTV

In the case of KTV, discursive strategies constructing a cross-border Kurdish identity inflect the discursive field of the regional Kurdish nationalism of the KDP with its own language and signs. All Kurdish satellite TV stations belong to regional and autonomous Kurdish organizations. In other words, pan-Kurdism lacks a distinct discursive field of its own mediated by satellite television. Thus, within the same discursive field of the dominant Kurdish regional nationalism, which KTV discourse is a prime example of, individuals who support pan-Kurdism appropriate pieces of that discourse to legitimize their own ideology.

This theoretical position, however, invokes several questions: is KTV management aware of the presence of pan-Kurdish ideology within its discourses? If so, why is it allowed? What are the cultural and political implications of a strong pan-Kurdish sentiment for the KDP, Iraqi Kurdistan, and other Kurds?

It is safe to suggest that the presence of pan-Kurdish discursive practices is not a secret to KTV management. There are times when pan-Kurdish sentiments are flagged on KTV quite explicitly. For example, on January 7, 2007, in the live program, *Rapirsî* (Opinion Survey), audiences were asked to call in and express their views on the following question: "Has KTV been successful in carrying out its national message?" In defining KTV's "national message," the host of the show read the following from a text:

> At the time when the entire Kurdish nation from all parts of Kurdistan was hoping to find themselves on KTV screen, KTV chose to carry a message that would satisfy a large segment of the people of [Iraqi] Kurdistan and also Kurdish nation in other parts of Kurdistan and the diaspora. (Talib, 2007, my translation)

The host of *Rapirsî* is very explicit about the "national message" of KTV: KTV is committed to represent Kurds from everywhere, to become the image and voice of Kurdishness, and to facilitate discourse practices of defining Kurdish identities.

Some suggestions can be made as to why KTV, which is owned by a regional and Iraqi Kurdish organization, promotes a cross-border Kurdish identity. Giving voice to a cross-border Kurdish identity on KTV is not only inevitable but also beneficial for KTV. Van Bruinessen (2000a) observes that a pan-Kurdish sentiment has existed in Kurdistan for a couple of centuries, even though, until recently, it was only an elitist preoccupation (p. 10). Horowitz (1992), pointing out that Kurdish organizations have sought regional autonomy or secession for separate Kurdistans since the Second World War, suggests: "It is no secret that a good many Kurds advocate the creation of a Kurdistan out of portions of several independent states" (p. 122). Given the fact that cross-border Kurdish sentiments are deeply rooted in the Kurdish psyche, it may not be in the interest of KTV to prevent its expressions. KTV is not the sole definer of Kurdish identity; there are several other Kurdish satellite TV stations, such as Roj TV, which advocate pan-Kurdism. In other words, KTV faces competition from other satellite TV channels to capture the attention of the largest audiences in Kurdistan and Kurdish diasporic communities. To satisfy its audiences, KTV allows its discourse to be inflected with the ideas and signs of pan-Kurdism.

Having a wider audience among the Kurds from other parts of Kurdistan is beneficial to KTV or, to be more precise, to its owner, the KDP, with Barzani as its leader. Iraqi Kurdistan has always felt threatened by the powerful neighboring states of Turkey and Iran, which have sizable Kurdish populations of their own and are not interested in having a powerful Kurdish state in their neighborhood, because they believe that the existence of an autonomous Kurdistan will motivate other Kurds to demand the same thing. To prevent any serious threat against Iraqi Kurdistan (i.e., military incursion into Iraqi Kurdistan), the KDP seeks the support of other parts of Kurdistan. In the case of imminent threats from the neighboring states, the KDP could use its influence among the Kurds of other parts of Kurdistan to put pressure on their respective states not to intervene in the Iraqi Kurdistan's affairs. For example, in April 2007, the top military general of Turkey threatened that Turkish armed forces would enter the Kurdistan-Iraq territory in pursuit of PKK rebels, who are presumably stationed in the mountains of Iraqi Kurdistan. Masoud Barzani was reported by *Reuters* as saying that, "Iraqi Kurds would interfere in Turkey's mainly Kurdish cities if Ankara interfered in northern Iraq" (Aqrawi, 2007, para. 2).

It seems that Barzani had good reason to believe that attacks on Iraqi Kurdistan would not be without reaction from other Kurds. For example, in April 2007, in response to Turkey's apparent intention of incursion into Iraqi Kurdistan, Hilmi Aydogdu, the leader of the largest Kurdish-based "legal" party in Turkey, the Democratic Society Party, said: "Any attack on Kirkuk [Kurdistan-Iraq] would be considered an attack on Diyarbakir [the largest Kurdish city in Turkey]" (Turks Charge Kurd, 2007, para. 8). This example illustrates that Barzani deems important the support that the governing body in Iraqi Kurdistan has gained from Kurds living outside Iraqi Kurdistan. The KDP uses KTV to strengthen this support by disseminating discourses, images, and symbols that appeal to many Kurdish nationalists around the world, who aspire to establish a Greater Kurdistan state. Thus, alongside a regional Kurdish identity, KTV subtly fosters discursive constructions of a cross-border Kurdish identity.

SOCIOCULTURAL ASPECTS OF THE KURDISH INTERNET

My analysis of the Kurdish Internet has revealed that the medium facilitates a number of discursive strategies contributing to the construction and reproduction of a cross-border Kurdish identity, along with local and regional identities. More importantly, the analysis has shown that the Internet has given voice to those whose views and ways of constructing Kurdish identity are often at odds with both the nationalist discourses of the major Kurdish organizations and the discourse of the nation-states of Turkey, Iran, Iraq, and Syria. Furthermore, in an unprecedented way, the Internet has facilitated a continuous and largely healthy dialogue among the Kurds from various regions and diasporic communities. However, this observation must be contextualized in light of the economic and political situation of the Kurds and Kurdistan.

Whereas expressions of cross-border Kurdishness and the construction of a greater Kurdistan are usually subtle on KTV, they are explicit and prevailing on the Internet. There are powerful and emotionally charged symbols and linguistic constructions that are shared by the vast majority of online Kurdish discourses. Among these are the Kurdish flag, the map of the Greater Kurdistan, images of a common memory that is both glorious and painful, images of common national heroes, and a great preoccupation with Iraqi Kurdistan from all walks of life. The fate of the Iraqi Kurdistan has become a shared and common concern and hope for most Kurds and, thus, a force of bonding.

Internet Access in Kurdistan

Despite the role of the Internet in the articulation and dissemination of Kurdish identity constructs, the Internet is not as accessible as satellite television for the Kurds, for both economic and sociopolitical reasons.[4] The World Bank has declared that electronic media such as the Internet "put unequal beings on an equal footing and that makes it the most potent democratizing tool ever devised" (Bernal, 2006, p. 176). Many researchers have also acknowledged the significant role that media can play in processes of political transformation, but they have also warned against believing in technological determinism:

> Communications and information technologies can be potent tools in fostering political transformation, although they remain to varying degrees dependent on political institutions and other nonmedia factors. Empowerment through information has been greater in recent years from the growing pervasiveness and influence of satellite television, the Internet, cell phones, and other such devices. The Internet, for instance, has been put to work by news organizations, governments, nongovernmental organizations (NGOs), terrorist groups, bloggers, and others and has had impact on political processes. Democratization does not, however, come easily, and it is important to resist the temptation to assume that technology can, in and of itself, transform political reality. (Seib, 2007, p. 1)

The Kurdish case proves Seib's assertion.

For a long time, Kurdistan has been among the most underdeveloped regions in Turkey, Iraq, Iran, and Syria (McDowall, 2004). Underdevelopment in Kurdistan seems to have had a direct impact on the extent to which people own computers or are technically literate enough to use them. The vast majority of Kurdish people cannot be consumers of information or entertainment on the Internet, let alone producers of Internet content (Sina, 2007b). Lacking either advertising revenue or financial support from public institutions, until recently, many Kurdish websites were technically unsophisticated or short-lived (Sina, 2007b).Use of the Internet among Kurds started in Kurdish diasporic communities. Even today, Kurds living in Europe and North America by far make up the majority of webmasters, bloggers, forum, and chat-room administrators and moderators.[5] The Kurds living in Kurdistan face several difficulties when it comes to using the Internet. The digital divide, the difference between the haves and have-nots regarding having access to the Internet, certainly applies to Kurdistan. There are still millions of people who do not have personal computers in their homes. Of those who have computers, fewer people have access to the Internet, as is often the case with most of the Middle East, particularly outside the capital cities (El Gody, 2007). When available, Internet connection is slow and, at the same time, expensive (Mills, 2002).

Kurdish Internet and Censorship

Researchers have underscored the freedom of expression that many diasporic communities enjoy on the Internet (Bernal, 2006).[6]

However, Internet users face censorship both inside and outside Kurdistan. As Mills (2002) notes, many states impose censorship on Internet usage, to prevent political and social activism. Kurds from Turkey and Iran and Syria, in particular, have often reported to suffer from this state practice of curtailing freedom of expression. On April 6, 2004, *Index Online* reported that "[t]wo Kurdish-language news websites based in Germany—www.amude.com and www.qamislo.com—which provide news, pictures, and video clips of demonstrations by the country's Kurdish minority, were banned by the government of Syria in mid-March" (Index Online, 2004, para. 2). According to the same source, at the time, Syria only had two ISPs and they were both controlled by the Syrian government. The censorship measures can take various forms. Sometimes, specific websites are filtered and stopped from being viewed inside a country. Other times, there may be persecution or arrest of journalists, bloggers, or people who contribute materials from the Kurdish regions to websites and online activities. On December 31, 2003, Reporters without Borders reported that a Syrian Kurdish student named Shagouri was arrested "for sending an e-mail newsletter from a banned site www.thisissyria.net" (para. 3). According to the source, Shagouri was kept in solitary confinement and tortured for at least seven months.

Kurdish online activities are also troubled by hacking and online intrusion. On numerous occasions, individuals who identify themselves as Turkish interrupt discussions in progress in chat rooms. These individuals sometimes highjack the microphone in a chat room or they start text messaging, insulting Kurds. In addition, hacking on Kurdish websites has become routine. In 2007, close to a dozen popular websites were hacked, such as Dengekan, Kurdgoal, Kurdish Media, and Rizgarî online. The hacking is also extended to non-Kurdish websites that acknowledge the existence of Kurdistan and its flag. For example, in February 2007, the website EU Minority was hacked, apparently because it carried a page titled "Poster of 100 European Nations" containing the Kurdish flag as a representation of Kurdistan and Kurds of Turkey. As an explicit declaration of the website being hacked, the map of "the European minorities" was replaced with a colorful map of Turkey. These virtual violent activities have turned the Internet into a symbolic battleground between Kurdish and Turkish ultra-nationalists. On September 18, 2007, the online Kurdish news portal Renesans reported that within one week, "in retaliation for Turkey's attacks on Kurdish websites, a group of Kurdish hackers, 'Gold Hackers,' hacked 100 official/governmental

Turkish websites with the domain .gov.tr" (Menaf, 2007, para. 5, my translation).

The Proliferation of the Internet in Kurdistan

Despite the limitations and barriers that the Kurdish Internet has been facing, there has been considerable growth in Kurdish online activities. In the early 2000s, there were just over two dozen websites launched from the Kurdish region, while in 2007 the number of websites, blogs, and forums launched from Kurdish regions, particularly Iraqi Kurdistan, has reached the thousands. There has been a proliferation of Internet cafes in Kurdish towns in Turkey, Iraq, and Iran. As early as 2003, a reporter from the city of Hawler, Iraqi Kurdistan, confirmed that, "while most Kurdish families cannot afford to buy a computer, Internet cafes are quickly catching on" (Kurds Retain Link, 2003, para. 10). In the past few years, news and information about newest developments and courses offered in the area of information technology (IT) have found their way into Kurdish periodicals and publications in the region.[7]

Other indicators point to the presence of cyber activities in the cultural, social, and political dimensions of Kurdish identity. This is the case inside Kurdistan, but even more so outside Kurdistan. Other forms of Kurdish media, such as print, television, and radio, more and more rely on websites for news and general information, as well as a channel for strengthening their contact and communications with audiences (e.g., Qadir, 2007; No 'Legal' Demonstration, 2005). The vast majority of periodicals, radio, and TV stations publicize their website addresses and email accounts. Some prominent periodicals such as the weekly *Hawlati*, published in Iraqi Kurdistan, started to rerun selections from Kurdish websites as early as 2004 (e.g., *Le malperekanewe*, 2004, p. 16). A quick survey of websites, forums, and weblogs that invite viewers to leave comments in reaction to the contents of these sources (e.g., Renesans, Kurdistan Net) indicates that the number of people who talk, listen, watch, read, and write from Kurdistan has increased considerably.

The vast majority of Kurdish online activities initiated and maintained from the West are manifestations of what Anderson (1992) has called long-distance nationalism. In the age of globalization, nationalism in general and minority nationalism in particular is not confined to the borders of a nation-state or the territorial boundaries of a nation. Nationalism at home is often linked to nationalism abroad, or what has been termed long-distance nationalism (Anderson, 1992;

Schiller & Fouron, 2001). If one can think of the homeland as home, in this day and age, one could say that home is no longer where one lives but more frequently "where one leave[s]" (Morley, 2000, p. 54). Following Schiller and Fouron (2001), long-distance nationalism can be defined as:

> a claim to membership in a political community that stretches beyond the territorial borders of a homeland. It generates an emotional attachment that is strong enough to compel people to political action that ranges from displaying a home country flag to deciding to 'return' to fight and die in a land they may never have seen. (p. 4)

Lord Acton, the British historian-politician, has been quoted as saying, "exile is the nursery of nationality" (Anderson, 1992, p. 3).

Some exilic people find themselves trapped in a third space so to speak, somewhere between the hostland, where they live now, and the homeland, where they originally come from. Although the immediate reference of exile is a geographical location other than the homeland, it is also "a process of becoming, involving separation from home, a period of liminality and in-betweenness that can be temporary or permanent, and finally incorporation into the dominant host country" (Naficy, 1993, p. xvi). In other words, exilic life or life in diasporas engenders what might be termed a crisis of identity. Long-distance nationalism appears to be a response to this crisis, especially for two groups: those who are lost in the in-betweenness of the host country and the homeland, and those who resist any sort of assimilation into the culture and way of living of the host country. Some exilic people seem to take comfort in the ideology of long-distance nationalism, in the idea of still belonging to a place, a culture, and a people that they can identify with without much difficulty, as they see it, and that they dream of returning to one day. Participating in long-distance nationalism, whether in the form of preserving home's cultural values or in the form of involvement in the politics of the homeland, seems to offer some exiled people the means to keep the memory of home fresh in their imaginations. This way, the community, group, or the nation continues to be imagined. As Kaiser (2002) observes, "[r]emembered places have, of course, often served as symbolic anchors of community for dispersed people" (p. 244).[8] In addition to basic traditions such as family connections, folk literature, and cultural objects, the media play indispensible roles to keep the images of the homeland reinvented endlessly (see Vertovec, 1999; Karim, 2003).

Diasporas have become arguably the best friends of the Kurds. Mountains of Kurdistan are no longer the only friends of the Kurds, although they may remain as their last. Diasporas have been home to the early ideas of Kurdish nationalism (McDowall, 2004), the first Kurdish periodical *Kurdistan*, the first Kurdish-owned satellite television station, and the first websites. On the one hand, diasporas reproduce the fragmentations of Kurdish identity; they have been safe havens for Kurdish regional organizations, and sub-Kurdish cultural and linguistic communities that might be confined to a village or town of the homeland. But diasporas have also become places of convergence, cultural and political revival, and collective identity formation. Diasporas have become pan-Kurdish communicative spaces. Rebwar Fatah, the director of the most prominent pro-Kurdish English website, reports that his website www.kurdmedia.com, which is only in English, has not only influenced the overall perception of Kurdish identity among non-Kurdish observers but also the Kurdish elites and politicians throughout Kurdistan (Ghazi, 2007; R. F., personal communication, June 2010). One of the main moderators of the chat room Kurdistan United, with the nickname Aram Ahmed, says that the room is visited by "a considerable number of Kurdish youth from the homeland" and many more from diasporic communities, and he credits the chat room with raising awareness about critical issues that concern Kurds from "all parts of Kurdistan" (Aram A., personal communication, July 6, 2007). Examples of critical issues mentioned by Ahmed include publicizing human rights violations committed by the states straddling Kurdistan and also by the Kurdish administration in Iraqi Kurdistan, exposing corruption among Kurdish political parties and "non-patriotic" attempts that instigate disunity in Kurdistan, and protesting honor killing and other forms of violence against Kurdish women.[9]

Kurdish online activities confirm more important observations that have been made by analysts with respect to the place of the Internet in the processes of group identity formations and reifications. Discourse practices on the Internet are saturated with dichotomies (e.g., Mills, 2002; Erikson, 2007). On the one hand, the Internet helps dispersed peoples to imagine themselves as nations and enables the disenfranchised to amplify their voices and further their causes. On the other hand, because online activities can bypass the limitations that states and major corporations impose on communicative spaces, individuals end up sharing less information and, instead, they become more selective as to what to read, watch, and listen to (Mills, 2002). In other words, we do not need to consume information in groups as much as we did or still do when watching television or movies. Now, we can select our own news feeds and blogs to read on our personal computer profiles.

This is certainly the case for Kurdish Internet users. The webmaster of the most popular Kurdish Internet directory observes that often people select websites to visit based on ideological affiliations or personal interests (Sina, 2007b). Furthermore, Kurdish Internet users are fragmented along linguistic lines. The vast majority of Kurds from Iran and Iraq may never visit websites of Kurds from Turkey because these websites are either in Turkish or a different Kurdish variety written in a different alphabet system. Instead, there are websites that use English as either their prime medium (e.g., *Kurdish Media*) or in conjunction with Kurdish, Turkish, Persian, or Arabic (e.g., *Peyamner*). These websites seem to be able to overcome the linguistic fragmentation more effectively than web sources that are only in Kurdish (Erikson, 2007).[10]

The Internet is a mass medium, especially when used for broadcasting, that fosters conformity but also diversification, at the same time. While it links and reconnects populations dispersed globally, it fosters the formation of smaller and smaller communities locally (Becker & Wehner, 2001). The Kurdish Internet is no exception. However, there is no reason for believing that the Kurds may become further fragmented to the extent that they may not see themselves as a nation anymore as a result of using the Internet. Prior to using the Internet, the Kurds were deeply fragmented already. The evidence presented in this study indicates that, in collaboration with other mass media, particularly satellite television, the Internet has started to bring millions of dispersed Kurds closer to each other. It cannot be denied that, due to language fragmentation, the Internet's full potential for facilitating communication among the Kurds has not been sufficiently realized. However, as the Internet's audio-visual features improve on social networking tools such as YouTube and Facebook, it will become easier for Kurds from different speech varieties to share more of their experiences, without depending entirely on the written text or even the verbal language.

It is also important to note that some of the fragmentations that the Internet fosters ought to be celebrated. The amplification of local and sub-local voices, for example those of Hawrami and Zazaki speakers, is among them. Similar to the discourse of Kurdish identity on KTV, this discourse is not homogenous on the Internet, either. The Internet has not been, and it may never be, a homogenous force fostering a unified Kurdish language and culture. However, the Internet has furthered a system of signification through which the Kurds from different countries and diasporic communities have started to advance the construction and reproduction of a shared Kurdish history, culture, territory, national symbols, and a present and future. At the same time, the Internet has fostered the revitalization and maintenance of more regional and local Kurdish identities.

Summary

This volume has focused on the interface between national identities, discourses, and communication technologies. I have investigated the ways the Kurds use satellite television and the Internet to reproduce, disseminate, and articulate discursive and semiotic constructions of their collective identities. Situating my research within the interdisciplinary approach of Critical Discourse Analysis, I have carried out analyses of television and the Internet discourses at three levels. At the discourse practice level, I have mapped the types of television programs and Internet constituents used for the practices of identity construction. At the textual analysis level, I have carried out multimodal and microanalyses of verbal language, images, and music. Finally, at the sociocultural level, I have explained findings from the previous levels of analysis in light of the historical and political contexts that bear upon the discursive constructions of identity.

Investigation of Kurdish media discourses in processes of identity formation reveals that Kurdish identity is simultaneously pan-Kurdish and regional, cultural and political, individual and collective. Although there is not one single Kurdish identity, it can be said that within the last decade or so, Kurds from everywhere have started to know more about themselves and their "Others" than they have ever known. They have started to communicate dialogically. Thus, it is safe to suggest that a strong pan-Kurdish identity has started to emerge alongside several regional identities.

I am not suggesting that satellite television and the Internet are the only factors, or the main factors, in stimulating this development in Kurdish identity. Many cultural and sociopolitical changes in the region have contributed to this change.[11] The emergence, growth, and use of satellite TV and the Internet are interwoven with the cultural and sociopolitical events and structures that have had some connection with the Kurds and Kurdistan. Nor do I wish to suggest that a strong cross-border Kurdish identity could lead to the establishment of an independent Greater Kurdistan. This possibility remains extremely remote. Nonetheless, it is important to remind ourselves that all nations are first imagined before they are built on the ground, and, even then, they continue to be re-imagined and reconstructed in language, images, and sounds that connect us. Satellite television and the Internet have provided the communicative spaces for the Kurds to do just that.

Given the complexity of the sociopolitical context that bears upon the formation of Kurdish identity, it is not possible to predict for certain how far this new identity formation will go and what the sociopolitical consequences will be. One major reason for this uncertainty is that when human beings come into contact, they do not just start sharing similarities, they also notice differences. Kurds have lived under different hegemonic cultures for at least a century. Seeing their fellow Kurds on television or communicating with them on the Internet after all this time might make them realize how different they are from each other, instead of bringing them closer. More communication might actually cause them to abandon aspirations for the establishment of a Greater Kurdistan state or belonging to a cross-border Kurdish identity. Thus, for instance, Iranian Kurds might realize that they share more with the rest of the Iranians than with Kurds from Turkey or Syria. On the other hand, people often politicize their identities when they are rejected, oppressed, and persecuted for who they are. The Kurds might continue to look at their cultural and linguistic differences in a positive light, as long as their rights are denied by the states where Kurds live.[12] At least in the near future, if not for longer, the shared experience of oppression will continue to provide a fertile ground for satellite television and the Internet to foster the formation of a stronger collective and national identity.

The strengthening of a collective sense of belonging among the Kurds may have two positive effects. First, it may prevent the Kurds from being used as pawns against each other by the host states and others. Also, the host states may realize that if they do not treat their Kurds fairly, irredentism, the attempt to make a state out of Kurdish regions from four nation-states, might grow stronger.[13] The formation of a pan-Kurdish identity seems to be in the interest of everyone and, thus, should be welcomed as a positive development. In 1997, when the Zapatistas used the Internet to amplify their voice to the world successfully, it was suggested that the Internet helped the Zapatistas shed more ink than blood in making themselves heard. It is hoped that the use of satellite television and the Internet alongside other sociopolitical factors will have similar consequences for the Kurds and for other oppressed groups, as well.

RESEARCH IMPLICATIONS

This study has implications for furthering our understanding of the interface between media, identities, and discourses. I will discuss these implications under the three headings: communication technologies, national identities, and positive critical discourse analysis.

Communication Technologies

The findings in this study indicate that, far from being agents of homogenizing the world, satellite television and the Internet have enabled non-state actors and marginalized minorities to reify both their regional/local and their cross-border identities in unprecedented ways. The findings also underscore the differences between the two media in their resourcefulness for semiotic and discursive constructions of identity. Television is primarily an aural and visual medium, transcending literacy barriers; the Internet, while offering communication in these two modes, is heavily dependent on the written mode. On television, identity is defined and articulated within the overall ideological framework and political interests of the owners, for example a dominant Kurdish political party. On the Internet, however, disenfranchised groups and individuals can also participate in practices of identity construction and bring to light nuances of Kurdish identities.

The findings also show that a comprehensive analysis of media discourses in the processes and practices of identity formation must take into account not only the form and content of the media but also the sociocultural and sociopolitical contexts within which media discourses are produced and consumed. What each medium is capable of is closely connected to the context. In the late 1700s, the printing press contributed to the formation of the modern nation-states; today, the electronic media are used by minorities and nations without a state of their own in their projects of building communities and collective identities. Furthermore, mass communication technologies and cross-border connections among peoples of the world have made it much more difficult for authoritarian states to ignore the rights of their national and minority groups and their demands for recognition.

National Identities

The nation-state ideology that conceives of a nation as homogenous and unified in every sense is no longer tenable (see Erikson, 2007). In each nation, there is a multiplicity of group identities from national to ethnic, cross-border to local, and religious to linguistic. This is particularly true of a nation without a state, such as the Kurds. Schlesinger (1991) suggests that "the stateless nation is judged to be of special significance as a prototype of potentially innovative forms of post-nation-state affiliation, as an exemplar of flexible networking, and as offering multiple identities and allegiances to its inhabitants" (p. 267). Discursive representations of a stateless nation, such as the Kurds, illustrates that the electronic mass media are suitable communicative spaces for the construction, articulation and dissemination of multiple national and ethnic identities.

Positive Critical Discourse Analysis

The findings also show that a positivist approach to discourse is not capable of taking into account the contentions with which discourses are saturated. Adapting a dialogic analysis of discourse is a more effective analytical approach to delineate the multiplicity and heterogeneity of identities. The CDA approach adapted in this study has proven to be effective in accounting for important aspects of media discourse, such as content and form, in addition to the sociocultural and sociopolitical contexts within which identity constructions are produced and consumed. The approach accounts for the complexity of identity construction in media discourses that are saturated with contentions and nuances. CDA started, and it has largely remained, as a research approach aimed at making transparent the discourse and ideologies of the powerful in order to create discourse awareness among the oppressed. However, in recent years, it has been suggested that CDA needs to go beyond this by investigating other types of discourse practices such as social movements, human rights activities, and identity construction practices (Luke, 2002). Beyond making the ideologies of domination transparent, discourse analysts also must examine how emancipating discourses work and what others can learn from these discourse practices that successfully resist or transcend attempts at domination and control (Martin, 2000). It is hoped that this study has contributed to this line of research.

This study has shown that CDA is a productive research approach for studying an oppressed people's practices of national identity construction as mediated by electronic mass media and their discourses. Previous research investigating the discursive constructions of identities articulated and disseminated via satellite television and the Internet has been scarce. Electronic mass media discourses, given their rapid progress and development and their sophisticated ways of producing and disseminating words, images, and sounds, should become indispensable parts of studies that attempt to expand our understanding of the complexity and dynamism of identities. Further research on the interface between identity, media, and discourse, using a critical and interdisciplinary approach like CDA, is needed to appreciate the hybridity of media discourses, the multiplicity of identities, and the heterogeneity of communities. It is hoped that further study will contribute to our understanding of what identities are, how and why they are created, who creates them, and what the implications of their reproductions and constructions might be.

Appendix 1: Semantic Macro-Areas of National Identity and Linguistic Realizations

Semantic Macro-Areas of National Identity

(1) The discursive construction of a common *past* and *history* including (a) myths of an ancient origin that indicates not only the uniqueness and purity but also continuity and timelessness of the nation (Hall, 1992), (b) shared memories of tragic but proud past experiences and also shared memories of a glorious past, (c) a common political history.

(2) The discursive construction of a collective and shared *present and future*. This includes expressions of " 'citizenship,' 'political achievements,' 'present and future political virtues/values' " (de Cillia et al., 1999, p. 159).

(3) The discursive construction of *national symbols* and *"invented traditions"* (Hobsbawm, 1988). These include national symbols such as national anthems, flags, maps, rituals, and public ceremonies, all of which "make historical confusion and defeats understandable; they transform disorder into community" (Wodak et al., 2009, p. 24).

(4) The discursive construction of a *common culture* which encompasses various aspects of a community's life such as religion, arts, music, sports, and everyday culture such as clothing and food.Under the heading "a common culture," Wodak et al. (2009) include language. However, since language plays such a central role in defining Kurdish identity, I have treated language under a separate heading.

(5) The discursive construction of a common *language*. Discursive practices under this heading could include several features such as: (a) the ways that languages or speech varieties of a nation are labeled so as to signal the recognition of language diversity or suppress such realities; (b) the ways that language or languages are used with respect to vocabulary, pronunciation and grammar (e.g., practices of language purification, standardization and homogenization). A nationalist discourse often attempts to suppress language diversity among a people

but at the same time aims for widening the gap between languages, between one's national language and others'.

(6) The discursive construction of a *common territory*. In addition to a clearly defined homeland, a nationalist discourse also encompasses particular physical aspects of the territory such as landscapes (e.g., mountains), architecture, and nature, in general, particular features of the physical landscape such as mountains, architecture, historical sites, and so forth.

Linguistic Realizations

Naming Practices

Different names, titles, and labels given to people, objects, and concepts, indicate the attitudes and beliefs of the speakers and writers towards them (Fowler et al., 1979). Names not only identify but they could also define things and people; they not only indicate the degree of intimacy with but also distance from people, places, and things. Studying the use of naming in the addresses to the nation in Poland, Galasiński and Skowronek (2001) observe that the practice did not only enable politicians and religious leaders refer to places and persons, rather the speakers used specific naming "to construct an ideologically preferred reality. Proper names were used to serve the political purpose of the day" (p. 63).

When it comes to the discourse of national identity, naming the nation and what is believed to be national characteristics and symbols are among the prime naming practices. Billig (1995) says, "[s]omehow, in ways difficult to articulate, the magic of 'our' name matters to 'us' deeply, whichever nationality 'we' are: it indicates who 'we' are, and, more basically, *that* 'we' are. In the secular age, the name of the nation is not to be taken in vain" (p. 73, emphasis in original; see also Shnirelman, 2006; Nicolaisen, 1990). For Bourdieu (1991), naming oneself is "the typically magical act through which the particular group—virtual, ignored, denied, or repressed—makes itself visible and manifests, for other groups and for itself, and attests to its existence as a group that is known and recognized" (p. 224). Clearly, naming practices have been indispensable parts of discourses of nationalism. Discussing naming practices in the nationalist discourses of the Québécois and Aboriginal peoples in Canada, Jenson (1993) states, "[n]ationalist movements are social movements involved in the definition of a collective identity; they make choices about names" (p. 337).

Pronouns

As Fowler et al. (1979) suggest, "personal pronouns always deserve notice" (p. 201; see also Wodak et al., 2009; Higgins, 2004); personal pronouns have proven very fruitful in analyzing discourses of national identity. Billig (1995) observes that "nationalism is, above all, an ideology of the first person plural.

The crucial question relating to national identity is how the nation 'we' is construed and what is meant by such construction" (p. 70).

Tense

Another central component of the modal function of language is tense (Fowler et al., 1979). Different uses of tense are neither arbitrary nor neutral; they indicate different orientations toward the phenomena that are talked or written about. For example, present tense "signals certainty, unquestionableness, continuity, universality" (p. 207). Fairclough (2001), in a similar vein, suggests that the simple present tense form "is one terminal point of expressive modality, a categorical commitment of the producer to the truth of the propositions" (p. 129). Dunmire (1997) cites Fleischman asserting that "the greater the likelihood that a situation will be realized, i.e. the closer to 'reality' the speaker perceives it as being, the closer to 'now' (=present) will be the tense used to represent it" (p. 234). In contrast, the past tense will be used when things are desired to remain in the past and not to be of current concern. As Fowler et al. suggest, "Temporal 'distance' nearly always conveys modal 'distance'" (1979, p. 207).

Metaphors

According to Lakoff and Johnson (1980), "the essence of metaphor is understanding and experiencing one kind of thing in terms of another" (p. 5, see also Fairclough, 2001, p. 119). For example in the sentence, *he spends time with her family*, English speakers understand the importance of time in terms of their common understanding of the value of money, which can also be spent, saved, or wasted. A crucial point to be raised here is that there is no apparent connection between time and money, but what brings them together is the perception that is based on cultural assumptions and also feelings that are mostly shared between humans from the same culture. On the importance of metaphor in our discursive practices, Lakoff and Johnson (1980) state that, "Since much of our social reality is understood in metaphorical terms, and since our conception of the physical world is partly metaphorical, metaphor plays a very significant role in determining what is real for us" (p. 146). In other words, we understand the world and conceptualize reality in part in terms of metaphors. As Wodak et al. (2009, p. 44) illustrate, metaphors play an important role in "the mental construction of nation" by implying in-group "sameness and equality," on the one hand, and out-group differences and inequality, on the other. Finally, it is also important to note that metaphors are context and culture-sensitive. For example, the expression *time is money* might be quite alien to another culture where people are less preoccupied with time. The cultural and context sensitivity of metaphors have implications for the study of the discursive construction of national identity. Metaphors that contribute to the formation of imagined communities could be different from one context to the next.

There are different kinds of metaphors one of which is personification. According to Wodak et al. (2009), "[p]ersonification attributes a human form to an abstract entity and thus constitutes a widely-used mean of realizing a constructive strategy, demanding, for example, identification with an anthropomorphized nation" (p. 43). Drawing on Billig (1995), Chouliaraki (1999) observes that "[p]ersonification and the concomitant attribution of intense human feelings to the nation metaphorize relations within the nation as relationships of kinship, of family, thus further forging a sense of imagined community among its members" (p. 49). The family metaphor has been fruitful to construct and reinforce not only solidarity and in-group unity but also out-group differences and distancing. Bloor and Bloor (2007) contend that, "[l]exical items are important here [e.g., brother, children, sister, father, mother] because their use trigger[s] conceptual image: the family as a self-contained group of loving and mutually supportive members united against the outside world" (p. 77).

Presuppositions

A presupposition is "a proposition that is tacitly assumed to be true for another proposition to be meaningful" (van Dijk, 1993, p. 251). A presupposition is an assertion that is implied rather than explicitly and overtly stated. Consider this example from van Dijk (1993), which had originally appeared in a British paper: "we have to be more brisk in saying no, and showing the door to those who are not British citizens and would abuse *our hospitality* and *tolerance*" (p. 256, my emphasis). In this example, it is presupposed that the British are "hospitable" and "tolerant," therefore, claims of mistreatment that might be put forward by minorities become irrelevant and unfounded. In situations like this, presuppositions can be "manipulative" and ideological, although there are other times when they can be "sincere" (Fairclough, 2001, p. 154). Presuppositions can be ideological when "what they assume has the character of 'common sense in the service of power'" (p. 154). In addition to their ideological significance, presuppositions also deserve attention in discourse analysis because they are crucial features of the intertextuality of texts (Fairclough, 1995b). In other words, presuppositions are features of texts that have been constructed before, in other times and in other texts but, nonetheless, they have become integrated parts of the meaning-making structure of the text in question.

Over-lexicalization

Over-lexicalization or "over-wording" (Fairclough, 2001, p. 115) refers to a high level use of words and lexical items that are synonymous, near-synonymous, or semantically close enough to contribute to the construction of an idea, theme and point of preoccupation. For a critical analysis of discourse it is important to consider over-lexicalization, because this linguistic tool "points to areas of intense preoccupation in the experience and values of the group which generates it, allowing the linguist to identify peculiarities in the ideology of that group" (Fowler et al., 1979, pp. 211–212). Fairclough (2001) calls this analytical tool over-wording and defines it as "an unusually high degree of wording often involving many words which are near synonyms. Over-wording shows preoccupation with some aspect of reality—which may indicate that it is a focus of ideological struggle" (p. 115).

NOTES

1 INTRODUCTION

1. Globalization is understood as "the movement of objects, signs and people across regions and intercontinental space. The globalization of culture entails the movement of all three" (Held et al., 1999, p. 329).
2. Hobsbawm (1990, p. 182) predicted: "the world history of the late twentieth and early twenty-first centuries... will inevitably have to be written as the history of a world which can no longer be contained within the limits of 'nations' and 'nation-states,' as these used to be defined, either politically, or economically, or culturally, or even linguistically. It will see 'nation-states' and 'nations' or ethnic/linguistic groups primarily as retreating before, resisting, adapting to, being absorbed, or dislocated by, the new supranational restructuring of the globe."
3. It has been suggested that the establishment and maintenance of even larger and transnational communities such as the European Union are dependent on mass communication (Schlesinger, 1999). Schlesinger maintains that the supranational economic and political practices of the EU have started to erode the function of the nation-state, which has been "the key framework for the practice of democratic politics and the exercise of citizenship" (p. 264). The EU, however, is primarily "class inflicted" and undemocratic. Thus, in order to democratize the EU, according to Schlesinger, there is the need for "supranational communication." In other words, the democratization and, thus, the survival of the ideal EU as a supranational but still European entity is only possible through the utilization of "supranational" means of communication, something that is not yet in place.
4. Some notable attempts made in response to this concern are Billig (1995), Madianou (2005), Schlesinger (1999), and Wodak et al. (2009).
5. Kurdish population estimate varies. It might be safe to arrive at the following figures based on McDowall (2004), and Hassanpour and Mojab (2005): 13.5 million in Turkey; 7 million in Iran; 4.5 million in Iraq; more than 1 million in Syria; about 1 million in Europe, North America and Australia; and about 400,000 in the Caucuses, especially Armenia.

6. Armenia, which used to be a part of the USSR, is sometimes included in the list of the countries where parts of Kurdistan is said to be located. However, the vast majority of Kurds refer only to *çiwar parçey Kurdistan* (four parts of Kurdistan), straddling Turkey, Iraq, Iran, and Syria.

7. According to McDowall (2004), "the term Kurdistan was first used in the twelfth century as a geographical term by the Saljuqs" (p. 6). However, "Kurdistan has been virtually wiped from the map in the twentieth century. Only in Iran is a single, truncated province labelled Kordistan [*sic*]. This cartographic obliteration has its origins in politics. No country, with the partial exception of the old Soviet Union, has been keen on promoting Kurdish identity" (Ciment, 1996, p. 75; see also McDowall, 2004, p. 3).

8. Kurdish national identity is understood as a shared collective identity denoting feelings of belonging to Kurds and Kurdistan, but at the same time feelings of difference from neighboring nationalities, such as Turks, Arabs, and Persians.

9. An alternative term for cross-border or trans-state would have been "transnational." However, following van Bruinessen (2000b), I am using cross-border/trans-state and sometimes pan-Kurdish identity instead of Kurdish transnational identity. Van Bruinessen suggests: "The term 'transnational' is commonly used to refer to various types of social relations and interactions that transcend 'national' boundaries...It is obviously an appropriate term to refer to the network of contacts and the complex of activities connecting Kurdish communities in Germany, Great Britain and Turkey, but I would object to its use for networks linking the Turkish, Iraqi and Iranian parts of Kurdistan because in the latter case the essential element of distance from the homeland is lacking" (para. 5).

10. Although Iraqi Kurds have been running their own affairs since 1991, it is no secret that they owe their success primarily to the involvement of the United States and its allies in Iraq.

11. The Kurdish patriotic poet Ahmad Khani, about 300 years ago, lamented Kurdish disunity. His observations are still echoed in recent studies of Kurds and Kurdistan (Romano, 2002; Ignatieff, 1993).

12. This is not to suggest that in the past expressions of a collective Kurdish identity had not existed at all. Pan-Kurdish nationalism ideology can be traced as far back as the late 1800s, for example in the verse of the Kurdish poet Hacî Qadir Koyî (Hassanpour, 2003b). The ideology has also seemed to be the driving force for several elitist Kurdish organizations such as the *Xoyîbûn* (Independence) party, the *Komeley Jiyanewey Kurd* (KJK) (The Society for Kurdish Revival), and the Kurdish Students Society in Europe, to name just a few. *Xoyîbûn* was founded in 1927 in Syria by Kurds who had been exiled from Turkey. The society's slogan was independence for

all Kurdistan (McDowall, 2004). The KJK established in the early 1940s in Mahabad, Iran, later became the Kurdish Democratic Party (KDP), which, with the help of the Soviet Army, established *Komari Mehabad* (the Mahabad Republic). The Barzani family, who joined the republic from Iraqi Kurdistan, provided considerable military support to the republic. Expressions of a collective Kurdish identity were also manifested in the Kurdish Students Society in Europe that emerged in 1956 involving Kurds from all parts of Kurdistan. These expressions of a pan-Kurdish ideology, however, were confined to small circles of elites or intelligentsias and were not materialized in any large segment of Kurdish societies. Until the mid-1990s, the Kurds did not have access to effective means of disseminating, sharing, and negotiating the idea of a collective Kurdish identity.

13. This sentence is incomplete: Even two decades ago, of course, it was possible to disseminate news within minutes via telephone. However, very few Kurds had access to telephone, compared to the number of people who have access to satellite television and the Internet these days.

14. It is also referred to as *Al Anfal* in Arabic. According to the Human Rights Watch-Middle East (1995, p. 21), the word *Anfal* means, "spoil,"(spoils of war), and it is the name of the eighth Sura of the Qur'an. In the Kurdish context the word Anfal was given by the Iraqi government at the time to a series of operations that its military forces carried out in Kurdistan-Iraq during 1987–1989.

15. The situation was a little bit different in Iran. Immediately after the incident, Iranian journalists were present at the scene. Being at war ,with Iraq, the Iranians disseminated the images to the world, as well. However, the world for the most part chose to either ignore the incident or to downplay it (Buloch & Morris, 1992; Sheyholislami, 2007).

16. "To be means to communicate dialogically" (Bakhtin, 1984, p. 252).

17. Communications technology played a decisive role in the Öcalan event, as Romano (2002) illustrates. However, one also needs to keep in mind that the effectiveness of the technologies perhaps owed a great deal to the sophistication of their user, *Partiya Karkerên Kurdistanê*—Kurdish Workers' Party—(PKK), which has been one of the most structured and ordered organizations in the history of Kurdistan.

18. Diaspora, which means dispersion, is derived from the Greek *diaspeirein,* meaning to scatter (Karim, 2003, p. 1). The term originally referred to Greeks who were away from Greece. Later, however, it started to become more associated with the Jewish communities who were exiled from the Palestine to Babylonia. In modern times, the term is commonly used to refer to immigrant communities, the

people and their current places of residence. Some scholars have presented a narrow notion of the word by linking diasporic populations to specific homelands. For example, for Connor (1994), "diasporas are people living outside of their homeland who have not assimilated to the host's identity" (p. 80). This definition, like many others, connects diasporas to an ancestral territory or a country other than the host-land. There are scholars, however, who suggest that "[a]ll diasporas do not have homeland myths at the centre of their consciousness" (Karim, 2003, p. 2). I understand diaspora as "a whole range of phenomena that encourage multi-locale attachments, dwelling, and traveling" (Clifford [1994], as cited in Karim, 1998, p. 4). To capture the political activism of diasporas, Hassanpour and Mojab (2005) talk about "diasporic nationalism" rather than long-distance nationalism.

19. Other studies have made this strong connection between traditional media (e.g., newspaper) and Kurdish nationalism (e.g., Hassanpour, 1992). However, in the subsequent chapters, I will illustrate why print, radio, or cable television could not be as effective as satellite television and even the Internet in fostering a cross-border and pan-Kurdish identity.

20. "Nationalism is a form of collective consciousness which both presupposes a reflective appropriation of cultural traditions that...spreads only via channels of modern mass communication...[This lends] nationalism the artificial traits of something that is to a certain extent a construct, thus rendering it by definition susceptible to manipulative misuse by political elites" (Habermas, 1994, p. 22).

21. For van Dijk (1998), ideology is "a shared framework of social beliefs that organize and coordinate the social interpretations and practices of groups and their members, and, in particular, also power and other relations between groups" (p. 8). This definition of ideology is similar to that of prominent researchers such as Eagleton, who has emphasised that "ideology should be reserved for shared ways of thinking that have a specific interest in gaining power" (Mcdonald, 2003, p. 29).This view of ideology suggests that ideologies are not held only by those in power but also by those who strive for power and pursue specific interests, or those who struggle for emancipation. Repressed groups can also have ideologies and could aspire to "specific interests in gaining power." An example of ideology is nationalism, which can exemplify both sides of ideology, as the worldview system of oppressors and the worldview of social movements, as well. According to Mann, nationalism is "an elaborated ideology shared by many people right across a territory" (as cited in Spencer & Wollman, 2002, p. 47). The ideology of nationalism "is organised around the core principle of prioritising the nation" (Sutherland, 2005, p. 188). Not only state nationalism or majority nationalism but also "nationalism

in stateless nations would qualify as clearly ideological, because it seeks the establishment of power" (Mcdonald, 2003, p. 29) and, more importantly, it is a "shared way of thinking" for mobilizing a shared social action such as the construction of a collective national identity and/or the establishment of a political entity. Viewing nationalism as an ideology, in fact, underscores the significance of communication technologies in nationalist projects and the production of national identities, because as Mann asserts, "if ideologies are to spread, they must be organized through specific channels of communication" (as cited in Spencer & Wollman, 2002, p. 47).

22. For Hobsbawm (1990), proto-nations are not full-fledged nations (nation-states) but they demonstrate the potential to be one. Hobsbawm recognizes the Kurds as an example of a proto-nation. What separates a proto-nation from a nation, which is synonym to nation-state for Hobsbawm, is the lack of a polity, a state. Proto-nations live on a large territory, share similar or closely related language varieties and other cultural traits and most importantly believe they share the same ethnic roots and similar ambition for a state and political recognition. Basically, what Hobsbawm calls "proto-nation" I have called nation in this study.

23. Deutsch reminds us that seeking fellowship with those who are similar ethnically or in nationality goes back to the time of antiquity: "Socrates enjoined upon his pupils the imperative, 'Know thyself,' and that Socrates' pupil, Plato, proposed that all Greeks should henceforth cease to plunder or enslave their fellow Greeks, but should rather do these things to the barbarians" (1966, pp. 184–85).

24. Guibernau (1999) says that "the re-emergence of nationalism in nations without states is directly related to the intensification of globalization processes which have proven capable of altering the political, economic and culture structures of current societies" (p. 20). Globalization, she argues, makes people aware of their differences with others, but at the same time it threatens them with its power and tendency to homogenize. It is the fear of homogenization and, thus, the loss of less powerful cultures that compels minority cultures to resort to identity construction practices.

25. The idea that identities are constructed is often said to be a "postmodern" position. Joseph (2004), however, believes that the notion is older than this and suggests that the misconception is rooted in lack of historical knowledge. To prove this, he quotes Jan Christiaan Smuts (1870–1950), the South African general and prime minister, in one of his books saying, "[M]y very self, so uniquely individual in appearance, is...largely a social construction" (p. 7).

26. Legitimizing identity is "introduced by the dominant institutions of society to extend and rationalize their domination *vis*-a-*vis* social actors" (Castells, 1997, p. 8). This fits Billig's (1995) view of the

nationalism of the nation-states as "banal nationalism" in which the job is carried out by the state apparatus.

27. Project identity building takes place "when social actors...seek the transformation of overall social structure" (Castells, 1997, p. 8). An example of this is the feminist movement.

28. According to Hall (2006), "[S]ocial movements characteristically take their character from the states with which they interact. Politically conscious movements tend to arise when states act in an arbitrary manner, whether in terms of taxation, repression, exclusion or conscription. This most certainly applies to nationalism" (p. 40). According to Hall, there are instances, for example in India, when satisfying nationalist demands of national groups and minorities has encouraged abandoning or delaying secessionist ambitions and movements and thus preventing conflicts, warfare, violence, and loss of life. Thus, it should not come as a surprise to learn that resistance identity is a prominent characteristic of the nationalist discourse of the minorities whose rights and demands are not respected (Guibernau, 1999, 1996).

29. This may not apply to most Iraqi Kurds who live in their autonomous region. It does, however, apply to Kurds in Turkey, Iran, Syria and diasporic communities.

30. More description of the data and methodology will follow.

31. I have drawn here on Hall (1980) who states: "Reality exists outside language, but it is constantly mediated by and through language; what we can know and say has to be produced in and through discourse" (p. 132).

2 Discourse, Media, and Nation

1. A summarized version of Wodak et al. (2009/1999) is presented in de Cillia et al. (1999). The 2009 publication, however, is a revised edition, with a new chapter reporting on new data ten years after the initial research.

2. Drawing on Bourdieu's work, Wodak et al. (2009) posit that "strategic action is oriented towards a goal but not necessarily planned to the last detail or strictly instrumentalist; strategies can also be applied automatically" (p. 32). Following Bourdieu, they "argue for 'soft, relative determinism'" to declare that actors are not completely free to act, and their actions are conditioned by "the socialisation of individual acting" (p. 32). Nonetheless, they are quick to assert that, despite this, individuals cannot be absolved from the responsibilities they aught to assume for their actions, including their discoursal activities. "For CDA, language is not powerful on its own—it gains power by the use powerful people make of it" (Weiss & Wodak, 2003, p.14). This is where these CDA researchers differ from some

extreme post-structuralist and post-modernist views claiming that all social constructions are purely discursive. The same applies to institutions, groups, and political entities involved in the construction, reproduction, and maintenance of national identities. Owners and webmasters of television stations and web pages are good examples. The degree of intention, however, may vary according to the type of data under analysis; for example, a political speech is often much more intentional and purposeful than a casual conversation among "ordinary" people.

3. Deixis (from Greek) means "pointing" with language (Yule, 1996, p. 9). "Any linguistic from used to accomplish this 'pointing' is called a deictic expression" (p. 9). Examples of deixis are: pronouns I or we (personal deixis), here or there (spatial deixis), and now or then (temporal deixis).

4. The term "Kurdistani" here refers to all who live in, are from, or share a sense of collective or/and national belonging to Kurdistan ("the land of the Kurds") regardless of their ethnicity or citizenship (i.e., Kurdistanis do not have to be ethnic Kurds). Kurdistanis could also come from diasporas.

5. McLuhan credits Innis (1951) as the "first" who explained "why print causes nationalism and not tribalism... Harold Innis was the first person to hit upon the *process* of change as implicit in the *forms* of media technology" (1962, p. 50, emphasis in original). McLuhan called his first major contribution (1962) "a footnote of explanation" to Innis's work.

6. Code here is understood "in the sense of a system of norms regulating linguistic practices" (Bourdieu, 1991, p. 45).

7. Although Anderson (1991), similar to McLuhan, underscores the importance of print in imagining the nation, he differs from McLuhan's view in that he believes that the creation of the nation was mediated through the communication means of print in its close ties with capitalism and the vernaculars, both of which contributed to the emergence of a mass readership and made the nation imaginable (p. 46). For some criticism of Anderson (1991), especially with respect to the suggestion that the nation is imagined in language, see Wogan (2001).

8. However, Gellner makes no reference to McLuhan.

9. This assertion from Anderson in built on a presupposition that there is no need for literacy with radio and television. Williams (1974) has likened the ability to watch television to being able to "watch and listen to people in our immediate circle, we can watch and listen to television" (pp. 131–132). Fisk and Hartley (2003), however, disagree, particularly with respect to television. They quote Diamond, who has suggested that "actually, television is a very demanding mode of communication. Television's information is ephemeral; there is no

way for the viewer to go back over material, in the way a newspaper reader or book reader can glance back over the page" (p. 16). Fisk and Hartley suggest that "we should not mistake an oral medium for an illiterate one. We have the example of Shakespeare to remind us that non-literate entertainment can be a demanding, and satisfying, as the most profound works of literature" (pp. 16–17).

10. In June 2010, according to the Internet world stats (internetworld-stats.com/stats7.htm), 27.3 percent the Internet use was in English.

11. For a brief account of the emergence of satellite technology among minorities and diasporic communities, see Karim (2003, pp. 11–15; 1998, pp. 11–14).

12. Imazighen are commonly referred to as Berbers in the West, but the author prefers the native term Imazighen (Almasude, 1999, p. 117). According to Almasude, Imazighen is the name of the people (or Berbers), Amazigh is the adjective as in "Amazigh cause," or "Amazigh person," and the name of the language family is Tamazight.

13. Several years ago when the vast majority of web pages, email communication, and online forums were in English, most commentators believed that this trend will lead to language homogenization (i.e., domination of English) and the death of smaller languages (see Thussu, 2000, p. 182; Warschauer, 2000, pp. 165–166).

14. For criticism of CDA, see (Widdowson, 2004, 1998).

3 Kurdish Identity

1. One could argue that all nations and national identities are fragmented along the lines of ethnic, religion, class, and socio-economic formation, gender, and dialect. Kurdish identity should not be an exception. However, nations with a collective identity, despite various internal differences, unite around a set of meaning-making resources that produce national identity. These resources include, among others, sociocultural attributes and values (traditions, language, religion, etc.), territory, narratives of the past, political aspirations, and the will to live together. These resources need to be communicated among prospective members of the nation, shared, and negotiated. The Kurds have lacked the means to do this, not just because of enduring so much injustice from the ruling regimes in Turkey, Iran, Iraq, and Syria, but also because of their own very deep fragmentations that for decades, if not centuries, made easy communication among them near impossible.

2. I am not suggesting that any Kurdish nationalist movement has started with the aim of being used against other Kurdish movements. This outcome rather has been the result of an imbalance in relationship between Kurdish movements and the states straddling Kurdistan.

3. Actually not all these myths are exclusive to the Kurds, especially the most common one, the story of Zahhak (*Zuhhak* in Kurdish). The myth of Zahhak, with some variations, is common among all ethnic groups and nationalities that once were a part of the Persian Empire, including Persians, Azerbaijanis, Tajiks, and so forth.

4. According to Hassanpour, there are scholars who have challenged this attempt to link Kurds to the Medes (1992; see also Kreyenbroek, 1992). Nonetheless, the importance of the claim may not be in its proximity to the truth but in its function in the construction of national identity.

5. Among the early notable Kurds, one can speak of two people, Sharaf Khan Bitlisi, the Kurdish prince who wrote the first history of the Kurds, *Sherefname*, in 1597, and Ahmad Khani, a Kurdish poet, who in his epic poem of *Mam u Zin* (*Mem û Zîn*), written in 1693–1694, conceptualized the idea of "Kurdish nation" distinct from the ruling nations of Arabs, Turks, and Persians (Hassanpour, 1992, p. 56).

6. Rivalry among Kurdish chiefs and *Hokkams* (governors), however, had a longer history, according to McDowall (2004): "[t]the pattern of nominal submission to central government, be it Persian, Arab or subsequently Turkic, alongside the assertion of as much local independence as possible, became an enduring theme in Kurdish political life" (p. 21).

7. The House of Ardalan was a Kurdish municipality ruling in Sine (Sanandaj), located in today's northwest Iran.

8. Eskandar Monshi (1557–1642), the official chronicler of Shah Abbas Safavid, has reported that 15,000 Kurds were deported from around the town of Urumiyeh (*Wirmê* in Kurdish), northwest Iran, to Khorasan province in the eastern part of Iran, where their ancestors continue to identify themselves as Kurds (see also Ivanov, 1925).

9. *Kajîk* is a pan-Kurdist society founded in 1959 in the Iraqi Kurdistan. It cannot be called a pan-Kurdish society since it is a primarily Iraqi Kurdish group. Among its leading figures were the well-known Kurdish linguist and nationalist Jamal Nabaz and the poet Ehmed Herdi (Ahmad Hardi). *Kajîk* called upon Kurds everywhere to unite and struggle for the independence of Kurdistan. The organization discredited the regional politics of the vast majority of Kurdish parties and renounced their aims of achieving autonomy within different states of Turkey, Iran, Iraq, and Syria. *Kajîk* no longer exists, but its ideas of pan-Kurdism live on and are reflected in various Kurdish nationalist discourses, including that of some regional organizations. Today, there are several small political parties and also some cultural organizations that share most of *Kajîk*'s ideas. Some examples of these organizations are: the Democratic National Union of Kurdistan (*Yekyetî Neteweyî Dêmokratî Kurdistan*): http://www.yndk.com/ , and Kurdistan National Congress: http://www.knc.org.uk/.

10. A number of scholars writing in English on the Kurds have mis-translated or even misunderstood the word *Kurdayetî*. For Dahlman (2002), "Kurdaity," means "Kurdishness" (p. 294). Similarly, Natali (2002) renders "*Kurdayeti*" as "Kurdish identity." In contrast, at least three of the most reliable sources on Kurds and Kurdish language (Hassanpour, 1992, p. 46; Sharafkandi, 1990, p. 629; Wahby & Edmonds, 1966, p. 80) have provided different and more reli-able definitions of the term *Kurdayetî*. They translate the word as "the Kurdish nationalist movement and ideology," "Kurdish patri-otic movement," and "to act in the interest of Kurdish people," respectively. Although it is arguable whether the two concepts of nationalism and patriotism are the same, the crucial point is that *Kurdayetî* refers to a movement or action that is carried out on behalf of the Kurds. It can also refer to an ideology or belief system that makes claims about Kurdish identity or Kurdishness. Ahmadzadeh (2003) also defines *Kurdayetî* as "Kurdish nationalism and strug-gling for the rights of the Kurds" (p. 245). These leave no doubt that in Kurdish the word *Kurdayetî* is not used to mean "Kurdish iden-tity" or "Kurdishness." C. J. Edmonds (1971, p. 88), in an article titled "Kurdish Nationalism," summarizes *Kurdayetî*'s main beliefs: "The Kurds constitute a single nation which has occupied its present habitat for at least three thousand years. They have outlived the rise and fall of many imperial races: Assyrians, Persians, Greeks, Romans, Arabs, Mongols, and Turks. They have their own history, language, and culture. Their country has been unjustly partitioned. But they are the original owners, not strangers to be tolerated as minorities with limited concession granted at the whim of the usurpers" (as cited in Hassanpour, 1992, p. 62).

11. Precisely for these reasons, Vali (2003) believes that Khani could not be called a "nationalist," but a "patriot" (p. 92). Van Bruinessen (2003) is also reluctant to call Khani a nationalist; nonetheless, he refers to him as "the father of Kurdish nationalism," because he believes that Khani's *Mem û Zîn* contributed to the emergence and development of Kurdish nationalist throughout Kurdistan.

12. Both van Bruinessen and Hassanpour believe that the emergence of Kurdish nationalism as a modern force was marked by the for-mation of first Kurdish political organizations. The first Kurdish organizations were formed in Turkey around the 1900s, and then in Iran during the Second World War, followed immediately by the establishment of KDP in Iraq. Although movements with nationalist tendencies are dated back to around the First World War, Kurdish nationalism as a mass movement only came to prominence in the 1960s in Iraq, followed by populous movements in Iran and then in the mid 1980s in Turkey.

13. Hassanpour (2003b) has contested Vali's reading of his position on the nature of ethnicity. Hassanpour says: "ethnicity is itself social,

constructed, contingent and changing, even in the most ethno-centrist nationalist theories and practices" (p. 147).

14. For debates on cultural and political nation and nationalism, see Hutchinson (1999) and Smith (1998, pp. 177–180).

15. "a 'state-nation' applies to a situation in which a state is arbitrarily designed ignoring the cultural and linguistic identities of the groups falling within its boundaries" (Guibernau, 1996, p. 115).

16. This, however, is not limited to the Kurdish case. Hall (2006) posits that "social movements characteristically take their character from the states with which they interact. Politically conscious movements tend to arise when states act in an arbitrary manner, whether in terms of taxation, repression, exclusion or conscription. This most certainly applies to nationalism" (p. 40).

17. Kurds also make up the majority of the population of three other provinces: West Azerbaijan, Kermanshah (*Kirmashan* in Kurdish), and Ilam.

18. In 1979, when the Iranian Revolution took place and Iranian Kurds started to gain a populous ethnic awareness, those interested in Kurdish print materials would pay a great deal of money to buy a Kurdish magazine or book smuggled over the mountains from the Iraqi Kurdistan. The publications, however, were often months old. The publications even were obtained and read by only a very small group of Iranian Kurds who could read and write.

19. "During the past half century, the Kurds of Turkey, Iran, Iraq and Syria—and not only those who migrated to the cities—have very clearly become more integrated into the economic, political, social and cultural life of these countries, although not always on equal terms with the dominant ethnic groups...the Kurds [in the four states] developed different tastes and attitudes" (van Bruinessen, 2000a, p. 52).

20. Kurdish nationalists, especially non-secular ones, have always taken pride in the famous Muslim Kurdish commander Saladin (in Kurdish pronounced *Selaheddin*) Ayyubi, who "decisively defeated the Crusaders and established the Ayyubid dynasty in Egypt, Syria and Iraq" (McDowall, 2004, pp. 22–23). It is safe to suggest that neither he nor other Kurdish heroes at the time gained fame in the name of *Kurdayetî* (Kurdish nationalism/patriotism) but in the name of Islam. This, however, has not prevented many Kurds from consid-ering Saladin a part of the Kurdish glorious past. It should be also stressed that religious affiliations in Kurdistan played important roles at the time when Kurdish emirates and principalities (fifteenth to seventeenth centuries A.D.) would often shift loyalties either to the Ottomans (Sunnis) or Iranian Safavids (Shi'ites) in order to preserve their hereditary rule (Hassanpour, 1992). Finally, one may argue that religion has been a factor in processes of Kurdish identity formation in Iranian Kurdistan. The vast majority of Iranian Kurds from those

regions that are known to be hotbed of Kurdish nationalism (e.g., the provinces of Kordestan and West Azerbaijan) are Sunni Muslim. The official religion of Iran, however, is a particular brand of Shi'ism (see Entessar, 2007, pp. 194–195).

21. "According to the conventional nation state ideology, the ideal state is homogenous, consists of one nation/ethnic group only, and has one language" (Phillipson et al., 1995, p. 5). Almost all the European nation-states were built on this premise and their practice was replicated elsewhere, for example in Turkey, Iran, and Syria, where the state in both theory and practice pursued the policy of imposing one national language, that of the dominant ethnic groups—Turkish, Persian, and Arabic, respectively—on multiethnic populations (see also Bourdieu, 1991; Cormack, 1993; Costa, 2003).

22. In Kurdish: *Mukrî, Soranî, Erdelanî, Suleymanî, Herkî, Jelalî,* respectively.

23. There are no consensuses on the naming of Kurdish varieties. Most Kurdish nationalists do not accept the naming that I have adapted here, following Hassanpour (1992) and Kreyenbroek (1992). For example, they prefer [Kurdish] North and [Kurdish] Central, instead of Kurmanji and Sorani, respectively, because they find the use of terms like Kurmanji and Sorani divisive. For a detailed survey of various approaches to Kurdish language typology, see Hassanpour (1992).

24. Hassanpour (1992) has conducted the most comprehensive study to date of the standardization processes of these two Kurdish varieties, especially Sorani or Central Kurdish.

25. For example, Sorani does not have gender case but Kurmanji does. For a brief account of these differences between Sorani and Kurmanji, see Hassanpour (1992).

26. Max Weinreich, a German linguist, is often quoted as saying, "a language is a dialect with an army and a navy" (as cited in Romaine, 2000, p. 13). Languages are traditionally perceived to belong to nation-states but dialects to ethnic groups and minorities.

27. Mutual intelligibility varies. Kurmanji (i.e., Badinani) and Sorani speakers of Iraqi Kurdistan who live in adjacent areas may easily communicate with each other. However, speakers of different Sorani dialects that are geographically far from each other (e.g., *Mukiryanî* of Mahabad and *Erdelanî* of Sine) may have difficulty understanding each other.

28. There are, however, those who also use the Latin-based alphabet writing system, as do the Kurds from Turkey.

29. There was some publishing in Turkey beginning in the 1960s.

30. Fernandes (2007, p. 46) reports on the following exchange between British MPs and Turkey's ruling party members during a meeting in Turkey in 2007. A British MP asks: "Will you add the Kurdish language into the [newly proposed 'civilian'] constitution as an

educational right and provision?" The ruling party's official replies: "Is there *a language* called Kurdish?...*It's not a real language*" (emphasis in original).

31. Article 15 of the current Iranian Constitution states, "The Official Language and script of Iran, the lingua franca of its people, is Persian. Official documents, correspondence, and texts, as well as textbooks, must be in this language and script. However, the use of regional and tribal languages in the press and mass media, as well as for teaching of their literature in schools, is allowed in addition to Persian" (International Constitutional Law, 1992). Article 15, however, has not been implemented in any significant way (Sheyholislami, forthcoming).

32. In 1970, a Kurdish "Scientific Board" was established in Baghdad. The board's contribution to the cultivation of Kurdish language and literature has been unparalleled in the history of the Kurds. However, after the resumption of war between the Iraqi central government and the Kurdish movement under the leadership of Mustafa Barzani in 1974, the Board's cultural activities slowed down considerably. Political relations between the Kurds and the government have often determined the status of the Kurdish language in Iraq.

33. "Secessionism is an attempt by an ethnic group claiming a homeland to withdraw with its territory from the authority of a larger state of which it is a part. Irredentism is a movement by members of an ethnic group in one state to retrieve ethnically kindred people and their territory across borders" (Horowitz, 1992, p. 119).

34. Although some scholars have made distinctions between "intelligentsia" and "intellectuals," in this study, following Collins (1990), I will use the two terms synonymously.

35. There was some impact of the event in the Iranian Kurdistan mainly due to the presence of the Iranian military in or around Halabja at the time. O'Leary (2002) recalls the event: "Between 40,000 and 50,000 people were living [in Halabja] at the time. The Iranian army had previously pushed Iraqi forces out of the area. During three days, the town and surrounding district were attacked with conventional bombs, artillery fire, and chemicals—including mustard gas and nerve agents (Sarin, Tabun, and VX). At least 5,000 people died immediately as a result of the chemical attack and it is estimated that up to 12,000 people died during those three days" (para. 5). After the bombardment, Iranian cameramen managed to film and take pictures of the horrific aftermath of the tragedy. The Iranian state television broadcasted video clips and still images in Iran, which were then redistributed by few international media outlets. It is interesting to note that the mainstream media in the West, for the most part, either ignored the incident or downplayed its seriousness (Sheyholislami, 2001, 2007).

36. The use of the term "Kurdistan" is still prohibited in Turkey. It is believed that the word is against "the indivisibility of the Turkish nation," and the "territorial integrity of the state" (Hassanpour & Mojab, 2005, p. 215).

37. A number of periodicals have been closed down (e.g., *Aso*, meaning horizon, banned in August 2005), Kurdish courses cancelled, and journalists and editors of Kurdish periodicals have either been put on trial or imprisoned (Amnesty International, 2007). In fact, *Mahabad*, a magazine that is named after the city where it is published, is the only known Kurdish periodical that has survived censorship in Iran.

38. An exception to this is *Parti Jiyan û Azadi Kurdistan* (Life and Freedom Party of Kurdistan), better known by its Kurdish acronym *PJAK*. It is a small organization which emerged on the political scene of Kurdistan-Iran several years ago, and it believes to be an offshoot of the PKK.

39. For example, Ivanov (1926) reports on the "transferring" of thousands of Kurds from the Kurdistan proper (in the western part of Iran) to Khorasan/Khurasan (a province located in the eastern part of Iran) in the sixteenth century: "some tribes of Kurds from Kurdistan proper were transferred as early as the middle of the sixteenth century. In the beginning of the seventeenth century a new party had arrived; some of these tribes still live there...some more of them arrived later on in the eighteenth century, under Nadir...At present there is no connection with the West [of Iran—Kurdistan], and the Khurasani Kurds are gradually undergoing 'Turkomanization'" (p. 150).

40. On the influence of the host countries on the dynamics of Kurdish diasporic communities, Wahlbeck (1999) observes that in Denmark due to the "assimilationist" immigration policies of the country Kurds seem to be less organized and isolated, and thus have much difficulty to integrate and settle. In contrast, Kurds of the U.K. take advantage of the "multicultural" policies of the U.K. towards immigrants and refugees; they are more organized, cooperative among themselves, and are more successful in finding employment (although most of them are low-paid jobs) and settling in the country.

4 Kurdish Media: From Print to Facebook

1. Nali's full name is *Mela Xidrî Ehmedî Şaweysî Mikaylî*. He has also been called Nalî *Şarezûrî*.

2. McDowall (2004) suggests that the newspaper moved to various European locations "possibly because the politically active Badr Khans wanted to be in closer touch with Ottoman exiles in Europe" (p. 90).

3. In light of research done after 1990s, this figure should be revised: the number is higher.

4. Two of the dailies in Iraqi Kurdistan, *Kurdistanî Niwê* and *Xebat,* are owned by the two dominant Kurdish organizations in Iraqi Kurdistan, the PUK and KDP, respectively. Other dailies that have emerged in recent years in Iraqi Kurdistan include *Hewlêr Post* and *Rojname. Azadiya welat* is a Kurdish daily newspaper that is published in Istanbul.

5. According to this source, the province of Kurdistan in Iran had the highest rate of illiteracy in the country's urban population (73.5 percent). The rate is a little bit lower for other Kurdish-populated provinces: Kermanshah, 62 percent, Ilam, 68.1 percent and West Azerbaijan 61.7 percent (p. 161). Hassanpour (1996) estimates the literacy rate in Kurdistan to be much higher, 50 percent by the mid-1990s (p. 66).

6. "…intellectuals as well as professionals, notable educators, are crucial to nationalism: so often, they propose the category of the nation in the first place and endow it with symbolic significance" (Smith, 1998, p. 92).

7. However, according to another source, Bianet, "On 25 January 2004, the Radio and Television Supreme Council (RTÜK) amended Article 4 of RTÜK Law No. 3984 and Law No. 4471, so as to allow 'the broadcast of traditionally used different languages and dialects used by Turkish citizens'." Institutions wanting to broadcast in Kurdish were given permission two years later, but with a daily limit of 45 minutes and a weekly limit of four hours. All programs must have Turkish subtitles. Radio stations are allowed one hour of Kurdish broadcasting daily and five hours weekly, also with mandatory translation (Bianet, 2007).

8. *Gün* is Turkish and it means day, daytime, or the sun.

9. The stations are not allowed to broadcast programs with content targeting children. All programming must be translated into Turkish (Bianet, 2007).

10. There have been conflicting reactions to Turkish government's possible motives for launching TRT 6 and the station's significance for Kurdish culture and language in particular and the overall Kurdish nationalist movement in Turkey (see Olson, 2009, pp. 107–114). At the time, the Turkish government viewed the initiative as a "smashing success" that would "[increase] the sense of belonging of [Turkey's] Kurdish ethnic citizens" (p. 114). However, Selahattin Demirtaş, a Kurdish member of the Turkish parliament, said that it was another "mask" put on by the Turkish government, "[b]ut the people [in Kurdistan—southeast Turkey] have not forgotten what they have experienced in the past. By putting on the TRT-6 mask, [the Turkish authorities—"they"] will not be able to hide their dirty faces" (p. 113). Olson has documented more reactions to TRT 6; however, he makes a gross mistake when he relies on an observer in Turkey who believes that "all of the

TV stations in Kurdistan-Iraq broadcast exclusively in Sorani" (p. 108). Thus, Olson concludes that "[u]ndoubtedly, the decision of the KRG to broadcast solely in Sorani was a policy to keep some distance between the Kurds of Turkey and Iraq and their respective nationalist movements" (p. 108). Here, I will show that the situation actually seems to be the opposite of what Olson suggests. The vast majority of Kurdish broadcasting in Iraq, especially those owned by the main political parties and also the Kurdistan Regional Government, has always aired programs in both major Kurdish varieties, including Kurmanji, which is spoken by the vast majority of Kurds in Turkey.

11. Hassanpour (1996) makes an important observation about the state-run Kurdish broadcasting and television services. Although the states have had their own ideological and political agendas for providing these services in Kurdish, it is quite plausible to suggest that Kurdish audiences could have filtered out, and continue to filter out, the host states' propaganda and enjoy Kurdish poetry, music, and folk literature. Having worked in at least two of these state-owned radio and television stations, I should say that this seems to be an accurate observation.

12. The PKK is considered a "terrorist" group by Turkey, the United States, the E.U., and a number of other states.

13. http://www.mmc.tv/

14. The fourth satellite TV channel belonging to Kurds from Iran is Aso Sat. Newroz TV with its main studio in Stockholm is also believed to be owned and operated by Kurds from Iran.

15. However, Roj TV and MMC TV can be viewed via live streaming service on the web.

16. Khaled Salih, a political scientist and one of the authors of the article I have quoted here, is able to provide inside knowledge with respect to the KDP because at the time of writing the article he was one of the advisors to the KRG in Hawler, Iraqi Kurdistan. For the past few years, he has been the official spokesperson for the KRG.

17. VOA reports that "[Iranian] authorities continue to detain Kia Jahani, a long-time contributor to the Kurdish-language television station, Kurdistan TV. He was arrested on February 24th [of 2007]" (*Voice of America*, 2007).

18. No official statistics are available on the exact numbers or percentage of people who had or have access to the Internet in Kurdistan. My observation is mostly based on my personal communication with people in the region about the status of media and communication in Kurdistan. My observation has also been informed by other forms of media reporting on the status of the Internet.

19. http://www.kurditgroup.org.

20. Amir Hassanpour has researched and written on the development of Kurdish media more than anyone else. However, in his 1996 article "[c]reation of Kurdish Media Culture," he does not cover the Internet (Hassanpour, 1996). This seems to indicate that at least prior to 1996, the Internet was not relevant among the Kurds. It is also important to note that Hassanpour wrote this particular chapter in mid-1994 but it was published in 1996 (A. Hassanpour, personal communication, August 15, 2008).

21. As an example, Romano (2002) reports that by using e-mail, the Kurds from Turkey managed to stage a simultaneous massive demonstration in the Western capitals in the wake of Abdullah Öcalan's kidnapping in Kenya, on February 15, 1999. Of course, one has to also take into account the popularity and usefulness of telephone in these circumstances. It is also worth noting that in the same article (p. 145), Romano suggests that Kurds from Montreal and Toronto had informed him that they were informed about Öcalan's arrest via MED-TV. It should be noted, however, that MED-TV's signals were never received by satellite dishes in North America. Video tapes of MED-TV were available in Canada at the time, but these were not fast enough to deliver the news.

22. In 2007, www.kurdishmedia.com was hacked by "Turkish sources," according to its director (Rebwar F., personal communication, May 19, 2007). The website's director and his colleagues started a fundraising campaign hoping to gather enough money to design a more secure website with the same title and mission. In the mid-2010, the website www.kurdmedia.com seemed as active as always.

5   Discourse Practices of Kurdistan TV (KTV)

1. The original text is in English.

2. In 1999 when the station started it produced and aired three hours of programs. This was soon increased to five, then eight, and finally to 24 hours a day (Hazim, 2004).

3. It should be noted that there are occasional irregularities in KTV's programs' airing time or durations.

4. Bahman Ghobadi, an Iranian Kurd, is the winner of the *Camera d'Or* at 2000's Cannes Film Festival for his film, *A Time for Drunken Horses*, set in a part of Kurdistan on the Iran-Iraq border. *Turtles Can Fly* and *Half Moon* are among his other internationally acknowledged movies.

5. Since the fall of Saddam Hussein, about 1,000 Korean military personnel have been stationed in Iraqi Kurdistan. They have been actively involved in building hospitals, schools, and other essential services in the region.

6. During the week of August 6–12, 2005, the following shows related to the past history of Kurdistan were broadcast: Kurdish principalities in 1515 as part of the history of the Greater Kurdistan, and the history of the ancient Sarim Bag Citadel located near the town of Naghada, Iran. Programs were also devoted to the demography and geography of several Kurdish populated cities in Iran such as Bookan, Sanandaj, and Marivan. In January 2007, Kurdish populated cities of Turkey started to be the focus of a series of programs called *Kurdistan, Bajar bi Bajar* (Kurdistan, city by city).
7. Kurdistan is also a popular name among the female Kurds.
8. This speaker, like most Kurds, uses the word *hunermend* (artiste) to refer mostly to musicians, singers, song writers, and musical instrument players.
9. In an interview with Zayele-Radio Sweden International, Husain Shukh-Kaman, better known as *Birayani Zézé* (Zeze brothers), a Kurdish singer from Iranian Kurdistan, who became famous in the 1960s, confirms Nadri's suggestion that in the past most people in Kurdistan "were mortified to sing. We [those that sang] were called *loti* [a derogatory term for wedding singer]. People would not even allow us to ask for the hands of their girls [Birayani Zeze laughs]...Singing was not something to be proud of at the time. But, now hundreds of people tell me that they wished they had my *huner* (artistic talent)" (Sina, 2007a).
10. The program's name later changed to *Rastewxo* (live) in summer 2007.
11. Given that the lessons on Kurdish are in the Kurmanji variety and also in the Latin-based alphabet, it is safe to suggest that these lessons are directed at Kurdish audiences in Turkey.
12. According to a report by the *Agence France-Presse*, high school and college students in Iraqi Kurdistan prefer to study English instead of Arabic as their second language (Young Iraqi Kurds, 2005, p. 12; see also O'Leary & Salih, 2005).
13. When communicating in different varieties, speakers occasionally run into difficulty understanding each other.
14. There have been exceptions to this assimilationist nation-building ideology, for example Switzerland, where four languages have been declared official.
15. It should be noted that since 2006, KRG has been under pressure from representatives of what has been called "Sorani chauvinism" to declare Sorani Kurdish (or central Kurdish) as the official language of Kurdistan-Iraq (Hassanpour, 2010a, 2010b). The suggestion which first emerged as a petition signed by 53 poets, writers, and journalists, mostly from Sulaimania, has faced fierce opposition by Kurmanji/Badinani and Hawrami speakers in addition to a number of Kurdish intellectuals and linguists (Sheyholislami, 2009b).

16. Although the typology civic vs. ethnic nation or nationalism has been criticized on several grounds (see Smith, 1998; Billig, 1995), it still proves to be very useful in conceptualizing some dichotomies in the discourses of national identity. Ethnic nationalism opens membership in a nation only to those who belong ethnically, for example linguistically or racially. Ethnic nationalism is said to be exclusive, emotional, and irrational (Ignatieff, 1993). The first home for ethnic nationalism is believed to be Germany, where the Romantics such as Herder and Fichte, "argued that it was not the state that created the nation, as the Enlightenment believed, but the nation, its people, that created the state. What gave unity to the nation, what made it a home, a place of passionate attachment, was not the cold contrivance of shared rights but the people's preexisting ethnic characteristics: their language, religion, customs, and traditions" (Ignatieff, 1993; see also Fichte, 1986). According to Smith (1998), ethnic nationalism has been the most common type of nationalism around the world. Conversely, civic nationalism is said to be rational, inclusive, and integrative. Within one territory and under the same political unit (i.e., state), civic nationalism accepts everyone who wants to join the community voluntarily, regardless of their ethnic characteristics (e.g., language, race, religion). This nationalism has been labeled civic, according to Ignatieff (1993), because "it envisages the nation as a community of equal, rights-bearing citizens, united in patriotic attachment to a shared set of political practices and values" (p. 4). Most scholars, who suggest this distinction between civic and ethnic nationalism, view the French Revolution as the prime example of civic type of nationalism. This type of nationalism is said to be dominant also in countries like Britain, the United States, Canada, and Australia. However, some scholars believe that all nation-states have been ethnic at the beginning, including France and Britain. Some have evolved into civic nations, but some have stayed as ethnic (e.g., Turkey). In all nations, there is a constant struggle between the two civic and ethnic tendencies. Kurdistan is no exception. (For more on civic vs. ethnic nation/nationalism, see Spencer & Wollman, 2002, pp. 197–217.)

6 Textual Analysis of KTV

1. Articles 62–64 of the Treaty of Sévres, which relate to this discussion, are reprinted in McDowall (2004, pp. 464–465).
2. There are important differences between the two naming practices: Northern Kurdistan (*Kurdistanî Bakûr*) and Kurdistan North/ North of Kurdistan (*Bakûrî Kurdistan*). Northern Kurdistan could refer to a distinct territory, which is not necessarily a part of a larger entity. However, Kurdistan North automatically invokes other parts

of the same territory, its south, east, and west. Kurdistan North indicates that the place that is referred to as such is a part of a larger territory, Kurdistan. However, it is not clear if all the users of the two terms, who often use them interchangeably, are aware of this subtle difference. It should be noted that Kurdistan North is more commonly used than Northern Kurdistan. I should also stress that some non-nationalist organizations and individual activists may use the language of pan-Kurdism when referring to parts of Kurdistan. They often do so as a sign of solidarity with the Kurds and because of their belief in the status of the Kurds as a nation entitled to self-determination. One has to see language use in context before making any judgment about it.

3. "Kurdistan region" is literal translation of *Herêmî Kurdistan*, which is the common label used to refer to Iraqi Kurdistan. The expression is so common that many times the word Kurdistan is omitted and people refer to Iraqi Kurdistan simply as *Herêm* (the region).

4. Guests from other parts of Kurdistan are seldom from organizations or groups that are known to have ideological differences with the KDP, for example Komala party and the PJAK (The Party of Free Life of Kurdistan) of Iranian Kurdistan, or the PKK of Turkish Kurdistan. Representatives of Kurdish organizations and societies from other parts of Kurdistan (e.g., the Kurdish Democract Party of Kurdistan-Iran) that appear on KTV are consistent with its owner's (i.e., KDP-Iraq) ideological outlook. It is important to note that none of the people who appear on KTV are from groups that are involved in armed struggle with the neighboring states. KTV is well aware that such endorsements will be interpreted as threats to the sovereignty of Iran and Turkey.

5. The Kurdish term is *Mezarê Nemiran* (Tombs of the Eternals) and it refers to the tombs of Mullah Mustafa Barzani, the father of the current Iraqi Kurdistan president, Masoud Barzani, and also the tomb of his brother, Idris Barzani. Foreign dignitaries and special Kurdish guests from other parts of Kurdistan or the diaspora often pay respect to the tombs when visiting Kurdistan, and these visits are occasionally reported in KDP media, including KTV.

6. By saying that he is ready to die under the same Kurdish flag under which he was born, Masoud Barzani means two things: first that he was born in Mahabad, Iranian Kurdistan, in 1946, when for the first time a Kurdish state was established. His father Mullah Mustafa Barzani, one of the most famous Kurdish leaders, had just been driven out of Iraqi Kurdistan with several hundred rebels (McDowall, 2004, pp. 241, 290). He took refuge with the Iranian Kurds in Mahabad. Although an alternative account put forward by the KDP claims that he went to Mahabad with the aim of helping the newly established Kurdish republic, a task that he and his 1,000 strong men carried out,

indeed. Mullah Mustafa Barzani was appointed as General Barzani and the commander of Kurdistan forces. During this stay of his father in Mahabad, Masoud Barzani was born. Second, Masoud Barzani implies that the flag he is standing next to today is the same flag that was hoisted on the roof of the Mahabad Republic's headquarters in 1946. This way he inserts the legitimacy of the Kurdish flag and his leadership, not just for Iraqi Kurdistan but for all Kurdistan. In a way, he presents himself as the inheritor of the Mahabad Republic and of Kurdish self-determination. What is missing in this imaginary thread, however, is the fact that the flag that today has been popularized as the Kurdish flag is different from the flag of the Mahabad Republic. During the time of the Mahabad Republic, the description of the Kurdish flag at that time was recorded vividly in a poem written by Hemin (1921–1986) (Sheykholislami, 1974), who was officially recognized as one of the "national poets" of the republic. There are some differences between the two flags, although the main colors of red, green, yellow, and white are the same. The current Kurdish flag popular particularly with Kurds in Iraq and Iran is a recent construct. Ignatieff (1993), who traveled to Iraqi and Turkish Kurdistan in the early 1990s, writes: "[Kurdistan] has no flag" (p. 182). He is correct, because at the time there was no common Kurdish flag that could be recognized by the majority of Kurds. There can be little doubt that the current flag is an invention of the Kurdish long-distance (diasporic) nationalism. It started to be displayed in Kurdish gatherings in the diaspora in the late 1980s (e.g., I saw this flag for the first time in 1988 during a Kurdish gathering in London, Ontario). One can suggest that in 1991, during the first Gulf War, Iraqi Kurds returning from diasporas for the first time introduced the current flag to Iraqi Kurdistan. Finally, the beginning of its popularization throughout Kurdistan coincides with the launching of the first Kurdish satellite television station MED-TV in 1995. It was only shortly after the launch of MED-TV that one could see in places like Mahabad (Iran) *desrey serchopî* (the handkerchief waved in the air by the one who leads a Kurdish dance) in the four colors of the Kurdish flag.

7. In 2003, after the Kurdish Students Association at Carleton University in Canada displayed a Kurdish flag in their display case, located in the tunnels of the university campus, the Turkish embassy in Ottawa complained to the Dean of Student Affairs office and asked for the removal of the flag. The Turkish embassy claimed that displaying the Kurdish flag, banned in Turkey along with the Kurdish language, violated and insulted the sovereignty of the Turkish state, even though the flag was displayed on the Canadian soil and thousands of miles away from Turkey (Leonard Liberande, personal communication, November 10, 2003).

8. In September 2006, Masoud Barzani, the president of Iraqi Kurdistan issued a decree banning the current Iraqi flag flying over any government building throughout Kurdish region. The move was translated as Iraqi Kurds' bid for declaring independence from Iraq (*Turkey wary as*, 2006). In June 2007, an 80 square meter Kurdish flag was officially raised over the Kurdistan regional parliament instead of the Iraqi flag. It is important to note that the Kurdish authorities have only opposed raising the current Iraqi flag because they say it is reminiscent of the atrocities that were perpetuated by the previous regime against them (*Kurdish flag hoisted*, 2007). They have asked that Iraqi flag be changed in a way that it would represent Iraq's ethnic, linguistic, and cultural diversity.

9. For example, a map of the Iranian "ethnic grouping" presented on BBC's website in spring 2006 created a war of words between the Iranian Azerbaijanis and Kurds. Azerbaijanis complained that the map had marked a large section of Azeri territory as Kurdish. Some prominent Azeris, including Reza Baraheni, the past president of PEN Canada, wrote to the BBC and urged them to change the map. Also, about 30 Azerbaijani organizations started collecting signatures to endorse a petition addressed to the U.N., some world leaders, and human rights organizations (*Prevent ethnic conflict*, 2006). The petition warned of an imminent conflict between the Kurds and Azerbaijanis. The dispute over the map continued for several months. This example nicely supports Kaiser's assertion that "[m]aps of the national homeland help to naturalize and historicize the images being created of the 'primordial nation' and its intimate connection to the sacred soil of its ancestral homeland" (Kaiser, 2002, p. 233).

10. Kurdistan does not have fixed and internationally recognized borders. Thus, there have been numerous maps of Kurdistan throughout history (O'Shea, 2004). Nonetheless, all the maps encompass territories within the countries of Turkey, Iraq, Iran, Syria, and even Armenia.

11. "The maps of Greater Kurdistan have been accepted by Kurds for so long that they have now a power of their own, they have become an espoused political aim as well as a commentary on ethnicity, spatial perceptions (which may now need to be adjusted to fit the map), historical ambition, and irredentism" (O'Shea, 2004, p. 186).

12. An obvious alternative to this text would have been *Ey Reqîb* or Ay Raghib (*O Enemy*), the Kurdish national anthem. But, Kurdistan TV does not air the anthem. In the past several years there has been much debate about the status of Ay Raghib. A group comprised of traditional nationalists view the anthem as sacred and intertwined with Kurdish national identity. This group believes that the anthem

should be maintained as it is. At least two other groups disagree. Religious groups have complained that the lyrics of the anthem disrespect the religious beliefs of the vast majority of Kurdistan people. For example, one of the lines says, "Both our faith and religion are our homeland" (*Diniman u ayinman her nishtiman*). The second group believes that Ay Raghib is ethnocentric and does not represent Kurdistan's ethnic and linguistic diversity. For example, the first line, which is also repeated several times throughout the anthem, says: "O Enemy! The Kurdish-speaking nation is still alive" (*Ey Reqib! Her mawe qewmi Kurd-ziman*). Also, there is resentment about the anthem's fictional history, which aims to construct the Kurds as descendants of "*Media*" and "*Keyxusrew*." It has been suggested that new lyrics should be written for the anthem and there have been attempts to accomplish this task, for example by the prominent Kurdish poet Şêrko Bêkes (Sherko Bekes) in 2006. The intriguing debate over Ay Raghib continues. However, providing a full account of the issue is beyond the scope of this study.

13. For example, during the parliamentary elections of 2005 in Iraq when Kurdish political parties were campaigning for have as many representatives as possible elected to the Iraqi National Assembly, this song was aired on daily basis. It has also been aired at times of national crisis, for example, whenever military threats, such as those by Turkey, against Iraqi Kurdistan have been portrayed as imminent.

14. Note that there are other versions of the song posted on YouTube such as this one that has been viewed about 4,000 times: http://www.youtube.com/watch?v=P59TGeI7J44.

15. Ahmad Askandari, an Iranian Kurdish social activist, who is also a Swedish citizen, tells a compelling story in an interview with the *Swedish Radio International, Kurdish Service* (Sina, 2005). In 2005, Askandari was invited to the Iraqi Kurdistan to attend a festival held by a women's forum promoting equity and equality in Kurdistan. He was awarded a special trophy by the forum for his activism in promoting Kurdish women's rights. On his way back to Sweden, at a Turkish checkpoint on the Iraqi-Kurdistan and Turkish border, Turkish border guards searched his belongings. As told by Askandari, the border guards destroyed the only Kurdish newspaper he had brought with him from Kurdistan. They made it clear to him that they did that because the newspaper contained the word "Kurdistan." Askandari describes vividly how the soldiers became "hysterical" when they saw the word "Kurdistan" also written on the trophy, a framed artwork, which he received from the women's forum. The trophy bore the phrase *Projy Yeksani, Hukumeti Herêmi Kurdistan* (Equality Project, Kurdistan Regional Government). Now the word Kurdistan did not just denote a geographical location but a political entity, a Kurdish government, as well. Askandari recalls how the soldiers shouted: "We

have told you people not to bring these things to our country. There is no such a thing as Kurdistan." The soldiers "violently," under their boots, trampled the trophy (Sina, 2005).

16. The Patriotic Union of Kurdistan, the second largest organization in Iraqi Kurdistan, has not become a significant contributor to this discursive shift.

17. Khaled Salih, the spokesperson for KRG in 2006, in a joint article with O'Leary writes: "Kurdistan and its parties are...as civic nationalist in disposition as the English, French, Danes, and Arab liberals, and unlike the latter they have proved themselves to be such in government. Within Kurdistan, minority rights in language, schooling, and religion have been protected. All citizens...are equals and treated as such. Kurdistani is not synonym with Kurd" (O'Leary & Salih, 2005, p. 34).

18. On the importance of family metaphor, Bloor and Bloor (2007) state: "Just as the family metaphor has been used to express solidarity and inspire unity, it has also been widely applied, sometimes explicitly, to reject other groups (p. 76)...Lexical items are important here [e.g., brother, children, sister, father, mother] because their use trigger[s] conceptual image: the family as a self-contained group of loving and mutually supportive members united against the outside world" (p. 77).

19. Fairclough (2001) calls this analytical tool over-wording and defines it as "an unusually high degree of wording often involving many words which are near synonyms. Over-wording shows preoccupation with some aspect of reality—which may indicate that it is a focus of ideological struggle" (p. 115).

20. This tune is close to pastoral music.

7   Discourse Practices of Kurdish Internet

1. In 1998, under the pseudonym Ashti, I started one of the first Kurdish websites, Mahabad Homepage, and maintained it for about two years on Geocities.com, which no longer exists after it was closed down by Yahoo in 2009. In the summers of 2001 and 2003, for about two months, on a weekly basis, I hosted a chat room dedicated to Kurdish literature and language on the Internet chat service Paltalk. In 2004, I started blogging in Kurdish sporadically and under more than one pseudonym. At the beginning of 2007, I started a multilingual filter blog on which I continue to provide links to online news and resources related to Kurdish communication and language.

2. Other notable Kurdish web directories include Kurdland and Kurdlinx. The first Kurdish Internet directory was Malper (webpage/website) that started in 1997. The word Malper, coined by Nasser Sina, the director of Radio Zayele, the Radio Sweden International-Kurdish

Service, has been widely accepted in all Kurdish speech varieties as a synonym for the English word website.

3. An exception to that is Nefel website, which carries a few Sorani titles but not in Latin-based alphabet rather than Arabic-based.

4. There is still no Kurdish broadcasting in Syria. Since 2002 there has been limited Kurdish broadcasting in Turkey that is run by the state.

5. MP3 is a digital audio encoding format. It is designed in a way that an audio file (e.g., a song) in this format requires much less amount of data.

6. The word *rojhelat* (the east) in the title of the website refers to eastern (Iranian) Kurdistan.

7. Only chat rooms that are offered at no charge have the limited capacity of 250 people.

8. It should be noted that this observation has been made before midnight Europe time, during which most Kurds living in Europe and the Middle East are online. After midnight, the usual *Paltalk* users are North American Kurds, who are much fewer in numbers.

9. 250 people per room is what the free module allows. Once one is subscribed to Paltalk.com and pays a small monthly fee, rooms' capacity reaches 1,000 people.

10. Aram Ahmad is the username and nickname of one of the main moderators (they are called administrators in Paltalk) of the chat room Kurdistan United.

11. A list of these weblogs were made available on Gulagenim's weblog (http://gulagenim.blogspot.com/2005_12_01_archive.html).

12. There are pro-Palestinian groups with more than 20,000 members.

13. www.facebook.com/group.php?gid=38949607225&ref=search.

8   TEXTUAL ANALYSIS OF KURDISH INTERNET

1. I have discussed these in details in the previous chapters.

2. The video clip has been removed. A possible reason for that could be the fact that the video in question generated a heated debate between some Kurds and those Assyrians who found, for very good reasons, the video offensive. A few comments evaluated the video as "racist" towards Assyrians, and a few more believed that the video misrepresented the Kurds.

3. For further information on whether Kurds are descendents of the Medes, see Izady (1994).

4. The video was posted on June 8, 2006, and in one year was viewed about 50,000 times, and it generated about 1,300 comments. Many of these comments are plain racial slurs exchanged between Kurds, Turks, and Armenians. Most comments in the form of postings

exchanged between Kurds and Turks were overtly racist. Until July 2010, the video was viewed 112,000 and it had generated more than 1,800 comments.

5. Most users who upload video clips on YouTube allow viewers to leave comments in reaction to the video. Viewers can also rate the video clip and report issues related to the appropriateness of the clip for the intended audience, as well.

6. Fewer Kurds prefer to think that there are *penc beş* (five parts) or *penc parçe* (five pieces), as opposed to four parts or pieces, of Kurdistan: Turkish, Iraqi, Iranian, Syrian, and Armenian/Azerbaijani.

7. The webmasters of at least two websites, IT 4 Kurd and Home 4 Kurd, have confirmed this observation (IT 4 Kurd Group, personal communication, February 21, 2008; Home 4 Kurd, personal communication, February 22, 2008).

8. This is not to suggest that the KDP's nationalist discourse could be immune from racist ideologies. However, winning the hearts and minds of the minorities in the region, such as Assyrians and Turkomans, has been very crucial in determining the balance of power in the region. KTV cannot afford to be racist but an unknown individual on the Internet can.

9. The post has been removed. However, it is reposted here: http://4. bp.blogspot.com/_f03HfUXIESU/TGxlmBzhBoI/AAAA AAAAABc/D3EyQ-1H9wY/s1600/forum_future+common. png

10. The directory Koord provides a list of these websites. koord.com/ weblanguage/fer_buni_kurdi.htm.

11. The Kurmanji Kurdish text says, *Kurdî binahiya çavên me ye. Kurdino zimanê xwe biparêzn!*

12. "Nothing suggests that Ghanaian nationalism is any less real than Indonesian simply because its national language is English rather than Ashanti" (Anderson, 1991, p. 133).

13. I hesitate to say that Kurdishness is imagined in the mother tongue for the majority of Kurds. It is well known that, because their language was banned for decades, Kurds from Turkey, including the leaders of the most nationalistic organizations (e.g., Abdullah Öcalan, the leader of the PKK), talk and write in Turkish most of the time. In this case, Kurdishness is imagined in Turkish. However, it is equally important to point out that even these organizations and leaders who cannot communicate in the Kurdish language put the right of the Kurds to be educated in their language at the top of their political demands.

14. Although some researchers only refer to the popularity of weblogs and how about 40,000 of them are created on daily basis, other scholars have noted that most of these blogs are abandoned after a short period of time (e.g., months or even days) (Miura & Yamashita,

2007). The fact that the two Kurdish blogs have been active for about six years is remarkable.

15. In Kurdish chatrooms, except for well-known people such as politicians, entertainers, and writers, most people do not identify themselves by their real names.

16. Previously, I have talked about some internal tensions among the Kurdish elites over the status of Kurdish varieties. On the one hand, there are those who consider Hawrami and Zazaki as languages distinct from Kurdish. At the other end of the spectrum, there are Sorani and Kurmanji elites who consider Hawrami and Zazaki as dialects of Kurdish. Finally, there are those who call for two things: (1) the right of the speakers to determine the status of their speech variety (i.e., its Kurdishness or otherwise); (2) the right to be educated in the mother tongue, regardless of whether the speakers consider their tongue to be a Kurdish variety or not (Sheyholislami, 2009b).

17. The lyrics of this anthem are by the late Ibrahim Ahmed, a well-known Kurdish poet, novelist, essayist, and politician who also happened to be Jalal Talabani's (Iraqi President) father-in-law.

18. Any firm judgement on the validity of this hypothesis should be based on solid fieldwork and research that seeks to investigate Kurdish speakers' experiences with exposure to different Kurdish varieties. Having said that, it should be stressed that Kurdish singers believe that singing in different Kurdish varieties brings those varieties closer to each other and it will make them more mutually intelligible. For example, Heval Ibrahim, a Kurmanji singer, is quoted as saying, "I think it is wonderful that Sorani singers sing in [Kurmanji] and [Kurmanji] singers sing in Sorani, because when Sorani singers sing in Kurmanji they manage to have their Kurmanji audience listen to the Sorani songs as well. Kurmanji audiences end up memorizing the Sorani songs and this way they start understanding Sorani...Today, most of the youth in [Kurmanji speakers region] can understand Sorani thanks to singers like Zakaria, Eyub Ali, Adnan Karim and many more who sing in both varieties" (Himmati, 2007, p. 17, my translation). Is this quote really saying that bilingual singing will make the varieties mutually intelligible, or is it simply claiming that it will increase bilingualism among the audience?

19. The making and reproducing of Kurdish calendar is another discursive strategy to construct Kurdish nation as primordial and ancient. The Kurdish year in the year 2007 was 2707.

20. The same search returned about 55,000,000 hits for "Canada," 5,000,000 for "Turkey," 700,000 for "Palestine," and 270,000 for "Nairobi."

21. There are maps of Iraqi Kurdistan but not in its entirety. These maps show the part of Iraqi Kurdistan that is administered by the Kurdistan Regional Government only, not all the regions of Iraqi Kurdistan

that are considered parts of Kurdistan in the Kurdish nationalist discourse. The map of the Greater Kurdistan, however, includes all the places with considerable Kurdish population. There are also maps that exaggerate greatly the size of the Kurdish populated territories. These maps have been even more controversial.

22. Halavais (2000) draws on Karl Deutsch's notion of communicative flows, which suggested that these flows (e.g., postal services) are measurable and they could indicate where the borders of the nation are drawn in the imagination of its members.

23. This finding illustrates the importance of Halavais' (2000) call: "an attempt to describe the social impacts of the Internet must include some indication of the structure of this medium" (p. 24).

9   DISCUSSION AND CONCLUSION

1. For example, since the fall of Saddam Hussein, Hoshyar Zebari, a high-ranking member of the KDP, has been the Iraqi foreign minister.

2. The KDP is not alone in being labelled as separatist; almost all Kurdish organizations and nationalists have gone through this experience.

3. In an interview with the Turkish newspaper, *Akşam*, Jalal Talabani, the second most influential Iraqi Kurd, and the current president of Iraq, declared: "I have never thought of establishing a Kurdish state or separating Kurdistan from Iraq" (Talabani: *Le jiyanimda*, 2005).

4. Although a much greater number of people in Kurdistan watch satellite television than use the Internet, it does not mean that satellite dish owners are free of persecution in Turkey, Syria, or Iran.

5. It should also be noted that the situation has improved considerably in Iraqi Kurdistan. Not only do more people have access to the Internet, but more people from the region launch websites and produce online contents. For example, according to www.alexa.com, the website www.kurdlinx.com, which is a directory of Kurdish sites and web sources, has 100 percent of its traffic from Iraq (read Iraqi Kurdistan and Iraq). The website, which is based in Kurdistan-Iraq, was launched in March 2006.

6. For example, Bernal (2006) notes that, "as a communicative space, cyberspace offers considerable freedom from censorship as well as from violence. In fact, I would argue that for Eritreans the possibility of exploring ideas without fear of official reprisal or violence is one of the underlying attractions of Internet commutations" (p. 166).

7. In 2004, the weekly *Hawlati* devoted at least one full page (out of 15–16 pages) to IT news and announcements. Similar pages can be found in periodicals published in Iranian Kurdistan (e.g., Said Shukri, 2006). In the same year, a book titled *Rêberî Saite*

Kurdiyekan (Guide to Kurdish Sites) was published in Suleimania, Iraqi Kurdistan.

8. The idea of returning home/homeland is often based on an image of the home as stable, unchangeable, and frozen in time and space. It is always questionable whether one can return to the *same* place one abandons. The homeland imagined in discourse may remain unchanged for a very long time, but this does not mean that it will also remain "the home" for everyone.

9. Ahmed reports that the chat room also helps to organize demonstrations and peaceful campaigns that sometimes have direct impact of sociocultural and political issues in Kurdistan. For example, Ahmed believes that *Kurdistan United* had a decisive role in mobilizing public opinion both in Kurdistan and diasporas to put pressure on the KDP to release a political prisoner, Kemal Said Qadir, a Kurdish-Austrian who was jailed in Iraqi Kurdistan because of insulting Masoud Barzani in his writings.

10. Erikson (2007) has made a similar observation: "It may actually be said that the Kurdish nation reaches its fullest, most consolidated from on transnational websites in the metropolitan languages of English, German, and French" (p. 9). I am personally not sure about the latter two, since the number of web sources using those languages are very few compared to those using English. Having said that, one needs to take Erikson's observation with a grain of salt, because it seems to be based on the assumption that a nation must be congruent linguistically, a position that I have tried to refute in this study. A nation can have more than one language (e.g., Switzerland, Canada, South Africa, and India), and by the same token a language can be shared among many nation-states (e.g., English among England, Canada, the United States, Australia, and India).

11. Among these events and changes is the immigration of Kurds from Turkey to the West in the 1960s and later in the 1980s following the Turkish military coup. Iraqi and Iranian Kurds joined Kurdish diasporic communities from the 1980s during and in the aftermath of the Iraq-Iran War. Another major change affecting the Kurds was the First Gulf War in 1991 and then the invasion of Iraq by the United States and its allies in 2003. The Kurds of Iraq have been governing themselves since 1992 and they have also become a source of hope for the Kurds from other countries. Finally, Turkey's application for full membership in the European Union submitted in the early 1990s was followed by some positive changes to the Kurdish issue in that country.

12. Even in such circumstances, when perceived threats of others may foster national unity, internal conflicts within a Kurdish community like the KRG that might be driven by unequal power relations based on class or gender are expected.

13. McDowall (2004) suggests: "Turkey, Iraq and Iran will be unable to repel the information offensive [from the new Kurdish media]. Furthermore, they will find that this [sic] form of assault on their centralized and ideological battlements much more threatening than guerilla operations" (p. 459).

REFERENCES

Ackah, W., & Newman, J. (2003). Ghanaian Seventh Day Adventists on and offline. In K. H. Karim (Ed.), *The media of diaspora* (203–214). London: Routledge.

Agence France Press (AFP). (2005, July 15). Rioting erupts in Iranian hotbed of Kurdish nationalism. Retrieved July 17, 2005, from www.payvand. com/news/archive/6-05.html.

Ahmadi, M. (2004). *Wéblogî Kurdî: Dîmane le gel Gulper̆* (Kurdish weblog: Interview with Gulper). Retrieved October 28, 2004, from wwww. dimane.com/index.php?subaction=showfull&id=1098976917&archive.

Ahmadzadeh, H. (2003). Nation and novel: A study of Persian and Kurdish narrative discourse. Uppsala: Uppsala Universitet.

Ainsworth, S., & Hardy, C. (2004). Critical discourse analysis and identity: Why bother? *Critical Discourse Studies, 1*(2), 225–259.

Alay Kurdistan. (2004, June 08). Mukryan. Retrieved July 2, 2004, from http://mukryan.blogspot.com.

Alinia, M. (2004). Spaces of diasporas: Kurdish identities, experiences of otherness and politics of belonging. Göteborg, Sweden: Göteborg University.

Almasude, A. (1999). The new mass media and the shaping of Amazigh identity. In J. Reyhner, G. Cantoni, R. N. St. Clari & E. P. Yazzie (Eds.), *Revitalizing indigenous languages* (117–128). Flagstaff, Arizona: Northern Arizona University.

Amnesty International. (2005). Syria: Kurds in the Syrian Arab Republic one year after the March 2004 events. Retrieved April 10, 2006, from http://www.amnesty.ca/Refugee/news/view.php?load=arcview&article =2366&c=Refugee_News.

———. (2007, February 16). Iran: Fear of torture or ill treatment/arbitrary arrest: Adnan Hassanpour. Retrieved March 10, 2007, from http: //asiapacific.amnesty.org/library/Index/ ENGMDE130172007?open&of=ENG-346.

Anderson, B. (1991 [1983]). Imagined communities: Reflections on the origin and spread of nationalism (Rev. ed.). London: Verso.

———. (1992). Long-distance nationalism: World capitalism and the rise of identity politics.Conference papers (Working paper 5.1). Conference on Nation, National Identity, Nationalism, September 10–12, 1992. University of California, Centre for German and European Studies.

Androutsopoulos, J. (2006). Multilingualism, diaspora, and the Internet: Codes and identities on German-based diaspora websites. *Journal of Sociolinguistics, 10*(4), 520–547.

Appadurai, A. (1996). *Modernity at large: Cultural dimensions of globalization.* Minneapolis, Minn.: University of Minnesota Press.

Aqrawi, S. (2007, April 14). Iraq Kurdish PM seeks to calm Turkey-Kurd tensions. *Reuters.* Retrieved April 15, 2007, from www.alertnet.org/thenews/newsdesk/L14502248.htm.

Ashuri, T. (2005). The nation remembers: National identity and shared memory in television documentaries. *Nations and Nationalism 11*(3), 423–442.

Associated Press. (2002, November 20). Turkey to air limited Kurdish programs. Retrieved June 10, 2006, from www.flash-bulletin.de/2002/eNovember21.htm#6.

Bakhtin, M. (1984). *Problems of Dostoevsky's poetics.*(C. Emerson trans.). Minneapolis: University of Minnesota Press.

Bakker, P. (2001, May). *New nationalism: The Internet Crusade.* International Studies Association Annual Convention, Chicago, IL. Retrieved May 20, 2003, from http://citeseerx.ist.psu.edu/viewdoc/download?doi=10.1.1.1 01.3066&rep=rep1&type=pdf.

Bargh, J. A., & McKenna, K. Y. A. (2004). The internet and social life. *Annual Review of Psychology, 55*, 573–590.

Barzani, M. (2003, December 26). Iraqi Kurdish claim for federalism: A Kurdish-Arab partnership. Retrieved October 24, 2004, from www.kurdistan.tv.

Be hoy bekarhênani rengî kesk u sor u zerd 8 mindalî Kurd le xwêndin dûr dexrênewe (Because of using the green, red and yellow colours eight Kurdish students are expelled from school) (2007, March 06). *Midya,* 280, p. 4.

Becker, B., & Wehner, J. (2001). Electronic networks and civil society: Reflections on structural changes the public sphere. In C. Ess (Ed.), *Culture, technology, communication: Towards an international global village* (67–85). Albany, NY: SUNY Press.

Bell, A., & Garret, P. (Eds.) (1998). *Approaches to media discourse.* Oxford: Blackwell Publishers.

Bendix, J., & Liebler, C. M. (1999). Place, distance, and environmental news: Geographic variation in newspaper coverage of the spotted owl conflict. *Annals of the Association of American Geographers, 89*(4), 658–676.

Benítez, J. L. (2006). Transnational dimensions of the digital divide among Salvadoran immigrants in the Washington DC metropolitan area. *Global Networks, 6*(2), 181–199.

Bernal, V. (2006).Diaspora, cyberspace and political imagination: The Eritrean diaspora online. *Global Networks 6*(2), 161–179.

Bianet.(2007, November 20). Diyarbakir broadcaster harassed over Kurdish-language programming; radio station on trial over song. *International*

Freedom of Expression Exchange. Retrieved November 21, 2007, from http://egypt.ifex.org/en/content/view/full/87783/index.html.

Billig, M. (1995). *Banal nationalism.* London: Sage.

Birch, N. (2003, October 3). Turkish Kurds, watching satellite TV, warily eye Kirkuk. *Eurasianet.* Retrieved October 24, 2004, from www.eurasianet. org/departments/insight/articles/eav041003_pr.shtml.

Bird, C. (2004). *A thousand sighs, a thousand revolts: Journeys in Kurdistan.* New York: Ballantine Books.

Bishop, H., & Jaworski, A. (2003). "We beat 'em": Nationalism and the hegemony of homogeneity in the British press reportage of Germany versus England Euro 2000. *Discourse & Society, 14*(3), 243–271.

Black, G. (1993). *Genocide in Iraq: The Anfal campaign against the Kurds: A Middle East Watch report.* New York: Human Rights Watch.

Bloor, M., & Bloor, T. (2007). *The practice of critical discourse analysis: An introduction.* London: Hodder Arnold.

Bourdieu, P. (1991). *Language and symbolic power.* J. Thompson (Ed.) (G. Raymond & M. Adamson, Trans.). Cambridge: Harvard University Press.

Breuilly, J. (1993). *Nationalism and the state* (2nd ed.). Manchester: Manchester University Press.

Brewer, J. D. (2006). Memory, truth and victimhood in post-trauma societies. In G. Delanty & K. Kumar (Eds.), *The Sage handbook of nations and nationalism* (214–224). London: Sage.

British Broadcasting Corporation (BBC). (1999, February 19). Kurdish arrests "reach 1000." Retrieved December 15, 2005, from http://news. bbc.co.uk/2/hi/europe/282492.stm.

Brubaker, R. (2004). *Ethnicity without groups.* Cambridge: Harvard University Press.

Bulck, H. V. d., & Poecke, L. V. (1996). National language, identity formation and broadcasting: Flanders, the Netherlands and German-speaking Switzerland. *European Journal of Communication, 11*(2), 217–233.

Bulloch, J., & Morris, H. (1992). *No friends but the mountains: The tragic history of the Kurds.* New York: Oxford University Press.

Calhoun, C. J. (1993). Nationalism and ethnicity. *Annual Review of Sociology, 19*, 211–239.

———. (1997). *Nationalism.* Minneapolis: University of Minnesota Press.

Castells, M. (1997). *The power of identity.* Oxford: Blackwell.

Chan, B. (2005). Imagining the homeland: The Internet and diasporic discourse of nationalism. *Journal of Communication Inquiry, 29*(4), 336–368.

Chouliaraki, L. (1999). Media discourse and national identity: Death and myth in a news broadcast. In R. Wodak & C. Ludwig (Eds.), *Challenges in a changing world: Issues in Critical Discourse Analysis* (37–62). Wien: PassagenVerlag.

Chouliaraki, L., & Fairclough, N. (1999). *Discourse in late modernity: Rethinking Critical Discourse Analysis*. Edinburgh: Edinburgh University Press.

Ciment, J. (1996). *The Kurds: State and minority in Turkey, Iraq and Iran*. New York: Facts On File, Inc.

Collins, R. (1990). *Culture, communication & national identity: The case of Canadian television*. Toronto: University of Toronto Press.

Connor, W. (1994). *Ethnonationalism: The quest for understanding*. Princeton: Princeton University Press.

Cormack, M. (1993). Problems of minority language broadcasting: Gaelic in Scotland. *European Journal of Communication, 8*, 101–117.

Cormack, M., & Hourigan, N. (Eds.) (2007). *Minority language media: Concepts, critiques, and case studies*. Clevedon: Multilingual Matters.

Costa, J. (2003). Catalan linguistic policy: Liberal or illiberal? *Nations and Nationalism, 9*(3), 413–432.

Clifford, J. (1994). Diasporas. *Cultural Anthropology, 9*(3), 302–338.

Crystal, D. (1997). *English as a global language*. Cambridge: Cambridge University Press.

Cunliffe. D. (2007). Minority languages and the Internet: New threats, new opportunities. In M. Cormack and N. Hourigan, N. (Eds.), *Minority language media: Concepts, critiques, and case studies* (133–150). Clevedon: Multilingual Matters.

Dahlman, C. (2002). The political geography of Kurdistan. *Eurasian Geography and Economics, 43*(4), 271–299.

Danish Council gives green light for Roj TV broadcasts. (2007, May 5). *Turkish Daily News*. Retrieved May 17, 2007, from www.turkishdailynews.com.tr/article.php?enewsid=72434.

Danet, B., & Herring, S. (2007). Multilingualism on the Internet. In M. Hellinger and A. Pauwels (Eds.), *Handbook of language and communication: Diversity and change* (554–585). New York: Mouton de Gruyter.

Dascal, M. (2003). Identities in flux: Arabs and Jews in Israel. In G. Weiss & R. Wodak (Eds.), *Critical discourse Analysis: Theory and interdisciplinarity* (150–166). New York: Palgrave Macmillan.

Davis, W. (2009). *The Wayfinders: Why ancient wisdom matters in the modern world*. Toronto, ON: House of Anansi Press.

De Cillia, R., Reisigl, M. & Wodak, R. (1999). The discursive construction of national identities. *Discourse & Society, 10*(2), 149–173.

Demertzis, N., Papathanassopoulos, S., & Armenakis, A. (1999). Media and nationalism: The Macedonian question. *Press/Politics, 4*(3), 26–50.

Deutsch, K. (1953). The growth of nations: Some recent patterns of political and social integration. *World Politics, 5*(2), 168–195.

———. (1966). *Nationalism and communication: An inquiry into the foundations of nationality* (2nd ed.). New York: M.I.T. Press.

Dixon, J., & Durrheim, K. (2000). Displacing place-identity: A discursive approach to locating self and other. *British Journal of Social Psychology, 39*, 27–44.

Dozens of DTP mayors face jail over Roj TV letter. (2007, April 4). *Today's Zaman*. Retrieved May 17, 2007, from www.todayszaman.com/tz-web/detaylar.do?load=detay&link=107375&bolum=103.

Drummond, P., Paterson, R., & Willis, J. (Eds.) (1993). *National identity and Europe: The television revolution*. London: BFI Publishing.

Dunmire, P. L. (1997). Naturalizing the future in factual discourse: A critical linguistic analysis of a projected event. *Written Communication*, *14*(2), 221–264.

Edebiyati Kajik (Kajik Literature). (n.d.). Compiled by HawreBakhawan. Retrieved January 30, 2007, from http://www.bakhawan.com/hawdocs/EdebiyatiKAJYK.pdf.

Edmonds, C. J. (1971). Kurdish nationalism. *Journal of Contemporary History*, *6*(1), 87–107.

Edwards, J. (2009). *Language and identity: An introduction*. New York, NY: Cambridge University Press.

Eggins, S. (2004). *An introduction to systemic functional linguistic* (2nd ed.). New York: Continuum.

El Gody, A. (2007). New media, new audience, new topics, and new rorms of censorship in the Middle East. In P. Seib (Ed.), *New media and the new Middle East* (213–234). New York: Palgrave MacMillan.

Entessar, N. (2007). Competing national identities: The Kurdish conundrum in Iran. In C. G. MacDonald & C. A. O'Leary (Eds.), *Kurdish identity: Human rights and political status* (189–200). Tallahassee: University Press of Florida.

Erikson, T. H. (2007). Nationalism and the Internet. *Nations and Nationalism*, *13*(1), 1–17.

Fairclough, N. (1995a). *Critical discourse analysis: The critical study of language*. London: Longman.

———. (1995b). *Media discourse*. London: Arnold.

———. (2001). *Language and power* (2nd ed.). New York: Longman.

———. (2003). *Analysing discourse: Textual analysis for social research*. London: Routledge.

Fairclough, N., & Wodak, R. (1997). Critical discourse analysis. In T. van Dijk (Ed.), *Discourse studies: A multidisciplinary introduction* (Vol. 2). *Discourse and social interaction* (258–284). London: Sage.

Fernandes, D. (2007). *The Kurdish and Armenian genocides: From censorship and denial of recognition?* Stockholm: Apec Förlag.

Fichte, J. G. (1986). *Addresses to the German Nation*.(R. F. Jones and G. H. Turnbull trans., G. A. Kelly Ed.). New York: Harper Torch Books.

Firouzi, T. (2005). *Kordestane Iran: Zire pousheshe televizyonhaye mahvareyi tahte setam va sarkoub e hokumate markazi* (Iranian Kurdistan: Under the coverage of satellite television, oppressed and suppressed by the central government). Retrieved November 13, 2005, from www.peiknet.com/1384/06mehr/page/312kord.htm.

Fishman, J. (1989). *Language and ethnicity in minority sociolinguistic perspective*. Clevedon: Multilingual Matters Ltd.

Fisk, J., & Hartley, J. (2003). *Reading television* (2nd ed.). London: Routledge.

Fowler, R. (1991). *Language in the news: Discourse and ideology in the press.* London: Routledge.

Fowler, R., Hodge, B., Kress, G., & Trew, T. (1979). *Language and control.* London: Routledge & Kegan Paul.

Fraser, S. (2007, April 10). Turkish prime minister warns Iraqi Kurdish leader not to threaten Turkey.*The Independent.* Retrieved April 20, 2007, from http://news.independent.co.uk/europe/article2437271.ece.

French court cancels Medya TV's broadcasting license. (2004, February 12). Retrieved January 10, 2005, from www.clandestineradio.com/crw/news. php?id=&stn=684&news=287.

Galasiński, D., & Skowronek, K. (2001). Naming the nation: A Critical analysis of names in Polish political discourse. *Political Communication, 18,* 51–66.

Galbraith, P. (2005). Kurdistan in federal Iraq. In B. O'Leary, J. McGarry & K. Salih (Eds.), *The future of Kurdistan in Iraq* (268–281). Philadelphia: University of Pennsylvania Press.

Geertz, C. (1973). *The interpretation of cultures: Selected essays.* New York: Basic Books.

Geisler, M. E. (2005). *National symbols, fractured identities: Contesting the national narrative.* Hanover: University Press of New England.

Gellner, E. (1983). *Nations and nationalism.* Ithaca, NY: Cornell University Press.

———. (1997).*Nationalism.* New York: New York University Press.

Ghazi, H. (Producer) (2007, August 20).*Ruwange* [Television Broadcast]. Copenhagen: Roj TV.

Ghobadi, B. (Director) (2004). *Turtles can fly.* [Motion picture]. Iran-Iraq: IFC Films.

Goodman, S. (1996). Visual English. In S. Goodman & D. Graddol (Eds.), *Redesigning English: New texts, new identities* (38–105). London: The Open University.

Griffiths, A. (1993). *Pobol y Cwm:* The construction of national and cultural identity in a Welsh-Language soap opera. In P. Drummond, R. Paterson & J. Willis (Eds.), *National identity and Europe: The television revolution* (9–24). London: BFI Publishing.

Guibernau, M. (1996). *Nationalisms: The nation-state and nationalism in the twentieth century.* Oxford: Polity Press.

———. (1999). *Nations without state: Political communities in a global age.* Oxford: Polity Press.

Gulagenim. (2002a, May 26). Retrieved March 15, 2004, from www. gulagenim.blogspot.com/2002_05_26_gulagenim_archive.html.

———. (2002b, July 04). Retrieved March 15, 2004, from www.gulagenim. blogspot.com/2002_07_04_ gulagenim_archive.html.

Gunter, M. M. (2005).The Kurdish minority identity in Iraq. In M. Shatzmiller (Ed.), *Nationalism and minority identities in Islamic societies* (264–281). London: McGill-Queen's University Press.

Guyot, J. (2007). Minority language media and the public sphere. In M. Cormack & N. Hourigan (Eds.), *Minority language media: Concepts, critiques, and case studies* (34–52). Clevedon: Multilingual Matters.

Habermas, J. (1994). Citizenship and national identity. In B. van Steenbergen (Ed.), *The Condition of Citizellship* (20–35). London: Sage.

Halavais, A. (2000). National borders on the World Wide Web. *New Media & Society, 2*(1), 7–28.

Hall, J. (1993). Nationalisms: Classified and explained. *Daedalus, 122*, 1–28.

———. (2006). Structural approaches to nations and nationalism. In G. Delanty & K. Kumar (Eds.), *The Sage handbook of nations and nationalism* (33–43). London: Sage.

Hall, S. (1980). Encoding/decoding. In P. Willman, S. Hall, D. Hobson & A. Lowe, Andrew (Eds.), *Culture, media, language: Working papers in cultural studies, 1972–79* (128–138). London: University of Birmingham.

———. (1992). The question of cultural identity. In S. Hall, D. Held & T. McGrew (Eds.), *Modernity and its futures* (273–316). Cambridge: Polity Press.

Hartley, J. (1978). Invisible fictions. *Textual Practice, 1*(2), 121–138.

———. (2004). Television, nation, and indigenous media. *Television & New Media, 5*, 7–25.

Hassanpour, A. (1992). *Nationalism and language in Kurdistan.* San Francisco: Mellon Press.

———. (1996). The creation of Kurdish media culture. In P. Kreyenbroek & C. Allison (Eds.), *Kurdish culture and identity* (48–84). London: Zed Books Ltd.

———. (1997). Language and television. In H. Newcomb (Ed.), *Encyclopaedia of television* (Vol. 1, 923–926). Chicago: Fitzroy Dearborn Publishers.

———. (1998). Satellite footprints as national borders: MED-TV and the extraterritoriality of sate sovereignty. *Journal of Muslim Minority Affairs, 18*(1), 53–72.

———. (2003a). Diaspora, homeland and communication technologies. In K. H. Karim (Ed.), *The media of diaspora* (76–88). London: Routledge.

———. (2003b). The making of Kurdish identity: Pre-20th century historical and literary discourses. In A. Vali (Ed.), *Essays on the origins of Kurdish nationalism* (106–162). Costa Mesa: Mazda Publishers.

———. (2010a). *Şovînîzmî Soranî û Efsanekanî: Beşî du* (Sorani chauvinism and its myths: Part one). *Farhang, 22*, 4–10.

———. (2010b). *Şovînîzmî Soranî û Efsanekanî: Beşî du* (Sorani chauvinism and its myths: Part two). *Farhang, 24*, 4–8.

Hassanpour, A., & Mojab, S. (2005). Kurdish diaspora. In M. Ember, C. R. Ember, & I. Skoggard (Eds.), *Encyclopaedia of diasporas: Immigrant and refugee cultures around the world* (Vol. 1, 214–224). New York: Kluwer Academic.

Hassanpour, A., Skutnabb-Kangas, T., & Chyet, M. (1996). The non-education of Kurds: A Kurdish perspective. *International Review of Education, 42*(4), 367–379.

Hastings, A. (1997). *The construction of nationhood: Ethnicity, religion and nationalism.* Cambridge: Cambridge University Press.

Hazim, R. (2004). *Întervûya digel Samî Ergoşî, spîkerê Kurdistan TV* (Interview with Sami Ergoshi, Kurdistan TV spokesperson. Retrieved January 15, 2005, from www.xweza.com/Digel%20Sami%20Ergoshi.htm.

Hearse, P. (1997, June 6). Kurdish satellite TV's second anniversary. *Green Left Weekly,* p. 27. Retrieved October 27, 2004, from www.greenleft.org.au/back/1997/276/276p27.htm.

Held, D., McGrew, A., Goldlatt, D., & Perraton, J. (1999). *Global transformations: Politics, economics and culture.* Stanford: Stanford University Press.

Heller, M. (1999) *Linguistic minorities and modernity: A sociolinguistic ethnography.* London: Longman.

Herman, E., & Chomsky, N. (2002). *Manufacturing consent: The political economy of the mass media* (2nd ed.). New York: Pantheon.

Herring, S. C., Kouper, I., Scheidt, L. A., & Wright, E. L. (2004a). Women and children last: The discursive construction of weblogs. In L. J. Gurak, S. Antonijevic, L. Johnson, C. Ratliff, & J. Reyman (Eds.), *Into the blogosphere: Rhetoric, community, and culture of weblogs.* Retrieved July 15, 2006, from http://blog.lib.umn.edu/blogosphere/women_and_children.html.

Herring, S. C., Sheidt, L. A., Sabrina, B., & Wright, E. (2004b). Bridging the gap: A genre analysis of weblogs. Proceedings of the 37th Hawaii International Conference on System Sciences.

Higgins, M. (2004). The articulation of nation and politics in the Scottish press. *Journal of language and politics, 3*(3), 463–483.

Himmati, H. (2007, September 18). *Sitranbêj Heval Ibrahîm: Êstaş methî Êraq dekem* (Singer Heval Ibrahim: I still praise Iraq). *Midya, 307,* 17.

Hobsbawm, E. (1988). Introduction: Inventing traditions. In E. Hobsbawm & T. Ranger (Eds.), *The Invention of tradition* (1–14). Cambridge: Cambridge University Press.

———. (1990). *Nations and nationalism since 1780: Programme, myth, reality.* Cambridge: Cambridge University Press.

Honeycutt, C., & Cunliffe, D. (2010). The use of the Welsh language on Facebook: An initial investigation. *Information, Communication & Society, 13*(2), 226–248.

Horowitz, D. L. (1992). Irredentas and secessions: Adjacent phenomena, neglected connections. In A. D. Smith (Ed.), *Ethnicity and nationalism* (118–130). New York: E. J. Brill.

Hroch, M. (2006). Modernization and communication as factors of nation formation. In G. Delanty & K. Kumar (Eds.), *The Sage handbook of nations and nationalism* (21–32). London: Sage.

Huchinson, J. (1999). Re-interpreting cultural nationalism. *Australian Journal of Politics and History, 45*(3), 392–407.

Huchinson, J., & Smith, A. D. (Eds.) (1994). *Nationalism.* Oxford: Oxford University Press.

Huckin, T. (2002). Textual silence and the discourse of homelessness. *Discourse & Society, 13*(3), 347–372.

Hult, F. M. (2010). Swedish television as a mechanism for language planning and policy. *Language Problems & Language Planning, 34*(2), 158–181.

Human Rights Watch-Middle East. (1995): I*raq's crime of genocide: The Anfal campaign against the Kurds.* New Haven: Yale University Press.

Iedema, R. (2000). Analyzing film and television. In T. van Leeuwen & C. Jewitt (Eds.), *The handbook of visual analysis* (183–204). London: Sage.

Ignatieff, M. (1993). *Blood and belonging: Journeys into the new nationalism.* New York: Farrar, Straus and Giroux.

Index Online. (2004). Syria: Access to two Kurdish websites blocked. Retrieved October 24, 2004, from http://www.indexonline.org /indexindex/20040406_syria.shtml.

Innis, H. (1951). *The bias of communication.* Toronto: University of Toronto Press.

Institut Kurde de Paris. (2005). Massud Barzani unanimously elected President of Iraqi Kurdistan. Retrieved December 16, 2005, from www. institutkurde.org/en/publications/bulletins/bulletins.php?bul=243#1.

Internet World Stats. (2007). Internet world users by language: Top 10 languages. Retrieved December 10, 2007, from http://internetworldstats. com/stats7.htm.

International Constitutional Law. (1992). Iran-constitution. Retrieved July 10, 2006, from www.servat.unibe.ch/icl/ir00000_.html.

Ivanov, W. (1926). Notes of the Ethnology of Khurasan.*The Geographical Journal, 67*(2), 143–158.

Izady, M. (1992). *The Kurds: A concise handbook.* Washington, DC: Taylor & Francis.

———. (1994). Are Kurds descended from the Medes? Retrieved December 20, 2006, from www.kurdistanica.com/english/history/articles-his /his-articles-08.html.

Jenkins, O. B. (2001). The Kurdish peoples. Retrieved July 10, 2006, from www.orvillejenkins.com/peoples/kurds.html.

Jenson, J. (1993). Naming nations: Making nationalist claims in Canadian public discourse. *Canadian Review of Sociology and Anthropology, 30*(3), 337–350.

Jones, E. (2007). The Territory of Television: S4C and the Representation of the 'Whole of Wales.' In M. Cormack & N. Hourigan (Eds.), *Minority language media: Concepts, critiques and case studies* (188–211). Bristol: Multilingual Matters.

Joseph, J. E. (2004). *Language and identity: National, ethnic, religious.* New York: Palgrave Macmillan.

———. (2006). *Language and politics.* Edinburgh: Edinburgh University Press.

Kaiser, R. J. (2002). Homeland making and the territorialization of national identity. In D. Conversi (Ed.), *Ethnonationalism in the contemporary world: Walker Connor and the study of nationalism* (229–247). London: Routledge.

Kane, A. (2000). Narratives of nationalism: Constructing Irish national identity during the Land War, 1879–1882. *National Identities, 2*(3), 245–264.

Karim, K. H. (1998). From ethnic media to global media: Transnational communication networks among diasporic communities. Paper for Strategic Research and Analysis: Canadian Heritage.

———. (2003). Mapping diasporicmediascapes. In K. H. Karim (Ed.), *The media of diaspora* (1–17). London: Routledge.

———. (2006). Nation and diaspora: Rethinking multiculturalism in a transnational context. *International Journal of Media and Cultural Politics* 2(1), 267–282.

Karner, C. (2005). The 'Habsburg dilemma' today: Competing discourses of national identity in contemporary Austria. *National Identities, 7*(4), 409–432.

KDP. (n.d.). General information about KDP. Retrieved October 15, 2005, from www.kdp.se/?do=what.

Kedouri, E. (1993).*Nationalism* (4th ed.). Oxford: Blackwell.

Kelly-Holmes, H., & Moriarty, M. (2009). Convergence and divergence in Basque, Irish and Sámi media language policing. *Language Policy, 8*, 227–242.

Kennedy, J. (2004). A Switzerland of the north? The nationalistes and binational Canada. *Nations and Nationalism, 10*(4), 499–518.

Knudson, J. W. (1998). Rebellion in Chiapas: Insurrection by Internet and public relations. *Media, Culture & Society, 20*, 507–518.

Kohn, H. (1944). *The idea of nationalism*. New York: Macmillan.

Koohi-Kamali, F. (2003). *The political development of the Kurds in Iran: Pastoral nationalism*. New York: Palgrave.

Kösebalaban, H. (2004). Turkish media and sport coverage: marking the boundaries of national identity. *Middle East Critique, 13*(1), 47–64.

Kress, G. R., & van Leeuwen, T. (1996). *Reading images: The grammar of visual design*. London: Routledge.

———. (2002). Colour as a semiotic mode: Notes for a grammar of colour. *Visual Communication, 1*(3), 343–368.

Kreyenbroek, P. (1992). On the Kurdish language. In In P. G. Kreyenbroek & S. Sperl (Eds.), *The Kurds: A contemporary overview* (68–83). London: Routledge.

———. (1996). Religion and religions in Kurdistan. In P. Kreyenbroek & C. Allison (Eds.), *Kurdish culture and identity* (85–110). London: Zed Books.

Kreyenbroek, P., & Allison, C. (Eds.) (1996). *Kurdish culture and identity*. London: Zed Books.

Kreyenbroek, P., & Sperl, S. (Eds.). (1992). *The Kurds: A contemporary overview*. London: Routledge.

Kurdish flag hoisted over regional parliament in north Iraq (2007, June 05). *Assyrian International News Agency*. Retrieved June 6, 2007, from www.aina.org/news/20070605141350.htm.

Kurdistan Television. (2006). About us. Retrieved March 10, 2006, from www.kurdistantv.net/info.asp?ser=20&cep=9.

Kurds retain link to cyber world (2003, January 22). Retrieved October 03, 2004, from http://old.krg.org/docs/articles/kurds-cyber-sarwat-jan-2003.asp.

Kutschera, C. (2005). Iran: A Kurdish awakening. Retrieved December 20, 2006, from www.chris-kutschera.com/A/Kurds-Iran.htm.

Kuusisto, A. K. (2001). Territoriality, symbolism and the challenge. *Peace Review, 13*(1), 59–66.

Kymlicka, W., & Patten, A. (2003). Language rights and political theory. *Annual Review of Applied Linguistics, 23*, 3–21.

Kymlicka, W., & Straehle, C. (1999). Cosmopolitanism, nation-states, and minority nationalism: A critical review of recent literature. *European Journal of Philosophy, 7*(1), 65–88.

Lakoff, G., & Johnson, M. (1980). *Metaphors we live by*. Chicago: University of Chicago Press.

Law, A. (2001). Near and far: Banal national identity and the press in Scotland. *Media, Culture & Society, 23*(3), 299–317.

Le dîdarî Barzanî u Muttekî da rega be helkirdinî alay Kurdistan nedra (The Kurdistan flag was not allowed at the meeting between Barzani and Mutteki). (2007, May 06). *Renesans News*. Retrieved May 06, 2007, from http://renesans.nu/articles.php?id=2377.

Le malperekanewe (From the websites) (2004, November 3). *Hawlati*, 16.

Lemke, J. (2002). Travels in hypermodality. *Visual Communication 1*(3), 299–325.

Luke, A. (2002). Beyond science and ideology critique: Developments in Critical Discourse Analysis. *Annual Review of Applied Linguistics, 22*, 96–110.

Luther, C. A. (2002). National identities, structure, and press images of nations: The case of Japan and the United States. *Mass Communication & Society, 5*(1), 57–85.

Lysaght, R. (2009). Language image in national minority language television idents. TG4 (Teilifís na Gaeilge, Ireland) and Whakaata Māori (Māori Television, New Zealand). *Estudios Irlandeses 4*, 45–57.

Madianou, M. (2005). *Mediating the nation: News, audiences and the politics of identity*. London: UCL Press.

Makhoudi, K. (Producer). (2005, August 10). *Kazîwe* [Television broadcast]. Tehran: Kurdistan TV, Tehran Office.

Malešević, S. (2006). Nationalism and the power of ideology. In G. Delanty & K. Kumar (Eds.), *The Sage handbook of nations and nationalism* (307–319). London: Sage.

Malmisanij, M. (2006a). The past and the present of book publishing in Kurdish language in Syria.Next Page Foundation. Retrieved July 15, 2007, from www.npage.org/article127.html.

———. (2006b). The past and the present of book publishing in Kurdish language in Turkey.Next Page Foundation. Retrieved July 10, 2007, from www.npage.org/article126.html.

Martin, J. R. (2000). Close reading: Functional linguistics as a tool for critical discourse analysis. In L. Unsworth (Ed.), *Researching language in schools and communities* (275–302). London: CASSELL.

Martin, J. R., & Wodak, R. (2003). Introduction. In J. R. Martin & R. Wodak (Eds.), *Re/reading the past: Critical and functional perspective on time and value* (1–18). Amsterdam: John Benjamins.

Martinec, R. (2000). Construction of identity in Michael Jackson's Jam. *Social Semiotics, 10*(3), 313–329.

Matras, Y., & Reerschemius, G. (1991). Standardization beyond the state: The cases of Yiddish, Kurdish and Romani. In U. V. Gleich & E. Wolff (Eds.), *Standardization of national languages: Symposium on language standardization,* February 2–3, 1991. Hamburg: UNISCO Institute for Education.

Mautner, G. (2005). Time to get wired: Using web-based corpora in critical discourse analysis. *Discourse & Society, 16*(6), 809–828.

May, S. (2008). *Language and minority rights: Ethnicity, nationalism and the politics of language* (2nd ed.). New York: Routledge.

Mcdonald, M. (2003). *Exploring media discourse.* London: Arnold.

McDowall, D. (2004). *A modern history of the Kurds* (3rd ed.). London: I. B. Tauris.

McKiernan, K. (2006). *The Kurds: A people in search of their homeland.* New York: St. Martin's Press.

McLuhan, M. (1960). Effects of the improvements of communication media. *Journal of Economic History, 20* (4), 566–575.

———. (1962). *The Gutenberg galaxy: The making of typographic man.* Toronto: University of Toronto Press.

———. (1964). *Understanding media: The extensions of man.* New York: Mentor Books.

Menaf, M.(2007, September 18). *Le yek hefte da hekerani Kurd 100 malperî fermî Turkiayan hak kird* (In one week, Kurdish hackers hacked 100 Turkish official websites) Retrieved September 20, 2007, from www.renesans.nu.

Meyrowitz, J. (1985). *No sense of place.* New York: Oxford University Press.

Miller, C., & D. Shepherd (2004). Blogging as social action: A genre analysis of the weblog. In L. J. Gurak, S. Antonijevic, L. Johnson, C. Ratliff, & J. Reyman (Eds.), *Into the blogosphere: Rhetoric, community, and culture of weblogs.* Retrieved January 15, 2007, from http://blog.lib.umn.edu/blogosphere/blogging_as_social_action_a_genre_analysis_of_the_weblog.html.

Mills, K. (2002). Cybernations: Identity, self-determination, democracy and the "Internet Effect" in the emerging information order. *Global Society*, *16*(1), 69–87.

Miura, A., & Yamashita, K. (2007). Psychological and social influences on blog writing: An online survey of blog authors in Japan. *Journal of Computer-Mediated Communication*, *12*(4), Retrieved November 27, 2007, from http://jcmc.indiana.edu/vol12/issue4/miura.html.

Mohtadi, A. (2005, January 01). *Wituwêjî xiwêneranî Dîmane le geļ Ebduļļay Muhtedî* [Dimane readers' interview with Abdullah Mohtadi]. Retrieved January 15, 2005, from www.komala.org/kurdi/vetvez/2005-01 -01AbaM-Dimaneh.htm.

Mojab, S. (2001).*Women of a non-state nation: The Kurds*. Costa Mesa, Calif.: Mazda.

Morley, D. (1992). *Television, audiences and cultural studies*. London: Routledge.

———. (2000). *Home territories: Media, mobility and identity*. London: Routledge.

———. (2004). Broadcasting and the construction of the national family. In R. C. Allen & A. Hill, *The television studies reader* (418–441). London: Routledge.

Muhammad, S. (2006, August). *Behruz Hesen: Debwaye dezga roshinbîrye-kanî Kurdistan saitêkî wekî [Pertûk] yandabimezrandaye* (BahruzHasan: Kurdistan cultural institutions should have established a website similar to Pertwk.com). *Kurdistan Report, 26*, 12.

Muhamad-Brandner, C. (2009). Biculturalism online: Exploring the web space of Aotearoa/New Zealand.*Journal of Information, Communication and Ethics in Society, 7*(2/3), 182–191.

Nabaz, J. (1976). *Zimanî yekgirtúy Kurdî* (The unified Kurdish language). Bamberg: W. Germany: National Union of Kurdish Students in Europe.

———. (1985). *Kurdistan u shorişekey: Zincîre witarêke salî 1971 be zimanî Almanî le Berlîn bo Kurd u dostanî Kurd xwêndrawetewe. Kurdo le Almanîyewe kirdúye be Kurdî* (Kurdistan and its revolution: A series of lectures delivered in German, in Berlin, in 1971 for the Kurds and friends of the Kurds. Translated into Kurdish by Ali Kurdo). Hewlêr (Irbil), Kurdistan-Iraq: Aras Publishing House.

Nafici, H. (1993). The making of exile cultures: Iranian television in Los Angeles. Minneapolis: Minneapolis University Press.

Nalî, M. X. E. S. M. (1976). *Dîwanî Nalî: Mela Xidrî Ehmedî Shaweysî Mikaylî*. (Collected Poetry of Nali: Mullah Khidir Ahmad Shawaysi Mikaili). [Edited] by Mala Abdulkarim Mudaris and Fateh Abdulkarim. Baghdad: Kurdish Academy Press.

Natali, D. (2002). Kurdayetî in the late Ottoman and Qajar empires.*Critique: Critical Middle Eastern Studies, 11*(2), 177–199.

Newrozi, R. (n.d.). *Panoramaya sed salji diroka rojnamevaniya Kurdi: 22, 04, 1898–22, 04, 1998* (A panorama of Kurdish journalism's story in one hundred years: 22, 04, 1898–22, 04, 1998). Retrieved May 12, 2006, from www.amude.net/kurdi/100-sal-rojnamevaniya-kurdi.pdf.

Nicolaisen, W. F. H. (1990). Place names and politics. *Names, 38*, 193–207.

No 'legal' demonstration prevented, Erbil governor says (2005, November 9). *The [Hawler] Globe*, 3.

O'Leary, B., McGarry, J., & Salih, K. (Eds.) (2005). *The future of Kurdistan in Iraq*. Philadelphia: University of Pennsylvania Press.

O'Leary, B., & Salih, K. (2005). The denial, resurrection, and affirmation of Kurdistan. In B. O'Leary, J. McGarry & K. Salih (Eds.), *The future of Kurdistan in Iraq* (3–43). Philadelphia: University of Pennsylvania Press.

O'Leary, C. (2002, December). The Kurds of Iraq: Recent history, future prospects. MERIA Journal, 6 (4). Retrieved April 14, 2005, from http://meria.idc.ac.il/journal/2002/issue4/jv6n4a5.html.

Olson, R. (1991). Five stages of Kurdish nationalism: 1880–1980. *Journal of Muslim Minority Affairs, 12*(2), 391–409.

———. (2009). *Blood, belief and ballots: The management of Kurdish nationalism in Turkey, 2007–2009*. Costa Mesa, CA: Mazda Publishers.

O'Shea, M. T. (2004). *Trapped between the map and reality: Geography and perceptions of Kurdistan*. New York : Routledge.

Peyamner News Agency (2005). Ême (About us). Retrieved December 15, 2005, from www.peyamner.com/Default.aspx?a=a.

Phillipson, R., Rannut, M., & Skutnabb-Kangas, T. (1995). Introduction. In T. Skutnabb-Kangas, R. Phillipson & M. Rannut (Eds.), *Linguistic human rights: Overcoming linguistic discrimination* (1–22). Berlin: Nouton de Gruyter.

Poster, M. (1999). National identities and communications technologies. *The Information Society, 15*, 235–240.

Prevent ethnic conflict. (2006). Retrieved July 14, 2006, from www.petitiononline.com/azeri.

Price, M. E. (1995). *Television: The public sphere and national identity*. Oxford: Clarendon Press.

———. (2001). Satellite broadcasting as trade routes in the sky. In Joseph M. Chan & Bryce T. McIntyre (Eds.), *In search of boundaries: Communication, nation-states and cultural identities* (146–167). Westport, CT: Abex Publishers.

Qadir, K. H. (1986). *Dîwanî Hacî Qadirî Koyî* (Collected poetry of H.Q.K.). Collected and edited by Sardar Hamid Miran and Karim Mistefa Sharaza. Baghdad.

Qadir, S. (17 July, 2007). *Interpol mêrdî shewboy destgîr kirduwe u britaniash deydatewe be kurdistan* (The Interpol has arrested Shewbo's husband and Britain will extradite him to Kurdistan). *Media, 14*. Retrieved July 20, 2007, from www.yndk.com.

Randal, J. C. (1997). *After such knowledge, what forgiveness? My encounters with Kurdistan*. New York: Farrar, Straus and Giroux.

Renan, E. (1990). What is a nation? In H. K. Bhabha (Ed.), *Nation and narration* (8–22). London: Routledge.

Reporters without Borders. (2003, December 31). Internet-user held in solitary for seven months for e-mailing a newsletter. Retrieved October 24, 2004, from http://www.rsf.org/article.php3?id_article=8941.

Ricento, T. (2003). The discursive construction of Americanism. *Discourse & Society, 14* (5), 611–637.

Riggins, S. H. (1997).The rhetoric of othering. In S. H. Riggins (Ed.), *The language and politics of exclusion* (1–30). London: Sage.

Riley, D. (2005, April 14). Number of blogs now exceeds 50 million worldwide. Retrieved May 20, 2005, from www.blogherald.com/2005/04/14/number-of-blogs-now-exceeds-50-million-worldwide.

Romaine, S. (2000). *Language in society: An introduction to sociolinguistics* (2nd ed.). New York: Oxford University Press.

Romano, D. (2002). Modern communications technology in ethnic nationalist hands: the case of Kurds. *Canadian Journal of Political Science, 35*(1), 127–149.

———. (2006). *The Kurdish nationalist movement: Opportunity, mobilization, and identity.* Cambridge: Cambridge University Press.

Ryan, N. (1997 March). Med-TV newsflash. *Wired,* 4–9.

O'Leary, B., & Salih, K. (2005). The denial, resurrection, and affirmation of Kurdistan. In B. O'Leary, J. McGarry & K. Salih, *The future of Kurdistan in Iraq* (3–43). Philadelphia: University of Pennsylvania Press.

Said Shukri, I. (2006, July). *Kanî Kamputêr u erke ferhengiyekanî* (Kani Computer and its cultural responsibilities). *Mahabad: Social, Cultural and Literary Magazine, 64,* 40–41.

Salih, B. (Producer) (2010). *Serdar Ezîz bas le ciyawaziyekanî nêwan rojnamegerî le Kurdistan u rojawa dekat* (Sardar Aziz talks about the differences between Journalism in Kurdistan and in the West). *Bernamey Ferheng û Torey Kurdî.* Voice of America, Kurdish Service.

Sami, K. (2006). *Seid Ehmed Rewandizî le dîdarî Kurdistan Anline da* (Said Ehmed Rewandizî in an interview with *Kurdistan Online*). Retrieved May 20, 2007, from www.chopy.net/hewallekan/66-2006/seyid%20ahmed-kurdonlain.htm.

Schaap, F. (2004). Links, lives, logs: Presentation in the Dutch blogosphere. In L. J. Gurak, S. Antonijevic, L. Johnson, C. Ratliff, & J. Reyman (Eds.), *Into the blogosphere: Rhetoric, community, and culture of weblogs.* Retrieved July 15, 2006, from http://blog.lib.umn.edu/blogosphere/links_lives_logs_pf.html.

Schiller, N. G., & Fouron, G. E. (2001). *Georges woke up laughing: long-distance nationalism and the search for home.* Durham, NC Duke University Press.

Schleifer, Y. (2006, April 21). Denmark, again? Now it's under fire for hosting Kurdish TV station. *The Christian Science Monitor.* Retrieved June 10, 2006, from www.csmonitor.com/2006/0421/p01s01-woeu.html.

Schlesinger, P. (1991). *Media, state and nation: Political violence and collective identities.* London: Sage.

———. (1999). Changing spaces of political communication: The case of the European Union. *Political Communication, 16,* 263–279.

Seib, P. (2007). New media and prospects for democratization. In P. Seib (Ed.), *New media and the new Middle East* (1–17). New York: Palgrave Macmillan.

Sharafkandi, A. R. (1990). *Henbane Borine: Ferhenge Kordi-Farsi* (Henbane Borine: Kurdish-Persian Dictionary). Tehran: Soroush.

Sheikhani, S. (2004). Iraqi Kurdish satellite channels: From media obscurity to the dream of international broadcasting. *Translational Broadcasting Studies, 12.* Retrieved December 10, 2006, from www.tbsjournal.com /kurdish.htm.

Sheyholislami, J. (2001). Yesterday's "separatists" are today's "resistance fighters": A critical discourse analysis of the representation of Iraqi Kurds in the *New York Times* and the *Globe* and *Mail.* Unpublished master's thesis, Carleton University, Ottawa, Ontario, Canada.

———. (2007). Yesterday's "separatists" are today's "resistance fighters": Mainstream media as agents of hegemony. In J. Bernardo, G. López & P. Sancho (Eds.), *Critical discourse analysis of the mass media of* communication (95–110). Valencia: Universitat de València.

———. (2009a). Minority language media: Concepts, critiques and case studies. [Review of the book with the same title, edited by Mike Cormack and Niamh Hourigan (2007). Clevedon: Multilingual Matters.]. *Canadian Journal of Communication, 34*(4), 757–759.

———. (2009b, November). *Language and nation-building in Kurdistan-Iraq.* 43rd annual meeting of the Middle Eastern Studies Association, Boston, Massachusetts, USA. Retrieved May 2010, from www.kurdishacademy.org/?q=node/712.

———. (Forthcoming). Kurdish in Iran: A case of restricted and controlled tolerance. *International Journal of the Sociology of Language.*

Sheykholislami, M. (1974). *Tarîk u rûn* (Dark and light). Baghdad: Peshewa Publishing.

Shnirelman, V. (2006). The politics of a name: Between consolidation and separation in the northern Caucasus. *Acta Slavica Iaponica, Tomus,23,* 37–73.

Siddiqui, H. (1999, February 21). Finding the mix of home and homeland. *Toronto Star,* A13.

Silverstone, R. (1999). *Why study the media?* London: Sage.

Sina, N. (Producer). (2005, December 19). Zayele [Radio Broadcast]. Stockholm: Radio Sweden International, Kurdish Service. Retrieved July 15, 2006, from www.sr.se/cgi-bin/International/programsidor/index. asp?ProgramID=2200.

———. (Producer). (2006, February 28). *Wituwêj le gel Shaho Husênî, yekêk le berpirsanî Tishk TV* (Interview with Shao Husseini, one of the Tishk TV's executives).Zayele [Radio Broadcast]. Stockholm: Radio Sweden

International, Kurdish Service. Retrieved April 10, 2006, from www.
sr.se/rs/red/grupp/kur/sounds/Zayele-TishkTV.ram.

———. (Producer).(2007a, January 01).*Wituwêj le gel Husên Shuxkeman*
(Interview with Hussein Shukhkaman). Zayele [Radio Broadcast].
Stockholm: Radio Sweden International, Kurdish Service. Retrieved
January 10, 2007, from www.sr.se/cgi-bin/International/programsidor
/artikel.asp?ProgramID=2200&Artikel=1246513.

———. (Producer). (2007b, February 12). Zayele [Radio Broadcast].
Stockholm: Radio Sweden International, Kurdish Service. Retrieved
February 15, 2007, from www.sr.se/cgi-bin/International/program-
sidor/index.asp?ProgramID=2200.

Skutnabb-Kangas, T., Fernandes, D. (2008). Kurds in Turkey and in
(Iraqi) Kurdistan: A comparison of Kurdish educational language policy in two situations of occupation. *Genocide Studies and Prevention,*
3(1), 43–73.

Smith, A. (1983). *Theories of nationalism* (2nd ed.). London: Duckworth.

———. (1991). *National identity.* Reno: University of Nevada Press.

———. (1996). LSE centennial lecture: The resurgence of nationalism? Myth
and memory in the renewal of nations.*The British Journal of Sociology,*
47(4), 575–598.

———. (1998). *Nationalism and modernism.* London: Routledge.

———. (1999). *Myths and memories of the nations.* Oxford: Oxford University
Press.

Somolu, O. (2007). 'Telling our own stories': African women blogging for
social change. *Gender & Development, 15*(3), 477–489.

Sorapure, M. (2003). Screening moments, scrolling lives: Diary writing on
the web. *Biography, 26*(1), 1–23.

Spencer, P., & Wollman, H. (2002). *Nationalism: A critical introduction.*
London: Sage Publication.

Steinberg, M. (1999). The talk and back talk of collective action: A dialogic
analysis of repertoires of discourse among nineteenth-century English
cotton spinners. *American Journal of Sociology, 105*(3), 736–780.

Straubhaar, J. (2002). (Re)asserting national television and national identity
against the global, regional and local levels of world television. In J. M. Chan
& B. T. McIntyre (Eds.), *In search of boundaries: Communication, nation-
states and cultural identities* (181–206). London: Ablex Publishing.

Sutherland, C. (2005). Nation-building through discourse theory. *Nations*
and Nationalism, 11(2), 185–202.

Taha, Y. (2006, October 10). *Be pêy failêki hizbî Be's, 43 pisporî perwerdeyî*
Kurd karyan bo nehêshtinî zimanî Kurdî kirduwe [According to a Baath
party's document, 43 Kurdish educators have worked towards terminat-
ing the Kurdish language], *Awene*, 1, 15, Retrieved October 15, 2006,
from www.awene.com.

Talabani: *Le jiyanim da birm le damezrandinî dewletî Kurdî yan ciyakird-
newey Kurdistan le Êraq nekirdotewe* (I have never thought of establishing a Kurdish state or separating Kurdistan from Iraq). (2005, June 19).

Peyamnêr News Agency. Retrieved June 25, 2005, from www.peyamner. com/article.php?id=13712&lang=kurdish.

Talib, N. (Producer). (2007, January 07). *Rapirsî* (Opinion Survey) [Television broadcast]. [Hawler, Kurdistan-Iraq]: Kurdistan TV.

Tewar. (2002, July 04). Retrieved March 15, 2004, from http://wera.blog-spot.com/2002/07/blog-post_04.html.

Thomas, G. (2007, June 12). Kurds: Grateful to America, want homeland. *The Christian Broadcasting Network.* Retrieved June 12, 2007, from www.cbn.com/CBNnews/174989.aspx.

Thussu, D. K. (2000). *International communication: Continuity and change.* London: Arnold.

Triandafyllidou, A., & Wodak, R. (2003). Conceptual and methodological questions in the study of collective identities: An introduction. *Journal of Language and Politics, 2*(2), 205–223.

Turkey renames 'divisive' animals. (2005, March 08). *BBC News.* Retrieved March 15, 2005, from http://news.bbc.co.uk/2/hi/europe/4328285. stm.

Turkey wary as Iraqi Kurds hoist Kurdish flag (2006, September 16). *Turkish Daily News.* Retrieved October 14, 2006, from www.turkishdailynews. com.tr/article.php?enewsid=54110&mailtofriend=1.

Turks charge Kurd with inciting hatred: Politician made remarks about Iraq. (2007, February 27). *The Washington Post.* Retrieved February 15, 2007, from www.washingtonpost.com/wp-dyn/content/article/2007/02/23 /AR2007022301909_pf.html.

Un, A. (2007, April 4). Kurdistan TV correspondents under pressure. *Bianet: Independent Communication Network.* Retrieved April 7, 2007, from http://eski.bianet.org/2006/11/01_eng/news94186.htm.

Vali, A. (1998). The Kurds and their "others": Fragmented identity and fragmented politics. *Comparative Studies of South Asia, Africa and the Middle East, 18*(2), 82–95.

———. (2003). Genealogies of the Kurds: Constructions of nation and national identity in Kurdish historical writing. In A. Vali (Ed.), *Essays on the origins of Kurdish nationalism* (58–105). Costa Mesa: Mazda Publishers.

Van Bruinessen, M. (1992). *Agha, shaikh and state: The social and political structures of Kurdistan.* London: Zed books.

———. (1999) The Kurds in movement: Migrations, mobilisations, communications and the globalisation of the Kurdish question. Islamic area studies, working paper series, no. 14. Tokyo: Islamic Area Studies Project Management Office.

———. (2000a). *Kurdish ethno-nationalism versus nation-building states: Collected articles.* Istanbul: The ISIS Press.

———. (2000b). Transnational aspects of the Kurdish question. Working paper, Robert Schuman Centre for Advanced Studies, European University Institute, Florence. Retrieved November 13, 2004, from www.let.uu.nl/~martin.vanbruinessen/personal/publications/transnational_Kurds.htm.

———. (2003). Ehmedî Xanî's Memû Zîn and its role in the emergence of Kurdish national awareness. In A. Vali (Ed.), *Essays on the origins of Kurdish nationalism* (40–57). Costa Mesa: Mazda Publishers.

Van den Berghe, P. (1995). Does race matter? *Nations and Nationalism, 1*(3), 357–368.

Van Den Bos, M., & Nell, L. (2006). Territorial bounds to virtual space: Transnational online and offline networks of Iranian and Turkish-Kurdish immigrants in the Netherlands. *Global Networks, 6*(2), 201–220.

Van Dijk, T. A. (1988). *News analysis: Case studies of international and national news in the press.* Hillsdale, N.J.: Lawrence Erlbaum Associates.

———. (1993). *Elite discourse and racism.* London: Sage Publications.

———. (1998). *Ideology: A multidisciplinary approach.* London: Sage.

———. (2001). Multidisciplinary CDA: A plea for diversity. In R. Wodak & M. Meyer (Eds.), *Methods of critical discourse analysis* (95–120). London: Sage.

Van Leeuwen, T. (2005). Multimodality, genre and design. In S. Norris & R. H. Jones (Eds.), *Discourse in action: Introducing mediated discourse analysis* (73–94). London: Routledge.

Vertovec, S. (1999).Conceiving and researching transnationalism. *Ethnic and Racial Studies, 22*(2), 447–462.

Voice of America. (2007, April 4). Iran's Kurdish media crackdown. Retrieved April 20, 2007, from hwww.voanews.com/uspolicy/2007-04-06-voa3.cfm.

Wahby, T., & Edmonds, C. J. (1966). *A Kurdish-English dictionary.* Oxford: Oxford University Press.

Wahlbeck, Ö. (1999). *Kurdish diasporas: A comparative study of Kurdish refugee communities.* London: Palgrave Macmillan.

———. (2002).The concept of diaspora as an analytical tool in the study of refugee communities. *Journal of Ethnic and Migration Studies,28*(2), 221–238.

Warschauer, M. (2000). Language, identity, and the Internet. In B. E. Kolko, L. Nakamura & G. B. Rodman (Eds.), *Race in cyberspace* (151–170). New York: Routledge.

———. (2001). Millennialism and media: Language, literacy, and technology in the 21st century. *AILA Review 14,* 49–59.

Watson, I. (Reporter) (2005, May 09). Neighboring Kurds travel to study in Iraq. National Public Radio. Retrieved May 10, 2005, from www.npr.org/templates/story/story.php?storyId=4528599.

Weiss, G., & Wodak, R. (2003). Introduction: Theory, interdisciplinarity and critical discourse analysis. In G. Weiss & R. Wodak (Eds.), *Critical discourse Analysis: Theory and interdisciplinarity* (1–32). New York: Palgrave Macmillan.

White, P. (2000). *Primitive rebels or revolutionary modernizers?The Kurdish national movement in Turkey.* London: Zed Books.

Widdowson, H. G. (1995). Discourse analysis: A critical view. *Language and Literature, 4*(3), 157–172.

Williams, L. (1999). National identity and the nation state: Construction, reconstruction and contradiction. In K. Cameron (Ed.), *National identity* (7–18). Exeter (Eng.): Intellect.

Williams, R. (1974). *Television: Technology and cultural form.* New York: Schocken Books.

Winter, J. (2007). *Lies the media tell us.* Montreal: Black Rose Books.

Wodak, R. (2006a). Critical Linguistics and Critical Discourse Analysis. In J. O. Östman & J. Verschueren (Eds.). *Handbook of pragmatics* (1–24). Amsterdam: John Benjamins.

———. (2006b). Discourse-analytic and socio-linguistic approaches to the study of nation(alism). In G. Delanty & K. Kumar (Eds.), *The Sage handbook of nations and nationalism* (104–117). London: Sage.

Wodak, R., de Cillia, R., Reisigl, M., & Mitten, R. (1999).*The discursive construction of national identities.* Edinburgh: Edinburgh University Press.

———. (2009).*The discursive construction of national identities* (2nd ed.). Edinburgh: Edinburgh University Press.

Wodak, R., & Ludwig, C. (1999). Introduction. In R. Wodak & C. Ludwig (Eds.), *Challenges in a changing world: Issues in Critical Discourse Analysis* (11–19). Wien: PassagenVerlag.

Wodak, R., & Meyer, M. (Eds.) (2001). *Methods of critical discourse analysis.* London: Sage.

Wogan, P. (2001). Imagined Communities reconsidered: Is print-capitalism what we think it is? *Anthropological Theory, 1*(14), 403–418.

Yang, G. (2003).The Internet and the rise of a transnational Chinese cultural sphere.*Media Culture Society 25,* 469–490.

Yavuz, M. H. (2005). Kurdish nationalism in Turkey. In M. Shatzmiller (Ed.), *Nationalism and minority identities in Islamic societies* (229–261). London: McGill-Queen's University Press.

Yoshimi, S. (2003). Television and nationalism: Historical change in the national domestic TV formation of postwar Japan. *European Journal of Cultural Studies, 6*(4), 459–487.

Young Iraqi Kurds choose English over Arabic. (2005, May 29). *The [Hawler] Globe,* 12.

Yumul, A., & Uzkirimli, U. (2000). Reproducing the nation: 'banal nationalism' in the Turkish press. *Media, Culture & Society, 25*(6), 787–804.

Zamdar, K. (Producer). (2005, August 12). *Şev Bêrî* [Television Broadcast]. [Hawler, Kurdistan-Iraq]: Kurdistan TV.

Zimmerman, A. (1994, July-August). Kurdish broadcasting in Iraq. *Middle East Report,* 20–21.

INDEX

Lightning Source UK Ltd.
Milton Keynes UK
UKOW06f1433311015

261830UK00006B/57/P

9 781137 563873